REASONING with DEMOCRATIC VALUES 2.0,

VOLUME 2

REASONING with DEMOCRATIC VALUES 2.0,

VOLUME 2

Ethical Issues in American History, 1866 to the present

David E. Harris
Anne-Lise Halvorsen
Paul F. Dain

TEACHERS COLLEGE PRESS

TEACHERS COLLEGE | COLUMBIA UNIVERSITY

NEW YORK AND LONDON

Published by Teachers College Press, 1234 Amsterdam Avenue, New York, NY 10027

Library of Congress Cataloging-in-Publication Data is available at loc.gov

Names: Harris, David E., 1945- author. | Halvorsen, Anne-Lise, author. | Dain, Paul F., author. Title: Reasoning with democratic values 2.0 : ethical issues in American history / David E. Harris, Anne-Lise Halvorsen, Paul F. Dain. Other titles: Reasoning with democratic values. | Ethical issues in American history Description: New York, NY: Teachers College Press, [2018] | Includes bibliographical references and index. Identifiers: LCCN 2018004264 |
ISBN 9780807759295 (pbk. : alk. paper) |
ISBN 9780807777084 (ebook)
Subjects: LCSH: United States--History. | Decision making—Moral and ethical aspects. Classification: LCC E178.1 .L82 2018 | DDC 973—dc23
LC record available at https://lccn.loc.gov/2018004264

ISBN 978-0-8077-5929-5 (paper)
ISBN 978-0-8077-7708-4 (ebook)

Printed on acid-free paper
Manufactured in the United States of America

25 24 23 22 21 20 19 18   8 7 6 5 4 3 2 1

I know that the values and the progress that we cherish are not inevitable, that they are fragile, in need of constant renewal. I believe what Dr. King said that the "arc of the universe is long but that it bends toward justice," but I also said that it does not bend on its own. It bends because we bend it, because we put our hand on that arc and we move it in the direction of justice, and freedom, and equality, and kindness, and generosity. It doesn't happen on its own.

—President Barack Obama

John F. Kennedy Profile in Courage Award Speech, May 7, 2017

Contents

Acknowledgments

We thank professors Alan Lockwood and Fred Newmann of the University of Wisconsin who inspired this work and who taught that values are an essential part of education for citizenship in a democracy. Our students have also been a source of inspiration for this work by demonstrating the sophisticated thinking that is possible when considering ethical values.

We also thank the following individuals for their assistance: Professor Mary Beth Norton of Cornell University for her critical review of a draft of the chapter about the Salem witch trials of 1692; Jesus Trevino for providing a copy of his original screenplay for the PBS documentary about Juan Seguín; Professor Jesus de la Teja of Texas State University for sharing his scholarship about Juan Seguín; Mark Barnett for permission to reprint his original portrait of Juan Seguín; Professor Peter Knupfer of Michigan State University for his assistance in finding answers to questions about John Adams's decision to defend the British soldiers accused in the Boston Massacre, the draft during The Civil War, and the disputed presidential election of 1876; Dr. Francisco Balderrama of California State University for his guidance and insights into the history of Mexican deportation during the 1930s; Gracelaw Simmons and Mary Kathryn Menck of the Royall House and Slave Quarters Museum for their assistance in discovering information about Belinda Sutton; Margot Minardi, assistant professor of history and humanities at Reed College, for her insights into the Belinda Sutton petition; Patrick Fahey and Christian Belina, archivist technicians at the Franklin D. Roosevelt Presidential Library in Hyde Park, New York, who personally provided expert and exhaustive assistance locating primary source documents about the 1938 voyage of the *St. Louis*, especially transcripts of phone conversations between Secretary of Treasury Henry Morgenthau, Jr., and Secretary of State Cordell Hull; Louise Kashino, who kindly granted permission to reprint a family photo of her husband, Shiro Kashino; Vince Matsudaira, who furnished a copy of his splendid documentary film about Shiro "Kash" Kashino and the 442nd Regimental Combat Team; Robert Asahina for his guidance in locating sources about Japanese Americans during World War II; filmmaker George Johnston for providing a copy of his documentary film about the 442nd Regimental Combat Team; Howard Hieshima of the Chicago Nisei Post of the American Legion for assistance in locating veterans of the 442nd Regimental Combat Team; and Bonnie and John Raines for granting a lengthy personal interview about their 1971 burglary of a Pennsylvania FBI office.

We extend our appreciation to Dr. Margaret Crocco, chairperson of the Department of Teacher Education at Michigan State University, for her encouragement of this project and to the Department of Teacher Education staff for its support of our writing. Our heartfelt appreciation also goes to Amanda Slaten Frasier and Maria Siciliano for their tireless and rigorous assistance with manuscript preparation.

We are deeply grateful to the staff of Teachers College Press at Teachers College/Columbia University, in particular Carole Saltz and Peter Sclafani, for initially supporting this project and guiding us thoughtfully as it progressed.

Finally, we acknowledge the support, patience, and encouragement of our families and friends who helped to sustain us during more than 4 years of research and writing.

David Harris, Anne-Lise Halvorsen, and Paul Dain

Dear Reader,

This book is intended to enrich study of American history. We have written true stories showing people making difficult decisions. These decisions involved basic values such as authority, the common good, diversity, equality, liberty, life, loyalty, promise keeping, property, and truth. We invite you to follow the stories of these decisions and make judgments about them.

In this volume there are 19 chapters. Each presents a story that brings you in contact with an ethical issue from U.S. history. For example, you will follow as journalist Nellie Bly falsifies her identity to investigate conditions for mental patients at Bellevue Hospital in New York. You will decide whether President Woodrow Wilson should have brought the United States into World War I. You will be a bystander as Michigan Governor Frank Murphy grapples with the General Motors sit-down strike. You will witness film director Elia Kazan's testimony before the House Committee on Un-American Activities during which he identified communists in the Hollywood film industry. You will accompany Bonnie and John Raines as they burglarize an FBI office in Pennsylvania. You will consider whether the U.S. government should pay reparations to African Americans.

Although these events took place in the past, the values continue to influence our lives. We believe that citizens of today must often make decisions involving the same values. That is why we have written this book.

Rational, responsible citizens face value issues and think carefully about them. Therefore, we have presented you with learning activities that will engage you in such thinking. Answers to these activities are presented in the Instructor's Manual for *Reasoning with Democratic Values 2.0*, available as an ebook from Teachers College Press.

More information about the Instructor's Manual, including samples of its content, and other aspects of *Reasoning with Democratic Values 2.0* is available on the website for these books at: www.rdv2.org.

We hope that you will enjoy the stories and gain a deeper understanding of the nation's remarkable history from reading and thinking about them.

Sincerely,
David Harris, Anne-Lise Halvorsen, and Paul Dain

Part VI

RECONSTRUCTION AND THE GILDED AGE
1866–1890

CHAPTER 21

Pioneer Suffragists

Elizabeth Cady Stanton, Susan B. Anthony, and Universal Suffrage

Elizabeth Cady Stanton and Susan B. Anthony

Courtesy of the Library of Congress.

Women in the United States finally won the right to vote in 1920. This long story has roots in Kansas. As a territory and then a state, Kansas played an important role in the history of voting rights for women and for African American men. The slave versus free state battle in the Kansas Territory, before statehood, foreshadowed The Civil War. After becoming a state in 1861, Kansas was the scene of the debate on citizenship rights prior to the passage of the Fourteenth Amendment (1868) and the Fifteenth Amendment (1870) to the U.S. Constitution. These amendments guaranteed formerly enslaved men the right to vote. Women, of any color, had to wait until passage of the Nineteenth Amendment in 1920 for the right to vote. Two of the reformers who fought for women's rights in the early and late 19th century were Elizabeth Cady Stanton and Susan B. Anthony.

The importance of Kansas in the great affairs of the nation began in 1854. In that year the U.S. Congress passed the Kansas-Nebraska Act that created two new territories from Indian lands: Kansas and Nebraska. The act gave the people in those territories the right to choose whether they would allow slavery. The choice was provided through popular sovereignty ("rule by the people"), the principle that the government's authority is created and sustained by the consent of its people. However, slavery had been illegal in this area since 1820, when the Missouri Compromise prohibited slavery in prospective states anywhere north of the 36° 30' parallel (this formed the boundary between Missouri and Arkansas).

The 1854 act plunged the nation into violent controversy. Kansas became a battleground over slavery. Most Southern Democrats welcomed an opportunity to extend slavery into the Kansas Territory. Most northern Republicans protest-ed opening Kansas to slavery. Antislavery northern emigrants from free states founded antislavery towns. Proslavery southern emigrants founded settlements that allowed slavery. Violence between the groups soon erupted in a series of bat-tles in what became known as Bleeding Kansas (or the Border War). The violence between the two sides continued in Kansas until 1859. In 1861, on the eve of The Civil War, the "free staters" achieved a hard-won victory when Kansas was admitted to the Union as a free state.

Bleeding Kansas in the 1850s heated up the debate on voting rights as well as human rights. During the Reconstruction period following The Civil War, the antislavery group (the abolitionists) insisted on suffrage for former male slaves (freedmen). *Suffrage* is the term for the right to vote. Some abolitionists even called for universal suffrage when they demanded that women, both Black and White, should be allowed to vote. *Universal suffrage* is the term for the right to vote for all, regardless of race, religion, property, gender, income, or other restrictions.

African American men had gained the right to vote in some states during the Revolutionary War with Great Britain. New York and North Carolina granted the vote to free African American men who met certain voting qualifications. African American men who owned property routinely voted in elections. The constitu-tions of Maine, Massachusetts, New Hampshire, and Vermont also granted the right to vote to freedmen. However, practice did not always follow law. In 1840, 93% of freedmen still lived in northern states that banned or restricted their right to vote.

Around the time of The Civil War, some states held a referendum (a di-rect vote by the electorate on a particular proposal) on African American men's suffrage. Voters in Minnesota and Iowa approved referendums in 1868 that gave African American men the right to vote.

With few exceptions, women still could not vote. One exception was the state of New Jersey. New Jersey's constitution of 1776 enfranchised all adult property owners (men and women). New Jersey laws passed in 1790 and 1797 referred to voters as "he or she." But in 1807, the New Jersey legislature reversed its earlier laws and took away the right to vote from women and African American men.

Eventually, the U.S. Congress took up the voting issue to bring some order to this legislative chaos. The Fourteenth Amendment, adopted in 1868, addressed voting in Section 2. It reversed the Constitution's three-fifths clause and declared that if the right to vote was "denied to any of the male inhabitants of such state, being twenty-one years of age, and citizens of the United States the basis of representation therein shall be reduced in the proportion which the number of such male citizens shall bear to the whole number of male citizens twenty-one years of age in such state." In other words, states would be penalized for denying the right to vote to African American men with a reduction of representatives in Congress.

Once again, however, practice did not always follow the law. Local and state restrictions still prevented African American men from voting in any elections. In response, in 1870, the U.S. Congress adopted the Fifteenth Amendment that states "the right of citizens of the United States to vote shall not be denied or abridged by the United States or by any State on account of race, color, or previous condition of servitude." The Fourteenth Amendment specifically mentioned "male citizens" regarding these rights. African American men had gained suffrage, but women still had not. Would women ever gain enfranchisement—that is, citizenship rights, especially the right to vote?

Kansas is an interesting case in the struggle for women's suffrage. No state had universal suffrage in 1867 when Kansas held the country's first referendum on women's right to vote and on African American men's right to vote. The electorate voted on two amendments to the constitution that the state legislature had approved: The first amendment proposed to eliminate the word *male* from the clause defining the qualifications of an elector. The second amendment proposed to eliminate the word *White* from the clause defining the qualifications of an elector. The voters (all White men) defeated both amendments.

In the campaign before this vote, interested groups in Kansas took sides on the two amendments, some in favor, others opposed. When the abolitionists who had fought so bravely against slavery during the years of Bleeding Kansas provided no support, two female activists from the American Equal Rights Association, an organization devoted to securing rights for all people, traveled from New York to Kansas to speak up for women's suffrage: Elizabeth Cady Stanton and Susan B. Anthony.

Elizabeth Cady Stanton (1815–1902) was born into a wealthy New York family. Her father, Daniel Cady, was a prominent lawyer and judge. From reading her father's law books and talking to his law clerks, Elizabeth took an early interest in the law. She was particularly interested in how few legal rights women had. Women could not own property, had no income of their own when it was accrued, and had no employment outside the home. Separated and divorced women had no custody rights to their children.

Until slavery was outlawed in 1827 in New York, many wealthy New York families, including the Cady family, used enslaved men and women for household work and child care. One of these enslaved people, Peter Teabout, took care of Elizabeth and her sister. In later years Elizabeth remembered that as a child she sat with him in the "Negro pew" of her church. Yet in all her work with women's voting, property, and income rights, Stanton never mentioned the celebrations that occurred on July 4, 1827, when African Americans, including Peter Teabout, were given their freedom in the state of New York. While she participated in abolitionist causes, her main lifelong interest was women's rights.

In 1840, Elizabeth Cady, age 24, married Henry Brewster Stanton, an abolitionist, lawyer, and journalist. Even at this young age, it was clear she had modern views on marriage. She refused to repeat the word *obey* in her wedding vows. She always insisted that she be known as Elizabeth Cady Stanton rather than Mrs. Henry Stanton.

Five years after Stanton was born, Susan B. Anthony (1820–1906) was born in Massachusetts to a Quaker farm family who owned a cotton factory. A story from her early childhood reveals her precocious attitude toward the rights of women. After watching the millworkers at the factory, she said to her father: "If Sally Ann knows more about weaving than Elijah, then why don't you make her overseer?" Her father replied that the millworkers would never accept a woman overseer.

There were more such experiences and stories. As a young teacher, Anthony was shocked to learn she was paid only one-fourth as much as the male teacher she had replaced. While still a teacher, she began to study algebra, a subject most people thought unfit for women. One evening, after she served homemade biscuits at dinner, her brother-in-law pointedly remarked: "I'd rather see a woman make biscuits like these than solve the knottiest problem in algebra." Anthony thought women could do both.

Gradually, Anthony developed a deep concern about the inferior legal status of women. She read newspaper accounts of the first women's rights convention, held in Seneca Falls, New York, in 1848. At the convention, 100 of the attendees signed the "Declaration of Sentiments," which called for the advancement of women. Anthony was particularly interested in Elizabeth Cady Stanton's demand for women's suffrage. As Anthony thought more about women's inability to own or inherit property, to enroll in college, and to claim joint custody of children, she came to a radical conclusion for the time. The only way to change these laws was to give women the right to vote.

Elizabeth Cady Stanton and Susan B. Anthony first met in 1851 at an anniversary meeting of the Seneca Falls Convention. This meeting was the beginning of a lifelong friendship. Although the two had very different backgrounds, they shared the same passion for women's rights.

The two women had a professional relationship as well as a warm friendship. Together they founded and led the American Equal Rights Association. From its founding in 1866, the association supported universal suffrage that would give African American men and all women the right to vote. Anthony also worked at the American Antislavery Society in New York. For 10 dollars a week, she arranged meetings, hung posters, and planned tours for the speakers.

During The Civil War, the country naturally focused more on slavery than on women's rights. In 1863, Stanton and Anthony founded an antislavery organization, the Women's Loyal National League. The league presented its antislavery petition, with almost 400,000 signatures, to the U.S. Congress. The petition is credited with helping pass the Thirteenth Amendment (adopted in 1865) that abolished slavery. The league was the country's first national women's political group.

The various activities by women during The Civil War bolstered Stanton and Anthony's suffragist movement. Many women, in both the North and the South, had to manage family farms and businesses when their husbands and sons enlisted as soldiers. Other women played a direct role in the conduct of the war. Anne E. Carroll advised President Lincoln on a military campaign. Dorothea Dix, the superintendent of army nurses for the Union Army, managed a large group of women nurses. Clara Barton, a hospital nurse during the war, founded the American Red Cross. Susie King Taylor, an African American who joined the 33rd Regiment of the First South Carolina Volunteers, worked as a nurse, laundress, and performed clerical duties.

Anthony, Stanton, and many others thought these wartime activities earned women the right to vote. Women had done "man's work," and had done it well. Yet women were advised to be patient. After The Civil War, it was the "hour of the Negro" ("Negro," though now outdated and considered offensive, was then a polite way to refer to people of African descent). Women must wait their turn as freed men were guaranteed citizenship and the right to vote.

The advocates for women's suffrage used four major legal strategies in their struggle: (1) legislative campaigning (i.e., working to change laws) at both the federal and state levels; (2) registering to vote and casting ballots by women, which was prohibited by law; (3) proposing a U.S. Constitutional Amendment instituting suffrage; and (4) litigating women's rights under the Fourteenth Amendment. Anthony and Stanton and the American Equal Rights Association worked with the first strategy at the state level.

They began in 1867 in Kansas where, along with the famous abolitionist and suffragist Lucy Stone, they campaigned for the two amendments to the state constitution on women's and African American men's suffrage described above. Not all abolitionists supported women's rights, but Stanton and Anthony supported universal suffrage for every citizen, regardless of race or gender. Campaigning in

Kansas was tough. Funds were low, travel by open carriage was slow and hazard-ous, and resistance was strong. As women from upper-class families, they found the rugged frontier life in Kansas a challenge. Drawing upon her diary, in her autobiography, Stanton reported that they ate "bacon floating in grease, coffee without milk . . . and bread or hot biscuit, green with soda." Often, they slept among bedbugs, pigs, or mice.

In addition to these challenges, Anthony had to overcome the stereotype people had of suffragists as meddlesome, sour old maids. When people met her, they formed a different opinion. She wore an elegant silk dress with a white lace collar and twisted her hair into a tidy knot. More important, she did not lecture her audiences. She spoke to them as equals.

Opponents of women's suffrage offered the same old arguments:

- God created separate roles for men and women.
- Women were already represented by men.
- Women were not strong enough for the physical tasks required of citizens (for example, military service and heavy labor).
- Women's work was the home and family, not "politicking" activities.
- Women were pure and delicate creatures, unsuited for the rough and tumble political world.

Partway through the Kansas campaign for universal suffrage, the support-ers' money ran out. Desperately, they wired George Francis Train, a Democrat in Omaha, for help: "Come to Kansas and stump the state for equal rights and female suffrage. The people want you. The women want you." Train replied by wire in colorful language:

> Right, Truth, Justice is bound to win. Men made laws, disfranchising Idiots, Lunatics, Paupers, Minors, and added Women as junior partner in the firm. The wedge once inserted in Kansas we will populate the nation with three millions *[sic]* voting women. Shall be with you as soon as our Editorial Party have shot their Buffalo, and seen the Rocky Mountains. Nebraska already allows women to vote in School Committee. If women can rule monarchies they should vote in republics.

Anthony replied the same day: "God bless you. Begin at Leavenworth Monday, Oct. 21st. Yes, with your help we shall triumph."

George Francis Train is an unusual character in the story of women's suffrage. He had made a huge fortune as an entrepreneur, financier, clipper-ship builder, and railroad promoter. Because he thought he might run for the U.S. presidency, he may have seen the Kansas campaign as an opportunity to raise his national pro-file. Train was very controversial, however. He was openly racist—he supported White women's suffrage but opposed suffrage for African American men.

Some suspected that Train's support for women's suffrage was insincere. He thought women's votes could offset the votes of African American men. He said: "Now black freemen have all power except the ballot. Give them that . . . and what chance has woman after?" and "Women first, and negro last, is my programme."

Although he raised money (as much as $3,000, or about $50,000 in today's dollars) and drew large crowds, his racism sickened Stanton and Anthony. They were abolitionists of long standing. Their friend and associate, Lucy Stone, threatened to resign from the American Equal Rights Association if Anthony and Stanton agreed to join Train on a statewide lecture tour. The prominent abolitionist William Lloyd Garrison claimed that Anthony and Stanton had lost their senses.

Eventually, Anthony and Stanton allied with the Kansas Democratic Party that supported enfranchisement for women but not for freedmen. In any case, Stanton now began to advocate more for women's voting rights than for the voting rights of freedmen and immigrants.

When both Kansas amendments were defeated at the polls, blame was quickly assigned. George Train was blamed. The linkage of the two suffrage issues was blamed. Yet one result was encouraging: One-third of the (White male) voters supported women's suffrage.

Another important public event in the battle for women's suffrage occurred in Rochester, New York, in 1872. Four days before Election Day, Anthony and several women tried to register to vote. After some resistance, they were allowed to register. Anthony then went door to door, urging other women to register. On Election Day, Anthony voted for Ulysses S. Grant for president. However, a federal marshal arrested her 3 weeks later for "criminal voting." She was tried, convicted, and fined without a jury trial. She refused to pay her bail to get out of jail. She said she would rather go to jail than pay the fine. When her lawyer secretly paid her bail, she was released. In an act of civil disobedience, she never paid the fine.

Anthony and Stanton led the National Woman Suffrage Association (NWSA), which had been formed in 1869 in New York after a policy split in the American Equal Rights Association over the Fifteenth Amendment. Anthony and Stanton, who led the NWSA, opposed the Fifteenth Amendment that gave African American men but not women the right to vote (they had also opposed the Fourteenth Amendment because of its inclusion of the word *male*, but they had not mobilized opposition to this amendment). They said the Thirteenth and Fourteenth Amendments granted African American men sufficient legal protections (given that the Fourteenth Amendment guaranteed enfranchisement to Black males). They argued that the Fourteenth and Fifteenth Amendments should be rewritten to include women's suffrage. Stanton wrote: "The prejudice against color, of which we hear so much, is no stronger than that against sex. It is produced by the same cause, and manifested very much in the same way."

Yet it is undeniable that Stanton's rhetoric became increasingly racist. She began to argue that women of wealth and education should use their votes to offset the votes of freedmen and immigrants. Some scholars claim that Stanton's emphasis on an "educated" body of voters was partly responsible for the adoption of voting literacy requirements in states in the South. For many years, African Americans who did not pass these literacy tests, often made more difficult for them, sometimes impossibly so, were not allowed to vote.

Civil rights leaders including Frederick Douglass criticized Stanton's views on the educated voter. Douglass also thought it was sufficient that fathers, husbands, and brothers, who could vote, represented mothers, wives, and sisters. Years later, Anthony said she regretted that her dear friend Stanton had taken this position on educated suffrage.

Other women followed in the two women's footsteps. In 1868, in Vineland, New Jersey, a group of 172 women, both Black and White, went to the polls—illegally—on Election Day. In 1870, the antislavery feminists Sarah and Angelina Grimke cast their votes in Hyde Park, Massachusetts. Between 1870 and 1872, over 100 women tried to register and vote in the District of Columbia and in the states of New Hampshire, Michigan, and California. When they were turned away from the polls, these women challenged the voting systems in the courts. For years, they were unsuccessful. From Pennsylvania to Illinois to California, the courts ruled against women's suffrage. It seemed little real progress was made on women's suffrage in 19th-century America.

Anthony and Stanton continued to work for women's suffrage. But they did not live to see their dream of women's suffrage realized.

When Elizabeth Cady Stanton and Susan B. Anthony died, in 1902 and 1906, respectively, women could vote in only four states: Wyoming, Utah, Colorado, and Idaho. A few years before her death, Anthony was asked if she thought all women in the United States would ever have the right to vote. She replied: "It will come, but I shall not see it. It is inevitable. We can no more deny forever the right of self-government to one half our people than we could keep the Negro forever in bondage."

Stanton and Anthony, whom historian Geoffrey Ward and filmmaker Ken Burns referred to as the two "uncompromising revolutionaries," died before all women age 21 and older gained the right to vote in the United States. In 1920, the Nineteenth Amendment, which enfranchised women, was adopted. More than 70 years after the 1848 Seneca Falls Convention, the women's suffrage movement had finally achieved the goal that Elizabeth Cady Stanton, Susan B. Anthony, and many others dreamed of.

The major sources for this chapter were:

Dubois, E. C. (1975). *A new life: The development of an American women's suffrage movement, 1860–1869* (Unpublished doctoral dissertation). Northeastern University, Boston, MA.

Ginzburg, L. D. (2009). *Elizabeth Cady Stanton: An American life*. New York, NY: Farrar, Straus, Giroux.

Holland, P. G. (1987). George Francis Train and the Woman Suffrage Movement, 1867–70. *Books at Iowa* 46, 8–29. Available at http://digital.lib.uiowa.edu/bai/holland.htm

Lutz, A. (1959). *Susan B. Anthony*. Boston, MA: Beacon Press.

Madsen, S. A. (1975). *The 1867 campaign for women's suffrage in Kansas: A study in rhetorical situation* (Unpublished doctoral dissertation). University of Kansas, Lawrence, KS.

National Public Radio. (July 13, 2011). For Stanton, all women were not created equal. Available at http://www.npr.org/2011/07/13/137681070/for-stanton-all-women-were-not-created-equal

Stanton, E. C., Anthony, S. B., & Gage, M. J. (Eds) (1882). *History of Women Suffrage*, Vol. 2, *1862–1876*. New York, NY: Fowler and Wells.

Ward, G. C., & Burns, K. (1999). *Not for ourselves alone: The story of Elizabeth Cady Stanton and Susan B. Anthony*. New York, NY: Alfred A. Knopf.

LEARNING ACTIVITIES FOR "PIONEER SUFFRAGISTS"

Facts of the Case

1. What were the two constitutional amendments voted on in the Kansas referendum?
2. What was the American Equal Rights Association, and what position did it take on the issue of suffrage?
3. Describe George Francis Train's role in the women's suffrage movement in Kansas.
4. Summarize the main provisions of the Thirteenth, Fourteenth, Fifteenth, and Nineteenth Amendments.

Historical Understanding

1. What effect did popular sovereignty have on the Missouri Compromise?
2. Why was Kansas referred to as Bleeding Kansas?
3. After The Civil War, what was the major political goal of the former abolitionists?
4. Why did many Republicans and former abolitionists withhold their support for women's suffrage after The Civil War?
5. What role did the Seneca Falls Convention have in the women's suffrage movement?

Expressing Your Reasoning

Should Susan Anthony and Elizabeth Cady Stanton have supported the adoption of the Fifteenth Amendment to the U.S. Constitution? Why or why not?

Key Concepts from History

What do the following have in common?

1. In 2015, 21 transgender women were murdered in the United States. Nearly all of them were women of color.
2. Latinas in the United States earn less money than White women and Latinos.
3. The death rate for poor White Americans is increasing at the same time it is falling for other groups. Among poor White Americans, the death rate is particularly high for those who are middle-aged with a high school education or less. The death rate increased by 134 deaths for every 100,000 people over the 14-year span from 1999 and 2013, compared to very little change among people with at least some college education.

Historical Inquiry

Are women currently denied the right to vote in any countries? Using online and other sources, test the hypothesis that women are denied the right to vote in some countries. Compose a short essay in which you accept or reject the hypothesis. Use evidence to support your conclusion. To begin your investigation, the following search terms will be helpful:

- Universal suffrage
- Women's suffrage

CHAPTER 22

The Last Battle of The Civil War
The Presidential Election of 1876

"A National Game That Is Played Out," Thomas Nast

A NATIONAL GAME THAT IS PLAYED OUT.

Harper's Weekly, December 23, 1876.

The Civil War began in 1861 and lasted until 1865 when President Andrew Johnson officially declared an end to the war. Vice President Johnson had become president upon the assassination of Abraham Lincoln on April 14, 1865. Although fighting had ended between Confederate and Union forces, a monumental task of reuniting and rebuilding the nation lay before the officials and political institutions of the United States.

The period following The Civil War is known as the Reconstruction Era. Reconstruction can be considered to have begun in 1863, even before the war's end, when President Lincoln issued the Emancipation Proclamation. The proclamation declared that all slaves living in the rebellious states were free. Also during 1863, Lincoln announced a plan to create governments in the southern states that were loyal to the Union.

Reconstruction ended shortly after the presidential election of 1876. Some historians refer to that contested election between Rutherford B. Hayes and Samuel J. Tilden as the last battle of The Civil War. The issues surrounding that presidential election were rooted in The Civil War and in the politics and policies of Reconstruction.

Union commander Ulysses S. Grant and President Abraham Lincoln both believed that The Civil War could be brought to an end only by a dedication to total war. This meant both fighting deadly battles and destroying the infrastructure of the Confederate States. As a result, many farms, homes, and railroads in the South were destroyed by Union troops.

In 1863, Lincoln favored moderate policies that would rebuild the South after the war and integrate the Confederate states and their citizens back into the Union. In March 1865, in his Second Inaugural Address, President Lincoln reflected on the need for conciliation with these enduring words:

> With malice toward none, with charity for all, with firmness in the right as God gives us to see the right, let us strive on to finish the work we are in, to bind up the nation's wounds, to care for him who shall have borne the battle and for his widow and his orphan, to do all which may achieve and cherish a just and lasting peace among ourselves and with all nations.

Not all members of Congress agreed with the conciliatory and moderate vision of the president. Within Lincoln's own Republican Party, there was a growing faction known as Radical Republicans. They favored harsh and punitive policies toward the former Confederate states.

Following Lincoln's assassination in 1865, and the end of the war, President Johnson attempted to continue a moderate approach to Reconstruction. In the election of 1866, however, the Radical Republicans gained control of their party in Congress. Over the objections of President Johnson, they passed laws that removed former Confederates from office in the South.

Radical Republicans favored full freedom, citizenship, and constitutional equality for African Americans. They established a Freedmen's Bureau to help the formerly enslaved adjust to freedom. The bureau sought to protect the legal rights of all African Americans. In addition, it assisted in establishing churches and schools for former slaves.

President Johnson's veto of the Civil Rights Act of 1866 was overridden by Congress. The act declared that all persons born in the United States were citizens regardless of their race, color, or previous condition of servitude.

The Radical Republicans were successful in enacting measures that removed civilian governments from the former Confederate states. The U.S. Army troops stationed in the southern states during Reconstruction protected newly formed state governments and oversaw elections in which Black citizens could vote and run for public office. Former Confederate officials were temporarily denied the right to vote or hold public office. As a result of these measures, 10 southern states had biracial governments with Black and White people both serving in elected positions for the first time.

In 1869, Ulysses S. Grant was elected as the 18th president of the United States. Like his two predecessors, he was a Republican. Grant would serve two full terms as president. He supported Radical Reconstruction (policies and laws favored by the Radical Republicans). President Grant used federal troops to enforce the laws enacted by Congress under Radical Republican control.

White supremacists, including the Ku Klux Klan (KKK), sought to deny equality to Black people. The KKK terrorized thousands of African Americans by committing rape, robbery, arson, and murder. The Grant administration used the Enforcement Acts to curtail racial violence and intimidation against Black Americans. These acts were passed in 1870 and 1871 by Congress to ensure equal protection of the law.

Southern White Republicans who supported the harsh Reconstruction policies of the Radical Republicans became known as Scalawags. Unlike so-called Carpetbaggers, who came from the North to help with Reconstruction (or to find less than honorable ways of enriching themselves), Scalawags were southerners. They fell out of favor among the White population, and southern Democrats grew in numbers and popularity.

In 1874, the Democratic Party gained control of the U.S. House of Representatives. A deep economic depression known as the Panic of 1873 had caused congressional Republicans to lose votes. Southern Democrats were also aided in the congressional elections by some northerners who had grown weary of Reconstruction. They argued that The Civil War was over and that slavery had ended, so it was time to leave the southern states to manage themselves.

As Republican congressional control ended, federal troops were gradually withdrawn from most, but not all, states in the South. White southerners used their newly regained legal and political power against African Americans by employing violence, discrimination, and intimidation. Hopes for Reconstruction with reconciliation faded.

In 1876, President Grant was serving his final presidential year. The Republican Party continued to have a majority in the Senate. The Democratic Party was enjoying its second year with a majority in the House of Representatives. The two major political parties prepared to nominate their candidates for the presidential election of 1876.

At their national convention, the Democrats nominated Samuel J. Tilden, the governor of New York, as their presidential candidate.

Samuel Tilden was born in 1814 to a politically active family in New Lebanon, New Jersey. He briefly attended Yale University before he entered law school at New York University. After graduating from law school, he became corporate counsel for New York City. Later, he grew wealthy from a highly successful law practice. Although an opponent of slavery, he had opposed Lincoln's candidacy in 1860, because he thought it would lead to the secession of southern states from the Union. Tilden went on to serve as the Democratic Party chair in New York and was elected governor in 1874.

Tilden was well known as a governor who fought corruption. Before his election, he had successfully opposed the corrupt New York City Democratic political machine, known as Tammany Hall and led by the notoriously powerful "Boss" Tweed. He was well positioned to be the Democratic candidate for president. President Grant's administration was rife with corruption. Seven cabinet departments had officials charged and convicted of fraud. It helped that Tilden was from a large state that had 35 electoral votes—the most of any state. In the 1876 election there were 369 electoral votes; a majority of 185 was needed for election. His wealth also enabled Tilden to spend large sums in support of his candidacy.

The Republican Party nominated Ohio Governor Rutherford B. Hayes as its presidential candidate. Hayes was born in 1822 in Delaware, Ohio. His father died 10 weeks before his birth. Hayes and his sister were raised by their mother. He entered Kenyon College at age 16 before attending Harvard Law School. After law school, he returned to Ohio as a lawyer. He despised slavery and defended fugitive slaves as their lawyer. Hayes became active in local politics and started the Republican Party in Cincinnati.

At age 30, Hayes married Lucy Webb. He worked for Lincoln's election as president in 1860. He volunteered to serve in The Civil War, and he was promoted from captain to lieutenant colonel and then to brigadier general. He participated in numerous battles and was wounded four times.

After the war, Hayes was elected to Congress from Ohio. As a member of Congress, he voted for the Fourteenth and Fifteenth Amendments. The Fourteenth Amendment to the United States Constitution addressed citizenship rights and equal protection of the law. The Fifteenth Amendment prohibited the denial of the vote on the basis of race, color, or a previous condition of servitude. These two Reconstruction Amendments to the U.S. Constitution were not popular in Ohio. Nonetheless, in 1867, Hayes ran for governor and was narrowly elected. Again by narrow margins, he was elected to two additional terms as governor.

At the 1876 Republican National Convention, after six ballots, Hayes finally received the necessary majority of delegate votes and was nominated as the Republican presidential candidate.

Tilden supported home rule for the three southern states of Florida, Louisiana, and South Carolina. They were the only three southern states remaining with federal troops protecting Republican-controlled state governments. Home rule for these states would mean withdrawal of those troops.

The 1876 presidential election was held on Tuesday, November 7. The winner of the popular vote in a state would receive all the electoral votes from that state. Each state had (and still has) electoral votes equal to its number of U.S. representatives plus its two senators.

The winner of the presidential election would be the candidate who received a majority of all electoral votes. There were 369 electoral votes in 1876. A simple majority of 185 was needed for election.

In the southern states of Florida, Louisiana, and South Carolina, the vote was too close to call. (In 1876, Florida had four electoral votes, Louisiana eight, and South Carolina seven.) Minus the disputed electoral votes in these three states and one electoral vote in dispute in Oregon, it appeared that Tilden had 184 electoral votes to Hayes's 166. Tilden was one vote short of the necessary electoral vote majority.

Hayes thought he had lost. He supposed that Tilden would win one or more of the three southern states that were still too close to call. On the night of the election, Tilden and his supporters were convinced they had won.

By chance, retired colonel Daniel Sickles, a Hayes supporter, but not a party official, decided after a night at the theater to stop by the Republican headquarters in New York City and check on the election returns. His calculations indicated that Hayes could win if he won Florida, Louisiana, and South Carolina. He telegraphed the party leaders in each of these states with this message: "With your state sure for Hayes, he is elected. Hold your state."

Lawyers and officials from both parties descended on the three states in question. Votes in each state were sent to their respective state election boards to verify their accuracy. The Republican Party had a majority of members on all three election boards. There were allegations that Democrats had prevented African Americans from voting in parts of the three states. There were countercharges by Democrats who accused the Republican-dominated election boards of not counting votes fairly. The historical evidence indicates that these allegations of both parties were true. Both parties also offered bribes and promised patronage to influence election officials.

In each of the three undecided states, the Republican-controlled election boards threw out enough Tilden votes to give Hayes the victory.

The Republican electors in the three states cast their votes for Hayes and, in each of the states, a Republican governor certified the legitimacy of the Hayes win. Each of the governors sent certificates to Congress confirming the electoral votes of their states. In Florida, South Carolina, and Louisiana, however, officials representing the Democrats sent competing electoral certificates awarding the states to Tilden.

To add to the electoral turmoil, a dispute over one electoral vote erupted in Oregon. Competing electoral certificates were sent to the United States Senate from Oregon, one by the Democratic governor and one by the state's secretary of state. With Tilden just one electoral vote short of a majority, the dispute in Oregon was important.

Two days before the electoral votes were to be cast, the U.S. Senate and House of Representatives each selected a committee to investigate the allegations in the disputed states. Both committees visited each of the states and took testimony. The Republican-controlled Senate committee ruled in favor of Hayes. The Democratic-controlled House of Representatives committee ruled in favor of Tilden.

The Twelfth Amendment to the Constitution requires the electoral votes to be opened and counted by the president of the U.S. Senate before a joint session of Congress. The Constitution does not provide guidance regarding what to do if there are competing electoral vote returns from a state.

A joint committee of Congress was established to find a solution. The committee proposed an electoral commission consisting of five Democratic members of Congress, five Republican members, and five justices of the Supreme Court. The commission would hear arguments from both sides of each state's disputed electoral returns.

After hearing these arguments, the commission would rule separately on each of the four states. A vote of eight of the 15 members would constitute a majority decision. The commission's decision in each of the four disputes would automatically be accepted by Congress unless it were rejected by a majority vote of both houses—an unlikely event considering each house was controlled by a different party. Both the House and the Senate approved the bill that was proposed by the joint congressional committee, thus establishing the Electoral Commission.

The appointment of five congressional Republicans and five congressional Democrats to the Electoral Commission was accomplished without a problem. Four of the five Supreme Court justices to be appointed were two Republicans and two Democrats. One additional justice was to be selected by these four justices. (Although Supreme Court justices are not identified formally as Republicans or Democrats, their political identification is usually well known because of the political party of the president who nominated them.)

The other justices selected Joseph P. Bradley as the fifth justice on the commission. The justices believed that even though Bradley had been appointed to the Supreme Court by Grant, he was still the least partisan of the remaining pool of justices.

The Electoral Commission began its work, as directed by law, in February 1877. Both Republican and Democratic lawyers presented arguments. Then lawyers for the commission made presentations. Once this process was completed, the 15-member commission discussed and then voted on the disputed electoral votes.

The Florida electoral vote dispute was the first to reach the commission. It quickly became evident that the central issue of all the disputes would be the scope of authority of the Electoral Commission. Democrats argued for allowing outside evidence to be introduced to probe whether the various state electoral boards had acted properly in rejecting certain votes. The Republicans argued against allowing outside evidence to be introduced. They believed it would lead to endless allegations that would delay or prevent resolution of the election disputes.

States' rights arguments were vigorously advanced. Traditionally, the Democratic Party was viewed as being more protective of the right of states to manage their own affairs. Republicans were viewed as the party that supported a more expansive authority for the national government.

Within the Electoral Commission these positions were reversed. The Republicans maintained that the states' certified election results should be respected, and that the federal government could only intervene if the certificates were forged or there were inaccuracies in the counting of the electoral votes by state election boards. The Democrats argued that the commission should be open to inquiring whether there had been electoral fraud or misconduct behind any given dispute.

After the commission heard the Florida arguments, each congressional member expressed his view regarding the arguments presented. The five justices then stated their opinions.

Justice Bradley's opinion was the most anticipated, because the opinions of the other 14 commission members divided evenly along party lines. Bradley stated that the Constitution did not allow the federal government to examine the vote within a state, or to count a state's electoral vote. He added that any challenges to a state's election boards had to be made before the electors actually voted on December 6. The commission's vote was eight to seven for not permitting outside evidence to be introduced. This decision ensured that Florida's electoral votes would go to Hayes. Bradley sided with the Republicans on the commission regarding the disputes in all four states.

Justice Bradley's vote was questioned by Tilden supporters, who alleged that he had suspiciously changed his opinion from supporting Tilden's arguments to those of Hayes. There is no historical evidence proving this; in replying to the allegations that he had reversed his position, Bradley acknowledged that he had written down arguments supporting both Tilden and Hayes. He explained that he had done this to clarify his thinking toward a correct decision. He firmly denied having received any visitors during the night in question.

The disputes in Louisiana and South Carolina were also decided in favor of Hayes by an eight to seven vote. The same reasoning was used: The commission could not permit going back to each state to obtain evidence of electoral fraud. Hayes would later be scornfully nicknamed "Old 8 to 7," "His Fraudulency," and "Rutherfraud B. Hayes, the Great Usurper." *The New York Sun* wrote, "A man whom the people rejected at the polls has been declared President of the United States through a process of fraud. A cheat is to sit in the seat of George Washington."

House Democrats believed the election had been stolen from Tilden, and Democrats representing the South threatened to delay or prevent a vote approving the commission's findings in favor of Hayes.

During December, January, and February, discussions took place between Hayes supporters and southern Democrats. In what is referred to as the Compromise of 1877, there were informal agreements, or understandings, made between southern Democrats and Hayes supporters. The agreements or understandings were made over a period of several weeks both before the commission began its work and after it had made its final decisions. This was done without the direct participation of Hayes, but he was kept well informed of events as they transpired.

Some moderate southern Democrats expected that a Hayes victory was inevitable, especially after Justice Bradley announced his decision in the Florida dispute. They were hoping to garner assurances that Hayes would look out for the interests of the South. In exchange, they were willing to allow an Electoral Commission ruling in favor of Hayes.

On the night of February 26, four southern Democrats met with five Republicans from Ohio at the Wormley House hotel in Washington, D.C. Hayes confidants announced that Hayes was ready to recognize the legitimacy of the newly elected Democratic governors in Louisiana and South Carolina. Southern Democrats in return relayed messages from Democrats in Louisiana that there would be no retribution against Republicans in their state and that the new state governments would pledge to recognize the political and civil rights of Blacks.

The terms of the unofficial compromise are elusive. There was no act of Congress, and there are no documents that outlined the elements of any bargain. The bargain did provide that in the House of Representatives a vote would be permitted that approved the commission's rulings in favor of Hayes. In exchange, federal troops would be withdrawn to their barracks in Louisiana and South Carolina, the only two states where they were still stationed. This meant the troops would no longer be present to protect the Republican-controlled state legislatures in those two states and the newly elected Democratic governors would take office. In addition, at least one southern Democrat would be included in the Hayes cabinet, Hayes would support a southern transcontinental railroad from Texas to the Pacific coast, and he would support legislation to help industrialize the South.

The central issue in the overlapping negotiations and agreements between the two sides was home rule for the southern states. The removal of troops from Louisiana and South Carolina cleared the way for home rule for all the southern states. Southern Democrats believed home rule would permit them to regain control of all the southern state governments. Behind the drive for home rule lay the belief of many Democrats that the Reconstruction policies had been a failure and that compromise over the electoral crisis was a convenient opportunity to bring an end to Reconstruction.

The promises made on behalf of Hayes made it clear that the new president would adopt a policy toward the South that was generous and conciliatory toward White men. Hayes and his supporters hoped this approach would relieve tensions with southern Democrats and lead to a smooth inauguration to begin his presidency.

Whether it was an agreement or just an understanding, the result of the Compromise of 1877 was that the Democrats from the South agreed to a vote and Hayes was elected president. Hayes received 185 electoral votes to Tilden's 184, just 2 days before the March 4 inauguration.

The result to the nation of Hayes's election was the end of Reconstruction and the abandonment of African Americans to a largely racist Democratic Party in the South. The presidential election of 1876 was the last before the Democratic Party came to dominate in the South. The noted historian, sociologist, author, and civil rights activist W. E. B. Du Bois wrote, "The Slave went free; stood a brief moment in the sun; then moved back again toward slavery."

The major sources for this chapter were:

Benedict, M. L. (1986). Southern Democrats in crisis 1876–1877: A reconsideration of reunion and reaction. *Journal of Southern History, 46*(4), 489–524.

Foner, E. (2002). *Reconstruction: America's unfinished revolution, 1863–1877.* New York, NY: HarperCollins.

Morris, R., Jr. (2003). *Fraud of the century: Rutherford B. Hayes, Samuel Tilden, and the stolen election of 1876.* New York, NY: Simon & Schuster.

Rehnquist, W. H. (2004). *Centennial crisis: The disputed election of 1876.* New York, NY: Random House.

Weston, M. (2016). *The runner-up presidency: The elections that defined America's popular will.* New York, NY: Random House.

LEARNING ACTIVITIES FOR "THE LAST BATTLE OF THE CIVIL WAR"

Facts of the Case

1. Why was the era following The Civil War called Reconstruction?
2. What Reconstruction measures were enacted by the Radical Republicans?
3. What were the electoral votes for Hayes and Tilden in the 1876 election once the Electoral Commission's decision was approved by Congress?
4. Why did Congress establish the Electoral Commission?
5. How did the Electoral Commission rule in the disputed election of 1876?

Historical Understanding:

1. Why was there animosity between the North and South, and between Republicans and Democrats, following The Civil War?
2. Why did the Radical Republicans oppose the moderate Reconstruction policies of Presidents Lincoln and Johnson?
3. What were the provisions of the Compromise of 1877 and what part did it play in ending the electoral dispute?
4. According to the Constitution, how are a president and vice president chosen if no candidate receives a majority of electoral votes?

Expressing Your Reasoning

Should President Hayes have carried out the promises made in support of his election? Why or why not?

Key Concepts from History

What do the following have in common?

1. In the Italian elections of 1948, the Truman administration, in cooperation with the Roman Catholic Church, secretly provided money to the Christian Democratic Party and other parties that were opposed to the Communist Party. The U.S. administration also made a number of economic concessions to the leaders of the Christian Democratic Party in order to advance their chances of doing well in the election. This was done legally through the National Security Act of 1947. The new law permitted the United States to engage in secret foreign operations, including electoral interference, during the Cold War, which followed World War II. The Christian Democratic Party was successful in the election and ended up forming a government.
2. In 1964, the United States government, acting through the Central Intelligence Agency (CIA), funneled over $3 million to Chilean political parties opposing the top presidential candidate, Salvador Allende. Allende was the leader of the Socialist Party of Chile, very closely associated with the Communist Party in Chile, and a supporter of Cuba, which at the time was considered a communist enemy of the United States. Much of the money was used by the CIA for radio and print advertising. Over 100 U.S. operatives were also sent to Chile to assist in secret activities to defeat Allende. Allende was defeated in the election.
3. In the presidential election of 2016 in the United States, various U.S. intelligence agencies all confirmed that Russia had intervened in the election. An intelligence community assessment stated:

Russian President Vladimir Putin ordered an influence campaign in 2016 aimed at the U.S. presidential election. Russia's goals were to undermine public faith in the U.S. democratic process, denigrate Secretary Hillary Clinton, and harm her electability and potential presidency. We further assess Putin and the Russian Government developed a clear preference for president-elect Donald Trump. We have high confidence in these judgments.

The election intervention took place through the hacking of computers of the Democratic National Committee and the personal account of John Podesta, Democratic nominee Hillary Clinton's campaign manager. The information was then leaked by WikiLeaks (an international nonprofit organization that publishes secret information, including classified documents from anonymous sources). Donald Trump was elected president in 2016 and was inaugurated in January 2017.

Historical Inquiry

In the 2016 U.S. presidential election, Donald Trump was elected president with his defeat of Hillary Clinton in the Electoral College by a vote of 304 to 227. Following the election, there were complaints about the Electoral College. Have there been proposals to reform the Electoral College?

Using online and other sources, test the hypothesis that there have been proposals to abolish or reform the Electoral College. Compose a short essay in which you accept or reject the hypothesis. Include in your essay how it is possible for a candidate to be elected by winning an electoral majority but losing the national popular vote. Use evidence to support your conclusion. To begin your investigation, the following search terms will be helpful:

- The history of the Electoral College
- Presidential elections
- Popular vote versus electoral vote

CHAPTER 23

Kill the Indian and Save the Man

Luther Standing Bear and the
Carlisle Indian Industrial School

Photo of Luther Standing Bear in 1891 (Photographer unknown)

Courtesy of the Library of Congress.

Luther Standing Bear's Indian name was Ota K'Te ("Plenty Kill" in the Lakota language). He was born in December 1868 at the Spotted Tail Indian Agency in Rosebud, South Dakota. This was one of several centers established by the U.S. government in the 19th century to manage trade with the Indian nations. His father was George Standing Bear, a Brulé Lakota chief. His mother was called Pretty Face. Ota K'Te's parents raised him, their first-born son, in the cultural traditions of the Lakota tribe. His father taught him how to hunt and how to be a warrior.

In 1879, when Ota K'Te was 11 years old, he saw a gathering of Native American warriors and a few White men at an agency building in Rosebud. The White men had come to Rosebud to enroll Native children in the Carlisle Indian Industrial School in Carlisle, Pennsylvania. Ota K'Te's father thought Carlisle could give his son the education and training a Native child needed to survive in the "White world."

With his parents' encouragement and approval, Ota K'Te enrolled at Carlisle. Many years later, he described his decision to enroll at the school:

> When I had reached young manhood the warpath for the Lakota was a thing of the past. The hunter had disappeared with the buffalo, the war scout had lost his calling, and the warrior had taken his shield to the mountain-top and given it back to the elements. The victory songs were sung only in the memory of the braves. So I could not prove that I was a brave and would fight to protect my home and land. I could only meet the challenge as life's events came to me. When I went East to Carlisle School, I thought I was going there to die; . . . I could think of white people wanting little Lakota children for no other reason than to kill them, but I thought here is my chance to prove that I can die bravely. So I went East to show my father and my people that I was brave and willing to die for them.

Captain Richard Henry Pratt, a Civil War veteran, founded Carlisle in 1879 under the authority of the U.S. government. Pratt had the support of Carl Schurz, secretary of the interior (whose permission he needed to use the site, a deserted military base, for the school), as well as the cooperation of the U.S. War Department and the U.S. Congress. Carlisle was the first federally funded, off-reservation Indian boarding school in the United States.

Pratt believed that the Native American nations should be "Americanized." One way to achieve this goal was to enroll Native children in boarding schools, located far from their families and tribes. At Carlisle, Pratt's aim was to teach American cultural values to the Indians and to strip away their tribal cultural values. He wrote: "Kill the Indian in him, and save the man."

Today Pratt's efforts to destroy Native culture and civilization appear racist, verging on cultural genocide. Yet Pratt thought he was acting in the best interests of the Indian nations. He wrote:

> We make our greatest mistake in feeding our civilization to the Indians instead of feeding the Indians to our civilization. . . . Why always invite and compel them to remain a people unto themselves?

As an "industrial" school, Carlisle educated and trained its students to work in the White world. The curriculum included academic subjects such as English, math, and history. Students also studied drawing and music. Many students played in the Carlisle Indian Band, which had an international reputation. Luther learned to play the military bugle and was even invited to lead the band across the Brooklyn Bridge at its grand opening in 1883.

Students at Carlisle also studied practical subjects such as farming and construction. They used their knowledge to build classrooms and dormitories. This training was intended to help them develop skills to advance in dominant society. However, most students returned to their lives on the reservations.

Pratt wrote that if each student "gets his living by the sweat of his brow, and demonstrates to the nation that he is a man, he does more good for his race than hundreds of his fellows who cling to their tribal communistic surroundings."

The threat to tribal culture did not begin with the Indian boarding schools. The threat began with the European colonization of North America in the 1600s. The threats were many and varied. The colonists infected the Native Americans with diseases such as smallpox, measles, and whooping cough—sometimes accidentally and sometimes intentionally. The Native Americans lacked both immunities to these diseases and the medicines to treat them.

The threat to Indian tribal culture increased as settlers expanded westward in the 1800s. The Homestead Act of 1862 gave settlers the right to 160 acres of federal land for a fee of only 10 dollars. This act opened the Great Plains to White settlements. Gradually, the settlers fenced off the tribal lands with barbed wire. Hunters and the U.S. Army slaughtered the buffalo herds that were Native peoples' lifeline. The transcontinental railroads cut across the Indian reservations. Tribes were coerced into signing treaties that were violated or broken.

The U.S. government followed a policy of Indian removal, whereby Native Americans were forcibly removed from their ancestral homelands in the southeastern United States to areas west of the Mississippi River. These forced removals of tribes such as the Cherokee, Muscogee, and Seminole were known as the Trail of Tears. Treaties confined Native people to land areas designated as "reservations."

Native Americans were not recognized as U.S. citizens in these years. The Fourteenth Amendment to the U.S. Constitution (ratified in 1868) guaranteed citizenship rights and equal protection under the law "to all persons born or naturalized in the United States" including former slaves. The Fourteenth Amendment would thus seem to apply to Native Americans, but because of puzzling wording in the amendment, this was not how it was interpreted.

In describing congressional representation for the states, Section 2 of the Fourteenth Amendment says people in the states should be counted, "excluding Indians not taxed." What does this phrase, "excluding Indians not taxed," mean regarding citizenship for Indians? No one could say exactly, because the amendment was unclear. Apparently, the phrase was intended only as guidance for census takers. Beginning with the 1830 census, the phrase was included in the instructions to U.S. marshals, who were charged with collecting census data. The marshals were to count all persons of a family except "Indians not taxed." The phrase was interpreted as denying Native Americans citizenship. (In 1924, Native Americans in the U.S. were granted full citizenship rights under the Indian Citizenship Act, also known as the Snyder Act.)

Because their members were not considered U.S. citizens, for years Indian tribes were treated as independent, sovereign nations. Reservations were established for them, enforced by the U.S. Army. Many tribes had to relocate to these reservations that were often far distant from their ancestral lands. History records the many bloody battles that followed as the Indians fought the U.S. Army and the settlers over rights to land. Perhaps the most famous of these conflicts was the Battle of the Little Bighorn (June 25–26, 1876) in what was then eastern Montana Territory, where members of several tribes killed every soldier under the command of Lieutenant Colonel George Custer as well as Custer himself.

Prior to contact with Europeans, the Native American population was estimated to be between 1-to-10 million. By the late 19th century, the estimate was 237,000. The U.S. government decided that the country had what it called an "Indian Problem." Native Americans were interfering with Western expansion. To solve this "problem," the federal government sought to assimilate Native Americans into Euro-American society by establishing boarding schools where Native children could acquire work training, and exchange their cultural values for dominant values.

The education model for Carlisle was, in part, that of the Hampton Normal and Agricultural Institute in Hampton, Virginia. In 1868, General Samuel Armstrong founded Hampton after The Civil War to provide moral training and practical, industrial education to African Americans (former slaves). Ten years after Hampton was founded, 70 male and female Native Americans were sent to Hampton. They had been imprisoned at Fort Sill, Oklahoma, at the end of the Red River War between the U.S. Army and the Southern Plains Indians. As an experiment, Pratt attempted to "civilize" these Native Americans at Hampton. Native American children attended Hampton until 1923 when the program there ended, due to controversy over racial mingling, particularly between Native American girls and Black boys.

When Ota K'Te arrived at Carlisle, he was shown a list of English names and told to pick a new name. Because he could not read English, he simply pointed at a name on the list. The name he picked was Luther. However, he was allowed to keep his father's surname. Thus, Ota K'Te became Luther Standing Bear.

Ota K'Te (now Luther) had to give up more than just his Indian name. His long hair was cut short to control head lice and because school leaders thought only savages had long hair. He also had to exchange his moccasins and buffalo-or-deer hide clothes for European-style high collars, stiff-fronted shirts, suspenders, leather boots, and, most uncomfortable of all, red flannel underwear. Luther described this underwear as "torture."

Everything at Carlisle was foreign to the Indian students. They could not speak their own languages; they had to speak English. They thought the food and dining habits were very strange. They were taught Christianity and were expected to attend church services. Carlisle followed a rigorous daily schedule that was timed by the clock. Students had to follow the rules and adopt required behaviors. Those who broke the rules were punished physically. Many of the students, trapped in "the White world" and separated from their families, found the Carlisle experience difficult and often traumatic.

Because Luther was a model student at Carlisle, Pratt asked him to recruit new students from the Indian reservation at Pine Ridge, South Dakota. Luther made a very favorable impression on prospective students and their families with his attractive appearance, his command of the English language, and his other skills.

Some students at Carlisle lived and worked with White people outside the school. For example, Luther Standing Bear worked at John Wanamaker's department store in Philadelphia. He became an outstanding employee. Wanamaker said he had never promoted anyone as rapidly. Years later, Wanamaker, as U.S. postmaster general, established a post office in Kyle, South Dakota, at Standing Bear's request.

Yet there were problems when Luther returned to his home on the Spotted Tail Agency in Rosebud, South Dakota. Some tribe members thought he had abandoned his culture and people. Others refused to shake his hand. It was even said that Luther "looked like a white boy dressed in eastern clothes."

Other Indian children who returned from Carlisle also found themselves straddling two worlds, and not fully accepted by either. It seemed the White world would not fully accept them because of their race, while some in the Native world rejected them for abandoning their tribal culture. Families were shocked when children pretended they could no longer speak the Lakota language. Families were also angry because of another shocking situation. Sometimes, when Indian children died at Carlisle, parents were not told of the deaths for many months.

Some students resisted the military-style regimen at Carlisle. These students refused to attend church and to obey the rules. Many wanted to leave Carlisle. One student, Ernest White Thunder, pleaded to return home. Like many other students, he was not granted permission. While at the school, he died from tuberculosis.

Upon returning home to the Spotted Tail Indian Agency in South Dakota, Standing Bear then worked as an assistant at the reservation's school. In 1891, he became the school's principal. He and his brother also opened a dry goods store on the reservation that sold clothing and other consumer products. They used the store as a place for public discussions on Indian treaties and current events.

In 1902, Standing Bear, his wife, and their six children went to England to join Buffalo Bill's Wild West Show, a popular traveling vaudeville show that romanticized the American frontier. The show featured cowboys, Indians, wild animals, horseback-riding tricks, and shooting competitions. Train holdups and famous battles were staged to the delight of audiences.

The founder of the Wild West Show, William Cody (known as Buffalo Bill), took the role of the "good guy" fighting the "bad guys" (outlaws and Indians). However, to some extent, Cody was more respectful of Indian culture and traditions than many other showmen. Although his show exploited the myth of the western frontier, Cody tried to preserve respect for Native culture. He described the Indians in his show as "the former foe, the present friend, the American." Pratt of the Carlisle School believed the shows portrayed Native Americans as savages and vulgar stereotypes, and led an unsuccessful campaign to discourage Native Americans from joining Wild West shows.

When Luther left the Wild West Show in 1905, he returned to South Dakota, where he was briefly Chief of the Oglala Lakota. Then he moved to Sioux City, Iowa, where he worked as a clerk in a wholesale company. In 1912, he went to Hollywood to work in the film industry. He appeared in many films and lobbied for the use of Indians in Native American movie roles.

Luther Standing Bear wrote several books and articles about his life and about Native American culture. His aim was to preserve Lakota heritage and sovereignty and to change U.S. policy toward Native Americans. Throughout the 1930s, Luther tried to promote legal and social rights for Native Americans.

In 1931, during the Great Depression, Luther returned to South Dakota. It had been 20 years since his last visit to his place of birth. To his sorrow, he found that his people were in a desperate situation. They lacked resources, even enough food. Disease in various forms was common. Perhaps most discouraging, he saw that his people had lost hope for a better life. He described his observations in his book *The Tragedy of the Sioux*:

> There is not and never has been a human attitude taken toward the Indian; no acknowledgement of his virtues; no friendly acceptance of his native abilities. He has been made to feel his segregation. Since the Indian wars ended the white man has so busied himself wresting riches from the land that its people have been forgotten. Forgotten save for a few friends and humanitarians whose sensitive souls are uneasy and irritated as long as the voices of the oppressed are audible.

In collaboration with John Collier (the commissioner for the Bureau of Indian Affairs, which was created in 1824 to manage Native American relations) and the Indian Rights Association, Luther tried to protect the religious and cultural traditions of Native Americans. One result of this work was the Indian Reorganization Act of 1934 (referred to sometimes as the Indian New Deal). The act restored the management of Indian land and mineral rights to the tribes, rejected the goal of assimilation of Native people into American society, and created a structure for tribal self-government.

Historians praise the Indian New Deal for helping Indians survive the Great Depression of the 1930s, and recognize Collier's energy and initiative. Yet they also criticize Collier for failing to acknowledge the diversity among the tribes, and argue that the Indian New Deal failed to stimulate economic progress or establish a usable structure for Indian politics.

In addition to Luther Standing Bear, other Carlisle students were models for a new generation of Native American leadership. During the school's existence, from 1879 to 1918, more than 10,000 Native American children from 140 tribes attended Carlisle. Carlisle's other most famous graduate was Jim Thorpe (1887–1953). Thorpe was a member of the Sac and Fox Indian nation and the first Native American to win a medal in the Olympics. He won Olympic gold medals in the 1912 pentathlon and decathlon. An all-around athlete, he also played professional football, baseball, and basketball.

Other graduates entered government service, attended law school, and found other kinds of employment off the reservations. However, these graduates and those like Luther and Jim Thorpe were exceptions. Most students did not graduate (one source indicates that only 158 out of the 10,000 attendees graduated). Nor did they assimilate into dominant society, which was the goal of the school. Instead, they returned home to life on the reservation. Many students who had been traumatized by the stripping of their culture, as well as mental, physical, and sexual abuse, had deep emotional scars that were difficult to recover from.

Indian boarding schools like Carlisle were founded all over the country. Carlisle was the model for 26 boarding schools managed by the Bureau of Indian Affairs and for hundreds of private boarding schools for Native American children. The goal of all these schools was to strip Native American boys and girls of their culture and assimilate them into mainstream White culture through education and training.

The 1928 Meriam Report, officially titled *The Problem of the Indian Administration,* documented the problems with boarding schools like Carlisle. The report was funded by the Rockefeller Foundation and was commissioned by the Institute for Government Research, a private organization dedicated to analyzing national public policy issues that would later become the Brookings Institution.

There was much criticism of the boarding schools in the report. The children's diet was poor, with few fruits and green vegetables and little milk. Medical services and sanitation were inadequate. Students were forced to work under the threat of harsh discipline. They were poorly educated. The report stated, "The survey staff finds itself obligated to say frankly and unequivocally that the provisions for the care of the Indian children in boarding schools are grossly inadequate." In its conclusions, the report recommended that Indian students should not be educated in separate schools. They would benefit far more from attending public schools with White students.

The schools, nonetheless, remained open. In 1969, more than 40 years after the Meriam Report was published, a report known as the Kennedy Report that examined conditions at Indian boarding schools declared Indian education a national tragedy. Only one-tenth of the teachers at boarding schools mentioned academic achievement as an important goal; instead, teachers still perceived their central role as "civilizing the native." In the 1970s, at their peak, about 60,000 Native American children were still enrolled in Indian boarding schools. Many such schools closed in the 1980s and 1990s. Yet, as recently as 2007, more than 9,000 Native American children lived at Indian boarding schools. It has taken a long time for society to understand what Luther meant when he wrote:

> "Civilization" has been thrust upon me since the days of the reservations, and it has not added one whit to my sense of justice, to my reverence for the rights of life, to my love for truth, honesty, and generosity, or to my faith in Wakan Tanka, God of the Lakotas.

Luther died on February 20, 1939, on the set of the film *Union Pacific*. He was buried in the Hollywood Forever Cemetery, far from his Lakota birthplace.

The major sources for this chapter were:

Adams, D. W. (1997). *Education for extinction: American Indians and the boarding school experience, 1875–1928.* Lawrence, KS: University of Kansas Press.

Bear, C. (2008, May 12). American Indian boarding schools haunt many. *National Public Radio.* Available at http://www.npr.org/templates/story/story.php?story-Id=16516865

Bear, C. (2008, May 13). American Indian school a far cry from the past. *National Public Radio.* Available at http://www.npr.org/templates/story/story.php?story-Id=17645287

Bosworth, D. A. (2011). *American Indian boarding schools: An exploration of global, ethnic, & cultural cleansing.* Mount Pleasant, MI: The Ziibiwing Center of Anishinabe Culture & Lifeways.

Work, H., & Lewis, M. (1928). *The problem of Indian administration: Summary and findings:* Washington, DC: Institute for Government Research. Available at http://www.alaskool.org/native_ed/research_reports/IndianAdmin/Indian_Admin_Problms.html

Hacker, J. D., & Haines, M. R. (2006). *American Indian mortality in the late nineteenth century: The impact of federal assimilation policies on a vulnerable population* (Working Paper 12572). Cambridge, MA: National Bureau of Economic Research. Available at http://www.nber.org/papers/w12572

Fear-Segal, J. (1990). Nineteenth-century Indian education: Universalism versus evolutionism. *Journal of American Studies, 33*(2), 323–341.

Pratt, R. H. (1973). The advantages of mingling Indians with Whites. In F. P. Prucha (Ed.), *Americanizing the American Indians: Writings by the "Friends of the Indian" 1880–1900*, pp. 260–271. Cambridge, MA: Harvard University Press.

Standing Bear, L. (1975). *My people, the Sioux.* Lincoln, NE: University of Nebraska Press.

Standing Bear, L. (1978). *Land of the spotted eagle.* Lincoln, NE: University of Nebraska Press.

Ziibiwing Center of Anishinabe Culture & Lifeways. (2011). American Indian Boarding Schools. Available at http://www.sagchip.org/ziibiwing/planyourvisit/pdf/aib-scurrguide.pdf

LEARNING ACTIVITIES FOR "KILL THE INDIAN AND SAVE THE MAN"

Facts of the Case

1. What were Colonel Pratt's ideas about Native Americans?
2. How was life at the Carlisle Indian Industrial School different from Luther's tribal life in South Dakota?
3. How did some Carlisle students resist the Carlisle Indian Industrial School's policies and rules?
4. What was Buffalo Bill's Wild West Show?
5. What did the Meriam Report conclude about education at the Indian boarding schools?

Historical Understanding

1. How did the U.S. government respond to the "Indian Problem" in the 19th century?
2. What were the provisions of the "Indian New Deal?"
3. Describe some of the experiences faced by Native American children when they returned home from the Indian boarding schools.

Expressing Your Reasoning

Should George Standing Bear and Pretty Face have agreed to send their son, Ota K'Te (Luther Standing Bear), to the Carlisle Indian Industrial School? Why or why not?

Key Concepts from History

What do the following have in common?

1. After World War I, Germany was forced to return the area of Alsace-Lorraine (where German was the main spoken language) to France. The French government then attempted to substitute state schools for the traditional church schools and to suppress the publication of German language newspapers.
2. Throughout the 19th and 20th centuries, Canada removed about 150,000 First Nations children from their homes and placed them in federally funded boarding schools. These schools, which were called Indian Residential

Schools, prohibited the children from speaking their native language and from wearing native clothing.

3. Japan ruled Korea from 1910 to 1945. From the late 1930s to 1945, the Japanese colonial government required schools in Korea to use the Japanese language. Korean students could not use their own language either inside or outside school. Koreans were also encouraged to take Japanese names. Korean-language newspapers were not allowed to publish.

Historical Inquiry

American Indian Code Talkers were Native Americans in the U.S. Marine Corps during World War II who transmitted secret tactical messages over military telephone or radio communication nets using codes based on their Native languages. Did their experience at the boarding schools help prepare Native Americans to become Code Talkers? Compose a short essay in which you accept or reject the hypothesis that their boarding school experiences helped prepare them to be Code Talkers. Use evidence to support your decision. To begin your investigation, the following search terms will be helpful:

- American Indian Code Talkers
- Navajo Code Talkers
- World War II and Navajo
- Native words Native warriors

CHAPTER 24

Telling a Lie to Discover the Truth

An Example in Investigative Journalism

Photograph of Nellie Bly, 1890

Courtesy of the Library of Congress.

In the early 19th century, people with mental disorders were cared for by family and friends. Sometimes small towns employed poor people to take charge of such people. Others were sent to workhouses (also called poor farms) or even jails. The causes of mental illnesses were poorly understood. It was commonly assumed that mental illness was incurable. Mental health treatment, to the extent it existed, was unregulated, underfunded, and harshly abusive. Confinement of the mentally ill in cages and basements in asylums and jails was not unknown.

By the mid-19th century, a wave of social reforms resulted in the abolition of slavery; the promotion of temperance (abstinence from alcoholic drink); and the founding of orphanages, prisons, and hospitals. In education, the common school movement led to the founding of organized systems of common schools. These systems were the first public school systems in the United States to provide free, universal, and nonsectarian education.

The tentative, initial steps in mental health treatment were other signs of this social reformist movement. Dorothea Dix (1802–1887), an author, former schoolteacher, and social activist, spoke out against the inhumane treatment of the mentally ill, especially those who were institutionalized in state hospitals. When Dix visited such hospitals, she was appalled to find that the patients (essentially inmates) were chained, poorly fed and clothed, and physically abused. Most Americans had no knowledge of these conditions; those who did know, such as administrators and even politicians, ignored them. However, as these conditions were publicized and medieval superstitions about the mentally ill were overcome, society gradually realized that cure of the mentally ill might be possible.

Dix traveled throughout the Northeast, Midwest, and South, investigating and writing about the conditions of the insane and working with various committees on legislative drafts and appropriation bills intended to improve mental healthcare. For example, she helped write the Bill for the Benefit of the Indigent Insane, or the Land-Grant Bill for Indigent Insane Persons, that, if it had passed into national law, would have granted federal land to the states on which to build and maintain asylums for the indigent insane. In 1854, after the bill passed both congressional houses, President Franklin Pierce vetoed it, and the Congress could not override his veto. Pierce's explanation of his veto was that the states, rather than the federal government, were responsible for social welfare, including care of the insane. There was no mental health-care federal legislation until 1946, some 90 years later.

Nevertheless, Dix's efforts led to the founding or expansion of more than 30 state psychiatric hospitals for the care and treatment of the mentally ill. However, mental health treatment remained underfunded and poorly staffed. In many cases, living conditions were still brutishly intolerable. Other than Dix, the mentally ill had few advocates who drew national attention to these problems. Then Nellie Bly (1864–1922) took up the cause that Dix had supported with her speeches, writings, and legislative pressure. Unlike Dix, Bly took a journalist's approach to uncovering facts and demanding change—an approach that involved a false identity and hidden motives.

"Nellie Bly" was born Elizabeth Jane Cochran in the small town of Cochran's Mills, Pennsylvania. Her father, Michael Cochran, was a wealthy land owner, judge, and businessman. His first wife died after the birth of 10 children, and Cochran remarried. Elizabeth was the third of five children born in this second marriage. She was described as the most rebellious, smart, and strong-willed of all the Cochran children. People called her "Pink" because she wore pink dresses instead of the dreary gray, brown, and black dresses the other girls wore. It was a nickname she always hated.

Elizabeth's early childhood was idyllic. The family lived in a beautiful house, with a large library, in Apollo, Pennsylvania, about 10 miles from her birthplace. She was an eager reader, and especially liked the library's collection of medical books. However, her father's death, when she was 6, left the family without a provider. Her mother then married John Jackson Ford, a Civil War veteran and occasional laborer. She later divorced him on the grounds that he was a violent drunk who abused the entire family. The experience made a lasting impression on Elizabeth. She realized how essential it was for women to be self-reliant and how important it was to support the vulnerable, especially women.

Elizabeth searched for a way to support herself and her family. In the late 19th century, few career options were available to women: factory work, farm work, domestic service for richer households, working for family businesses, nursing, and teaching. In the hope she could become a teacher, she enrolled at the State Normal School in Indiana, Pennsylvania, which offered teacher training. However, she left the school after one semester because she could not afford the fees.

She and her family moved to Pittsburgh in 1880. With 60,000 residents, Pittsburgh was Pennsylvania's second largest city. Still an avid reader, each day Elizabeth studied the *Pittsburgh Dispatch*, the city's oldest newspaper. She especially liked Elizabeth Wilkinson Wade's columns. Wade, using the pen name Bessie Bramble, was a strong supporter of women's suffrage (voting for women). Erasmus Wilson was another columnist who caught Elizabeth's attention. In his popular column, "Quiet Observations," Wilson, known as the Quiet Observer ("Q.O."), offered his opinions on a variety of topics. In reaction to his column titled "What Girls Are Good For," in which Wilson expounded on the proper role of women (i.e., having babies and caring for the home), Elizabeth sent an anonymous rebuttal to the newspaper attacking the column. She signed her statement as "Lonely Orphan Girl" and gave no return address. The *Dispatch's* editor, George Madden, liked its sincerity and spirit. He ran an advertisement in the paper, seeking the author's identity.

When Elizabeth identified herself as the author, Madden asked her to write a feature-length column on "the women's sphere." Her first column, published on January 25, 1885, was titled "The Girl Puzzle." She again used the pen name "Lonely Orphan Girl." The following excerpt is typical of the content and style of the column:

> Let a youth start as errand boy and he will work his way up until he is one of the firm. Girls are just as smart, a great deal quicker to learn; why, then, can they not do the same? As all occupations for women are filled why not start some new ones. Instead of putting the little girls in factories let them be employed in the capacity of messenger boys or office boys. It would be healthier. They would have a chance to learn; their ideas would become broader and they would make as good, if not better, women in the end.

These were powerful, even radical, words at this time. However, Madden was so impressed that he offered Elizabeth a regular column on the paper. Because it was customary that women use a pen name to disguise their identity, he gave Elizabeth the pen name "Nellie Bly." The name came from a song by Stephen Foster, a popular American songwriter of the mid-1800s. Now, known to the public as Nellie Bly, Elizabeth wrote "women's interest news"—the annual flower show and fashions. She also wrote profiles of well-known women.

As one might expect, Bly did not enjoy these assignments. In 1885, at age 21, she left the *Dispatch* after 9 months. She moved to Mexico and wrote a book, *Six Months in Mexico*, about her observations of the lives and customs of Mexican peoples during her travels. She briefly returned to Pittsburgh and the *Dispatch*, and then, in 1887 she applied for a position on Joseph Pulitzer's *The New York World*, which was New York's most successful (and most sensationalist) newspaper. She asked to report on a hot air balloon ascent sponsored by the newspaper, but was denied the assignment with the excuse that the ride would be too dangerous for a "lady." A few months later, Bly convinced her editor, John A. Cockerill, to allow her to travel from Europe to the United States in steerage class so she could describe the immigrant voyage firsthand. Although Cockerill denied her request, he was impressed with her daredevil attitude.

For her next assignment, she feigned insanity in order to be committed to the Women's Lunatic Asylum on Blackwell's Island in New York. A few months earlier, the *World* had specifically called for an investigation of mental health treatment at Ward's Island, a New York mental asylum, after two employees were charged with the manslaughter of a patient. The newspaper also wrote that this asylum was "disgracefully overcrowded." The newspaper expressed similar concerns about the Women's Lunatic Asylum on Blackwell's Island.

In proposing the assignment, Cockerill said to Bly: "You can try. But if you can do it, it's more than anyone would believe." It was an entirely novel assignment, well suited to Bly's ambition and character. Nellie Bly spent 10 days in the asylum disguised as a patient. Afterward, she wrote a series of articles for the *World* that were later published as a book called *Ten Days in a Mad-House*. Chapter 1, "A Delicate Mission," began with the following paragraph:

On the 22d of September [1887] I was asked by the *World* if I could have myself committed to one of the asylums for the insane in New York, with a view to writing a plain and unvarnished narrative of the treatment of the patients therein and the methods of management, etc. Did I think I had the courage to go through such an ordeal as the mission would demand? Could I assume the characteristics of insanity to such a degree that I could pass the doctors, live for a week among the insane without the authorities there finding out that I was only a "chiel [child] amang 'em takin' notes?" I said I believed I could. I had some faith in my own ability as an actress and thought I could assume insanity long enough to accomplish any mission intrusted

to me. Could I pass a week in the insane ward at Blackwell's Island? I said I
could and I would. And I did.

Before her commitment to the asylum, Bly sought advice about the legality
of her "delicate mission" from Henry D. Macdona, an assistant district attorney
of New York. Although Macdona advised against the assignment, when he saw
he could not dissuade Bly, he agreed he would give her immunity from prosecution, if necessary, after the publication of her experiences at the asylum. With this
assurance, Bly proceeded.

To gain admittance to the asylum, Bly wrote that she could "feign insanity at
the house of friends, and get myself committed on the decision of two competent
physicians, or I could go to my goal by way of the police courts." She chose the
latter route, not wanting to involve friends and physicians in her mission. She
secured lodging at a working-class boardinghouse, Matron Irene Stenard's Temporary Home for Women, using the false name Nellie Brown (so that the initials
would match her embroidered linen). After a few days' stay, she began acting
irrationally. She kept repeating, "I can't remember, I can't remember" about the
fate of her lost trunks, as well as affecting a distant, faraway look. Finally, after the
proprietors sent for a police officer, two policemen ("big, strong men") took her
to the courtroom of Judge Patrick G. Duffy.

After questioning Bly, and seeing that she was a well-dressed, well-man-
nered, pretty young woman, who seemed to have amnesia, Duffy decided she was
"somebody's darling" who had been drugged and brought to the city. He then
sent her to Bellevue Hospital for examination. At the hospital, Bly continued to
feign madness by acting strangely and refusing to answer questions. A doctor declared she was not drugged but suffered from hysteria. With this diagnosis of insanity, Bly was transported to the Women's Lunatic Asylum on Blackwell's Island.

As she was driven to the asylum, Bly thought she had "attained the object of
my work." The only potential concern was that Judge Duffy had invited reporters to his courtroom to see if they could learn her identity. Both the *New York
Sun* and *New York Times* published stories about this mysterious young woman.
The headline in the *New York Sun* was "Who Is This Insane Girl?" After 10 days,
Peter A. Hendricks, an attorney from the *World*, arranged Bly's release. She then
published her findings in articles in the *World* and in a book.

Bly's descriptions of life at the Women's Lunatic Asylum on Blackwell's Island were shocking. She wrote about the inhumane abuse of the patients by the
nurses; the wretched, inedible food; the lack of eating utensils; the absence of
reading materials; the hard, uncomfortable benches; the rats and cockroaches;
the human waste near the eating areas; and the freezing cold inside the buildings.
She observed no efforts to treat the mentally ill: just cruelty and neglect. Of the
baths, Bly wrote:

> Once a week the patients are given a bath, and that is the only time they see
> soap. . . . On bathing day the tub is filled with water, and the patients are

washed, one after the other, without a change of water. This is done until the water is really thick, and then it is allowed to run out and the tub is refilled without being washed. The same towels are used on all the women, those with eruptions as well as those without.

However, as terrifying and repellant as these experiences and observations were, Bly found she was treated far better than some patients who were very ill. Bly recounted the story of Bridget McGuinness, who was sent to the "Retreat," a confinement space for violent patients. Bridget was tied to the "rope gang" in which women were connected by wide leather belts to a long cable. McGuinness described the experience to Bly:

> The beating I got there were something dreadful. I was pulled around by the hair, held under the water until I strangled, and I was choked and kicked. The nurses would always keep a quiet patient stationed at the window to tell them when any of the doctors were approaching. It was hopeless to complain to the doctors, for they always said it was the imagination of our diseased brains, and besides we would get another beating for telling. They inject so much morphine and chloral [a sedative] that the patients are made crazy.

The *World* claimed her articles prompted Vernon M. Davis, an assistant district attorney for New York, to convene a grand jury to investigate the Women's Lunatic Asylum. At one point, Bly accompanied the grand jurors on a visit to the asylum. Evidently the asylum administrators had advance notice of the visit, because the jurors found the rooms sparkling clean and the food nutritious and edible. Bright new basins had replaced the washtubs that Bly had described. It seems the jurors were not deceived by this pretense, because they supported all the changes Bly recommended, especially those about employing more qualified and empathetic nurses, preparing and serving healthy meals, and appointing women physicians to supervise the nurses.

By now, politicians and the general public were demanding reform of institutions for the mentally ill. Bly wrote in her book:

> I am happy to be able to state as a result of my visit to the asylum and the exposures consequent thereon, that the City of New York has appropriated $1,000,000 more per annum than ever before for the care of the insane. So I have at least the satisfaction of knowing that the poor unfortunates will be the better cared for because of my work.

Bly's experience with immersion journalism at the Women's Lunatic Asylum launched her career as an investigative journalist. After her experience at the asylum, she reported on other examples of corruption and injustice such as police officers' mistreatment of prisoners, the lack of care for the poor, and the unsafe working conditions for laborers. In 1922, Elizabeth Cochran—"Nellie Bly"—died at age 57, leaving a legacy of reporting on society's ills.

At age 23, Nellie Bly had pioneered a new kind of undercover, investigative journalism that many followers, in various ways, have imitated. Because the focus of such journalism is the journalist's experience, the journalist can escape the limitations of so-called fair-and-balanced, or objective, reporting. Some critics use the term *stunt journalism* to describe such journalism, which uses tactics that may be illegal, unethical, or voyeuristic. Defenders, however, point to the results of their reporting that often exposes corruption, abuse, and injustice.

The main sources for this chapter are:

Bly, N. (1887). *Ten days in a madhouse.* New York, NY: Ian L. Munro Publisher.
Dickens, C. (1913). *American notes for general circulation.* London, UK: Chapman & Hall, Ltd. Available at: https://www.gutenberg.org/files/675/675-h/675-h.htm
Kroeger, B. (1994). *Nellie Bly: Daredevil, reporter, feminist.* New York, NY: Times Books.
Popova, M. (2014, April 30). What girl are good for: 20-year-old Nellie Bly's 1885 response to a patronizing chauvinist. Brain Pickings. Available at https://www.brainpickings.org/2014/04/30/nellie-bly-letter
Rosenkrantz, B. G., & Vinovskis, M. A. (1979). Caring for the insane in ante-bellum Massachusetts: Family, community, and state participation. In A. J. Lichtman & J. R. Challinor (Eds.) *Kin and communities: Families in America* (pp. 187–218). Washington, DC: Smithsonian Institution Press.

LEARNING ACTIVITIES FOR "TELLING A LIE TO DISCOVER THE TRUTH"

Facts of the Case

1. Who was "Nellie Bly"?
2. How did Bly become a journalist?
3. Describe the circumstances under which Bly entered the Women's Lunatic Asylum in New York.
4. What assurance did Nellie Bly have that she would escape prosecution?
5. Which mental asylum reforms resulted from Nellie Bly's reporting?

Historical Understanding

1. Describe the social reforms that began in the mid-19th century.
2. Describe the employment opportunities available to women in the late 19th century.
3. Describe the societal attitudes toward women in the late 19th century.
4. Describe the living conditions and treatment for the mentally ill in the late 19th century.

Expressing Your Reasoning

Was Nellie Bly justified in telling the lie that allowed her to enter the Women's Lunatic Asylum. Why or why not?

Key Concepts from History

What do the following have in common?

1. In 1903, the American journalist Ida Tarbell wrote a series of articles for *McClure's Magazine* that were later published in her book, *The History of the Standard Oil Company* (1904). In the book she exposed the use of a monopolistic trust by the Standard Oil Company; her reporting led, in part, to the Supreme Court's ruling that the Standard Oil Company violated the Sherman Antitrust Act, and then to the eventual breakup of the company.
2. In 1906, the American journalist Upton Sinclair published *The Jungle*, a book that described the unsafe and unsanitary work conditions of the U.S. meat-packing industry. This book led, in part, to the passage of the Pure Food and Drug Act and the Meat Inspection Act.
3. From 1998 to 2000, the American journalist Barbara Ehrenreich worked undercover in a series of minimum-wage jobs so that she could witness their working conditions, people's efforts to survive on low wages, and the effect on people's lives of the 1996 Welfare Reform Act. She published her observations in her book *Nickel and Dimed: On (Not) Getting By in America* (2001).

Historical Inquiry

Did the treatment and living conditions for people with mental illnesses improve after the publication of Nellie Bly's articles in the *World*? Using online and other sources, test the hypothesis that the treatment and living conditions for people with mental illnesses improved after the publication of Nellie Bly's articles in the *World*. Compose a short essay in which you accept or reject the hypothesis. Use evidence to support your decision. To begin your investigation, the following search terms will be helpful:

- Exposé of New York's Blackwell's Island asylum
- Conditions at Blackwell's Island asylum
- History of mental asylums in the United States

Part VII

INDUSTRIALIZATION AND REFORM
1891–1918

CHAPTER 25

Richest Man in the World
John D. Rockefeller and the Standard Oil Company

1917 Portrait of John D. Rockefeller, John Singer Sargent

John Davidson Rockefeller was the richest man in the history of the United States. None of his wealth was inherited. His money came from his ownership of the Standard Oil Company that he founded in the late 19th century. As an industrialist, his business tactics were very controversial and much criticized. In fact, Ida Tarbell, an investigative reporter, published a book in 1904 that claimed the company's business practices were unethical.

In 1911, the U.S. Supreme Court ruled that Standard Oil had become "a combination in restraint of trade" (monopoly) and thereby violated U.S. anti-trust law. For many people, Rockefeller was the most hated figure in American business.

Yet there was another side to Rockefeller. He was also one of the most generous philanthropists in history. (A philanthropist is an individual who donates money to public and humanitarian causes.)

Rockefeller was born on July 8, 1839, in Richford, New York. He was the second child in a family of six children. His father, "Big Bill" Rockefeller, was a tall, handsome man, known for his charm and lively sense of fun. Big Bill was also imaginative and resourceful. When he failed as a farmer and businessman, he became a traveling medicine man, a quack (fake or fraudulent) doctor, and even a magician—occupations behind his other nickname, "Devil's Bill." Big Bill often disappeared for long periods at a time. Using the fake name William Levingston, he married another woman and had a second family while still legally married to Rockefeller's mother. It is no surprise that Rockefeller would not respond to reporters when asked about his father years later. Historian Ron Chernow described Rockefeller as being as "steady and trustworthy" as Big Bill was "feckless and mercurial."

Despite his father's long absences and bad reputation, Rockefeller's rural New York upbringing was traditional. The family was never truly poor, as Big Bill supported Rockefeller's mother and his siblings, albeit inconsistently. Big Bill was respectable in some of his business practices; he believed in contractual obligations and paid his debts on time. But because he was known to take advantage of other people's confidence in him, few people trusted Big Bill. If Rockefeller can be said to have inherited some of his father's shrewdness, he inherited a calm temperament and common sense from his mother. She was thrifty and knew how to manage the family money. Rockefeller was a responsible son who helped with the chores and the care of the younger children. He even helped his mother with the family budget. He was also a very good student. Like his mother, he was very religious and did not smoke or drink alcohol.

In 1853, the Rockefeller family moved to Cleveland, Ohio. Rockefeller attended Cleveland's Central High School where he excelled in mathematics and music. He also learned to debate and could speak clearly and concisely. It was a skill that would prove useful as he entered the world of business. Even at a young age, Rockefeller had many interests and strong opinions. For example, he was outspoken in his criticism of slavery. After he graduated from high school in 1855, at age 16 (6 years before the start of The Civil War), he enrolled in a 10-week bookkeeping course at Folsom's Commercial College.

When he completed the bookkeeping course, Rockefeller looked for work at the large companies in the Cleveland area. Looking back, he described this 6-week search: "I went to the railroads, to the banks, to the wholesale merchants." After finding the "top man" at the various companies, he would begin his pitch confidently with this self-description: "I understand bookkeeping and I'd like to get to work." He was eventually hired as an assistant bookkeeper at the produce (fruits and vegetables) merchant and shipping firm Hewitt and Tuttle, on September 26, 1855. All his life, Rockefeller celebrated that day as "Job Day." Rockefeller had the right temperament and work ethic for a bookkeeper; he was hardworking, meticulous, and honest. He loved the precision behind the columns of numbers.

In this job Rockefeller witnessed the importance of transportation (i.e., the railways) and communication (i.e., the telegraph) in business. After 3½ years at Hewitt and Tuttle, he left the firm. He had learned all he could learn in this job. He was certain there were better opportunities elsewhere.

In 1859, now age 20, Rockefeller borrowed a small sum from Big Bill. With this loan, he formed a business partnership with a former classmate and neighbor, Maurice B. Clark. They called the firm Clark and Rockefeller. Like the owners of Hewitt and Tuttle, the two men set out to make their fortune in the produce business.

When The Civil War began in 1861, Rockefeller was a Republican, a Lincoln supporter, and an abolitionist. However, he did not enlist. Like many northern young men of wealth, Rockefeller bought his way out of the Union Army. The Enrollment Act of 1863 allowed a man who had been drafted into the army to pay a substitute $300 (about $6,000 in today's dollars) to take his place.

The substitutes were mostly poor and much in need of the $300. Rockefeller justified this action: "I wanted to go in the army and do my part. But it was simply out of the question. We were in a new business, and if I had not stayed it must have stopped—and with so many dependent on it." Rockefeller was the main support of his mother and his brothers and sisters. They could not depend consistently on Big Bill's support. A private in the Union Army was paid only $13 a month (around $250 in today's dollars). Many of the wealthy men who legally hired substitutes contributed to the war effort by providing the Union Army with transportation, clothing and shoes, and financing. Rockefeller was one of the men who donated money to the Union cause.

Throughout The Civil War, Clark and Rockefeller transported food and sold farm tools. The firm was hugely profitable. By 1862, the firm had an annual profit of $17,000 (about $400,000 in today's dollars). Rockefeller was on his way to becoming a very rich man. However, he was still looking for new investments and new opportunities. The next chapter in Rockefeller's life was to transform American business practices. Understanding that change invites a look into the history of oil and its role during the industrial era.

Electric lighting, as we know it today, was not invented until the late 19th century. Until almost the mid-20th century, streets, houses, and offices were lit by gas lighting. Gas lighting is artificial light produced by the combustion of a variety of fuels: camphene, whale oil, lard oil, and coal oil. None of them was ideal for consumers. Camphene, made from alcohol, was too expensive because of alcohol taxes. Whale oil was the most expensive fuel, at $1.30 to $2.50 (about $40 to $75 in today's dollars) a gallon. Although lard oil and coal oil were cheaper, they were smelly and of low quality.

In the 1860s, when kerosene was introduced as a lighting fuel, it quickly replaced all other fuel lighting sources. Kerosene was used in table lamps, hand-held lanterns, and street lamps. Kerosene is a liquid derived from petroleum, which is recovered by drilling deep into the Earth. Kerosene, which was less expensively priced at 60¢ (about $17 in today's dollars) a gallon, was far cheaper than any other fuel source. Natural gas, a fossil fuel also found in deep underground rock formations, was used for heating and cooking.

In 1859, Colonel Edwin Drake drilled a 69-foot oil well in Titusville, Pennsylvania, for the Seneca Oil Company. The company hired men (teamsters) to drive wagons pulled by oxen, horses, or mules to transport the oil to markets. Between 1862 and 1868, numerous oil-related businesses were formed in western Pennsylvania. These businesses included refineries (industrial complexes with extensive piping for purifying petroleum and natural gas, and producing kerosene from petroleum). These businesses flourished as the demand for kerosene lamps grew.

Rockefeller entered the oil business because of his association with Samuel Andrews, who was a friend of Maurice Clark. Andrews, a self-taught chemist, had experience in refining oil and knew about artificial lighting. In 1862, Andrews, Rockefeller, and Clark began an oil-refining venture. Each man contributed $4,000 (about $77,000 in today's dollars) as start-up capital. At this time, oil refining for Rockefeller was just a sideline business to his commodities activity. He may not have had a clear idea how important this new business would become.

In 1863, Rockefeller and his partners built an oil refinery in Cleveland, near the Cuyahoga River that flows into Lake Erie. The location for the oil refinery was well chosen, because it was next to the site where the Atlantic and Great Western Railroad planned a rail line. This line would directly link to Pennsylvania where the oil fields were. Rockefeller continually sought new ways to bring order and efficiency to the oil refinery business. As thrifty as ever, he kept tight internal control of costs. His bookkeeping training was again very useful.

In 1864, Rockefeller married his high school classmate Laura Celestia Spelman. When Laura graduated from high school, she had given a speech titled "I Can Paddle My Own Canoe" in which she stated that women must have minds of their own and criticized men for depriving women of culture and then blaming them for their dependency on men. She worked as a public school teacher and as an assistant principal. She and Rockefeller brought up their five children (four daughters and one son) to share their political, social, and religious views.

In February 1865, Rockefeller bought the Clark brothers' share of their jointly owned company for $72,500 (about $1 million in today's dollars). He and Samuel Andrews then formed a partnership called Rockefeller & Andrews. Rockefeller, always aware of the importance of dates in his life, described the day they began the partnership: "It was the day that determined my career." In 1867, Henry Flagler joined the partnership that was then renamed Rockefeller, Andrews, & Flagler. By 1868, the partners owned the largest oil refinery in the world.

On January 10, 1870, the partnership was incorporated as the Standard Oil Company, a joint-stock company, in the state of Ohio. In the articles of incorporation, Rockefeller was identified as the company president. In a joint-stock company, shareholders can buy and sell shares of the company's stock. At the time, joint-stock companies were common only in the railroad industry.

From his first entry into the business of oil refining, Rockefeller set out to dominate the industry. He took a two-pronged business approach of vertical and horizontal integration to achieve this goal. In vertical integration, a company expands its business into different stages of the same production or distribution path. In horizontal integration, a company either acquires or merges with one or more companies that produce the same goods or offer the same services.

Rockefeller also realized how important the railroads were for transporting his refined products to markets, especially markets in the eastern United States. In 1871, after three railroads merged to form the Southern Improvement Company, its president, Thomas A. Scott, partnered with Rockefeller in a secret deal. According to the terms of the deal, the railroad company would receive regular oil shipments, thus ending price wars and ensuring its profit. Standard Oil (and other refineries in the deal) would receive rebates on their railroad shipments in return for a guaranteed volume of shipments. The refineries not in the deal would be required to pay higher rates for their railroad shipments. Thus, Standard Oil would have a significant advantage over its competitors. When details of the secret deal leaked out, the "Oil Wars" broke out. Rioters painted skulls and crossbones on Standard Oil signs. Rockefeller received death threats. The independent refineries protested against this scheme and it never went into effect, but it had a lasting negative effect on Rockefeller's reputation.

When the scheme fell apart, he turned to the horizontal integration strategy. He secretly began acquiring many of Cleveland's other refineries in exchange for Standard Oil shares. He took a carrot-and-stick approach. The carrot was his promise: "Take Standard Oil stock, and your family will never know want." The stick was his threat to drive the refineries into bankruptcy if their owners did not take the offer. Many of these former competitors became very wealthy when the price of Standard Oil's shares rose. Some of these men even went to work for Standard Oil. Within 4 months in 1872, Standard Oil had acquired 22 of its 26 Cleveland competitors in what became known as the Cleveland Massacre.

By the 1870s, Standard Oil had nearly 90% of the oil refining capacity in the United States. The company borrowed from banks, reinvested its profit, controlled its costs, and re-used the refinery waste. It had 200,000 domestic wells, 4,000 miles of pipeline, 5,000 tanker cars, and more than 100,000 employees. Standard Oil was the largest oil refiner in the world.

In 1882, Rockefeller's lawyers created an innovative business structure called a trust. A business trust combines several large businesses with the intent to create a monopoly (in which one company or a group of companies controls an industry). The main advantage of the trust structure was that it protected individual corporation directors from lawsuits and public criticism. Nine trustees managed the Standard Oil Trust, which consisted of 41 corporations. Rockefeller, of course, was a trustee. Other companies soon adopted this business innovation and formed their own trusts.

In 1885, the trustees of Standard Oil of Ohio took advantage of New Jersey's more lenient corporate stock ownership laws and concurrently chartered the Standard Oil Company of New Jersey. A few families privately owned the new company.

By the 1880s, Standard Oil Trust was losing its dominance over the oil refinery business as competition from Russia and Asia increased. Furthermore, the use of kerosene lighting waned as electric lighting became available. Yet Standard Oil continued to be, in historian Ron Chernow's words, "an infallible moneymaker." Chernow describes one of Standard Oil's tactics as predatory pricing (setting prices low in an attempt to stifle competition); in states where the practice was outlawed, the ban, he reports, was difficult to enforce.

The general public and the press were increasingly hostile to Rockefeller's business practices. They understood that business trusts were used to gain industry monopolies. They also despised Rockefeller's enormous wealth and power, which they thought he had acquired unethically. For example, in 1880, the *New York World* claimed that Standard Oil was "the most cruel, impudent, pitiless, and grasping monopoly that ever fastened upon a country." The most damning exposé of Rockefeller and his business practices appeared in a series of newspaper articles by Ida Tarbell. She had a personal reason to expose Rockefeller's tactics. Her father, Franklin Summer Tarbell, was an oil producer and refiner who lost his business in the Cleveland Massacre.

Tarbell was a journalist for *McClure's Magazine*, a monthly periodical that is credited with starting the tradition of muckraking—the act of reform-minded American journalists who investigated corruption in business institutions and politics.

In November 1902, Tarbell published the first of 19 articles on the history of the Standard Oil Company in *McClure's Magazine*. In 1904, all her articles were published as a book called *The History of the Standard Oil Company.*

Tarbell's research methods were both scrupulous and revolutionary. She conducted interviews and read thousands of public documents. She even visited Rockefeller's Baptist Church. Her focus was always on Rockefeller's business practices and his personal character. She praised some of Rockefeller's qualities—his ability to learn from mistakes, his faith, his intelligence, his efficiency, his love of his family, and his knowledge of the oil industry.

She also described his less attractive qualities—his willingness to pursue special and unfair privilege (as demonstrated by the Southern Improvement Company scheme and predatory pricing tactics) and his ruthless eagerness to take business advantage. She described Standard Oil's espionage practices, its price wars (competition in which companies cut prices in order to increase their share of the market), and its blackmailing tactics (the act of demanding money from a person for not revealing compromising information about that person).

Across America, readers were fascinated by Tarbell's book. It provoked a huge backlash against Rockefeller and Standard Oil. Even Tarbell was shocked by the public's reaction. She protested that she was critical only of the company's way of doing business. She had no complaint against corporate profit if it was fairly earned in open competition. Rockefeller never spoke publicly about the book, although privately he called its author "Miss Tarbarrel." Nevertheless, it was noticeable that following the book's publication he made himself more available to the press. Yet Rockefeller's reputation as a businessman who was more than willing to make secret deals, crush competitors, and demand rebates followed him until his death. Despite his enormous charitable donations, many historians still claim that reputation was well earned.

The U.S. government also challenged the Standard Oil Trust that was created in 1882. In the late 1880s, after many states passed antitrust laws, members of the U.S. Congress proposed numerous antitrust bills. Rockefeller was most concerned with the bill proposed in December 1889 by John Sherman, U.S. senator from Ohio. A few years earlier, in 1885, Rockefeller had tried to purchase protection of his business interests with a donation of $600 (about $15,000 in today's dollars) to Sherman's election campaign. Senator Sherman rebuffed this attempt and repeatedly named Standard Oil in the debates on his bill. In 1890, the U.S. Congress passed the Sherman Antitrust Act. The act allowed certain competitive business activities but recommended that the federal government investigate trusts. The purpose of the Sherman Antitrust Act was to preserve a competitive marketplace that protects consumers from predatory business practices and monopolies.

In *Standard Oil Co. of New Jersey v. United States* (1911), the U.S. Supreme Court ruled that a business combination is illegal if it engages in "unreasonable restraint of trade." Standard Oil was found guilty of controlling the petroleum industry through abusive and anticompetitive actions, in violation of the Sherman Antitrust Act. As a result, the Court required Standard Oil to be divided into 34 geographically distinct firms that would compete with one another.

This ruling led to the formation of companies now known as Chevron, Pennzoil, ConocoPhillips, British Petroleum, and ExxonMobil. Rockefeller's complete dominance of the oil industry was at an end. His personal wealth, however, increased, because he and other stockholders received proportionate shares in each of the 34 companies. Now Rockefeller had almost $900 million (about $24 billion in today's dollars).

In retirement, Rockefeller seemed embarrassed by his reputation and by public hatred of his family and its wealth. To protect his children from the damage a great inheritance often causes, he began giving away some of his wealth. He followed the words of John Wesley, the English clergyman: "Gain all you can, save all you can, and give all you can." Rockefeller had always donated generously to churches (including African American churches) and had even once paid for an enslaved person's freedom. At age 16, he gave 6% of his earnings to charity (recorded diligently in his personal ledger). By age 20, he was donating 10% of his earnings to charity, mainly to his church.

Rockefeller also made donations to nonreligious institutions. He provided funding to the Atlanta Baptist Female Seminary in Atlanta for African American women. This seminary, which is now known as Spelman College (named after his wife, Laura Spelman Rockefeller), is one of America's premier HBCUs (historically Black colleges and universities). He also gave $80 million (over $2 billion in today's dollars) to the University of Chicago. In 1901, he founded the Rockefeller Institution for Medical Research, which became Rockefeller University in 1965. His General Education Board, founded in 1903, was established to promote education throughout the country, including education in Black schools in the South.

On May 14, 1913, after years of planning, Rockefeller donated $250 million (over $6 billion in today's dollars) for the formation of the Rockefeller Foundation. The foundation's stated mission was "promoting the well-being of humanity throughout the world." Today the foundation supports public health activities, medical training, and the arts. One of its most notable accomplishments was the funding of research leading to the development of a vaccine for yellow fever.

Some of the foundation's activities, however, were not to its credit. For example, the foundation paid for eugenics (the science of improving a human population by controlled breeding) research and supported an institute that conducted racial studies in Nazi Germany. The Rockefeller family and the foundation today denounce these activities even if, at the time, Rockefeller himself did not. The Foundation states its mission today as "advancing inclusive economies that expand opportunities for more broadly shared prosperity, and building resilience by helping people, communities and institutions prepare for, withstand, and emerge stronger from acute shocks and chronic stresses."

In his book *The Tycoons*, Charles R. Morris charges that Tarbell's reporting was inaccurate. He wrote: "Rockefeller didn't need to cheat to win world oil dominance; he was simply better at the business than anyone else." The historian Allen Nevins argued:

> We have abundant evidence that Rockefeller's consistent policy was to offer fair terms to competitors and to buy them out, for cash, stock, or both, at fair appraisals; we have the statement of one impartial historian that Rockefeller was decidedly "more humane toward competitors" than Carnegie; we have the conclusion of another that his wealth was "the least tainted of all the great fortunes of his day."

Rockefeller's two goals in life were to accumulate $100 million and to live to age 100. He easily achieved the first goal and nearly reached the second. He died on May 23, 1937, at age 97. When he died his personal fortune was $1.4 billion (about $24 billion in today's dollars), it equaled more than 1.5% of the total U.S. gross domestic product (GDP).

The major sources for this chapter were:

Chernow, R. (1998). *Titan: The life of John D. Rockefeller, Sr.* New York, NY: Random House.

Morris, C. R. (2005). *The tycoons: How Andrew Carnegie, John D. Rockefeller, Jay Gould, and J.P. Morgan invented the American supereconomy.* New York, NY: Times Books.

Nevins, A. (1953). *Study in power: John D. Rockefeller: Industrialist and philanthropist.* New York, NY: Scribner.

Tarbell, I. M. (1904). *The history of the Standard Oil Company.* New York, NY: McClure, Phillips & Co.

LEARNING ACTIVITIES FOR "RICHEST MAN IN THE WORLD"

Facts of the Case

1. Briefly describe Rockefeller's childhood experiences.
2. What personal qualities helped Rockefeller achieve great financial success?
3. How did Rockefeller avoid The Civil War draft?
4. How did Rockefeller enter the oil industry?
5. Describe vertical and horizontal integration.
6. What was the Southern Improvement Company scheme?
7. Describe Rockefeller's motivations for philanthropy.

Historical Understanding

1. Why was the oil industry a lucrative business in the 19th century?
2. What was the Sherman Antitrust Act?
3. What happened to the Standard Oil Company of New Jersey after the Supreme Court ruled it violated the Sherman Antitrust Act?
4. What effect did Ida Tarbell's *The History of Standard Oil* have on Rockefeller's public image?

Expressing Your Reasoning

Were John D. Rockefeller's competitive business methods justifiable? Why or why not?

Key Concepts from History

What do the following have in common?

1. Telmex is a Mexican telecommunications company that was founded in 1947. Telemex currently controls 90% of the Mexican landline telephone market. It also owns 90% of the telephone lines in Mexico City and 80% of the telephone lines in Mexico.
2. U.S. Steel, founded in 1901, was, at one point, the largest steel producer and largest corporation in the world. Several large steel companies combined to form U.S. Steel. In its first full year of operation, U.S. Steel manufactured 67% of all steel manufactured in the United States.
3. American Telephone and Telegraph Company (AT&T), founded in 1885, dominated the telephone service business throughout the 20th century. At times, it was the world's largest telephone company, with a network of subsidiaries known as the Bell System in the United States and Canada. In 1982, U.S. regulators required AT&T to divest itself of these subsidiaries and turn them into individual companies.

Historical Inquiry

John D. Rockefeller was a major philanthropist. Using online and other resources, test the hypothesis that John D. Rockefeller donated more personal wealth (calculated as percentage of total wealth) than any other American in history. Compose a short essay in which you accept or reject the hypothesis. Use evidence to support your conclusion. To begin your investigation, the following search terms will be helpful:

- Top givers United States
- Most generous philanthropists

CHAPTER 26

The Wobbly Giant
Conflict Between Labor and Capital on the Frontier

William Dudley Haywood

The members of the Industrial Workers of the World (IWW) union were commonly known as *Wobblies*. The origin of the term is unknown. Among the founding members of the IWW were William "Big Bill" Dudley Haywood and Eugene V. Debs, the five-time Socialist Party of America candidate for president of the United States. "Big Bill" Haywood was known as the Wobbly Giant. In 1917, *The New York Times* referred to him as "the most hated and feared figure in America." In contrast, Eugene Debs called Haywood "the Lincoln of labor."

William Dudley Haywood was born in 1869 in Salt Lake City, Utah. Utah was a territory of the United States at the time. It became a state in 1896. Though not especially big in size, Haywood earned his reputation and nickname, Big Bill, by the force of his beliefs and actions. When Bill was 3 years old, his father died. Bill's mother remarried in 1875 to a miner and moved into a mining camp where Bill received a limited amount of schooling. At age 9, Bill was whittling a piece of wood when the knife slipped out of his hand and flew into his eye. He lost his right eye and forever after would turn his face to the right when having his picture taken to hide the missing eye.

That year, his stepfather took him to his first job, in a mine. Later, he was indentured (bound by a work contract) to a local farmer. When he was 13, Bill began to work on his own at odd jobs. At 15, he moved from Utah to Nevada and joined his stepfather working in a mining camp. For the next 16 years, Haywood would work as a miner. He also engaged in homesteading and worked as a surveyor, cowboy, and real estate agent. In 1889, he married Nevada Jane Minor, the daughter of a rancher, and claimed to have returned to Utah. Two daughters were born to the couple. Bill spent time away from home in search of better employment. In 1895, he left the family in Utah and ended up in Silver City, Idaho, where he took a job as an underground miner.

Haywood lived in a tough frontier environment. Mining camps would come and go. Miners were frequently injured or killed while working for low wages. Lynching and street shootouts were often used as forms of frontier justice. Haywood said, "I accepted it all as a natural part of life."

But Haywood was befriended by an old miner who tutored him in the concept of the class struggle and the principle "that an injury to one is an injury to all." The concept is closely associated with Marxism (the political and economic theory advanced by Karl Marx and Friedrich Engels in their 1848 work entitled *The Communist Manifesto*).

Marxism was a reaction to capitalism. According to Marx, the ruling class (those who own the means of production) exploit the working class. Marxist theory predicts that class struggle will lead to violent revolution. After the revolution, according to Marxist theory, a new communist society with no social classes (classless society) will emerge. Central to Marxist ideology is the labor theory of value, which maintains that the value of a product should be determined by the amount of human labor used in its production.

In a capitalist society, trade and industry are controlled by private owners. (The communism of Karl Marx rejects a right to private property; the state should control property, especially the means of production.) According to capitalist theory, the owners of private companies, including their investors, are motivated by profit in what is called a free market. Within a free market, prices and wages are determined by supply and demand. With an increase in demand, prices rise. As demand decreases, prices fall.

The tutoring by the old miner resonated dramatically with Haywood on the day of the Haymarket Affair of May 4, 1886. The day began with a peaceful labor rally in Haymarket Square in Chicago to support workers striking for an 8-hour day. The demonstrators were also marching in memory of several workers who had been killed by police during street demonstrations the day before. Suddenly, a dynamite bomb was thrown by an unidentified person. Seven police officers and four civilians were killed. Many others were wounded.

Ten years later, in August 1896, Haywood attended a meeting in Silver City of the Western Federation of Miners (WFM). At the meeting, he heard a speech from the union's first president, Ed Boyce. The WFM had been formed in 1893 in Butte, Montana, to fight for better pay and working conditions for miners. The union was founded during a labor conflict in the Coeur d'Alene region of Idaho, where workers went on strike to protest working conditions in the mines. The governor of Idaho, Frank Steunenberg, called for action to put down the strike. Mine owners came together with state and federal officials to crush the strike.

Boyce urged workers in his Silver City audience to join the WFM. He told them that the union offered their only protection from injury, indigence, dependence, and exploitation. Haywood and many of his fellow miners were inspired to join the WFM and soon formed their own Local 66 (a local is a branch of a union). It was Haywood's first union membership.

Boyce led the WFM as a radical arm of the labor movement in the West. In that year, the union came into open confrontation with the American Federation of Labor (AFL), founded and led by Samuel Gompers. The AFL was a federation of various unions, each of which represented workers of similar skills, trades, or crafts. The AFL tried to avoid confrontation with owners and to work within the American system of capitalism.

By contrast, the WFM advocated a radical approach to unionism. Its members believed in industrial unionism, where membership was open to all workers in an industry, not only to skilled workers with a specific trade or craft. The WFM expected that all workers, regardless of their specific trade, would join one big industrial union under a single contract in order to maintain their employment. This contrasted with the AFL's closed shop concept that required all workers in the same trade to be part of separate trade unions with separate contracts for their various trades.

The WFM's policy was the greater threat to owners. Having one union for all workers gave that union more leverage when negotiating with the ownership of a company. A single strike of all workers with the same contract could shut down a company. The WFM's slogan was: "The longer the picket line, the shorter the strike."

Haywood suffered a mining injury that prevented him from continuing to work in the mines. He turned to full-time work on union activities in a paid position. In 1900, he became a member of the WFM's national executive board. Soon afterwards he became secretary-treasurer of the union, working with its new president, Charles Moyer.

Under the leadership of Moyer and Haywood, the union moved to a more radical approach to unionism—socialism. Socialism, like other expressions of Marxism, advocates that the means of production, distribution, and exchange of goods and services be owned collectively and regulated by the community as a whole. This socialist position on ownership of property clashed with capitalism. Mine owners saw the WFM and its leaders, Moyer and Haywood, as dangerous people who would spread discord among their workers and threaten profits.

Haywood was a very successful organizer for the WFM. By 1903, the WFM had close to 60 locals and its membership approached 40,000 workers. The movement began attracting new interest eastward into the Midwest, including the states of Minnesota, Wisconsin, and Michigan.

Haywood favored direct action. He wanted to use tactics and strategies that would openly confront owners. Direct action included strikes and demonstrations. Sometimes Haywood's rhetoric hinted at the use of illegal means to achieve the union's purposes, but Big Bill rejected violent confrontation. Frustrated when their demands and strikes were met with force by mine owners and by local and state law enforcement, some WFM members believed that it might be necessary to meet force with force.

Regardless of their differences with the AFL, Moyer and Haywood decided to join it. They believed their relatively small union would benefit from an alliance with the larger, stable, and more moderate AFL. The relationship, however, soured when the AFL failed to come to the aid of the WFM during a violent conflict with the Cloud City mine owners in Colorado. The WFM allied with the Socialist Party of America (SPA) and its founder Eugene Debs, instead of the AFL.

Late in 1904, WFM leaders and other labor radicals organized a national convention in Chicago that would produce a new revolutionary union. The new union created at the convention was (and still is) the Industrial Workers of the World (IWW). The Wobblies, as they were known, took an aggressive approach to union organizing. The first sentences of their constitution read, "The working class and the employing class have nothing in common. There can be no peace so long as hunger and want of food are found among the working people and the few, who make up the employing class, have all good things in life."

The IWW instituted a number of organizing and union innovations. They made agreements with other unions that prevented crossing one another's strike picket lines. They engaged in production slowdowns as a means of protest. They called the slowdowns "a collective withdrawal of efficiency by workers at the point of production." They were the first union to employ the "sit-down" strike at the workplace. The IWW was unique among the unions at the time in that it welcomed African American and immigrant workers into its ranks.

Only 1 year after the formation of the IWW, Big Bill faced big trouble. In 1900, Haywood had visited the Coeur d'Alene mine in Idaho, where in 1896, Governor Steunenberg had ordered the violent workers' strike to be quelled. Hundreds of striking workers had been jailed in railroad boxcars where they subsisted on bread and water and without blankets. Writing in the *Miners Magazine,* Haywood said:

That we condemn such arbitrary action of the said Governor of Idaho for the usurpation worthy of tyrants of the Middle Ages and that such a man is unworthy of the respect and support of all liberty loving people.

The WFM newspaper stated that Steunenberg would be held to account for his actions in the Coeur d'Alene affair.

On December 30, 1905, Frank Steunenberg was assassinated by an explosion as he opened the gate to the walkway of his home in Caldwell, Idaho. He had been a popular governor and a well-respected businessman in Caldwell. His murder caused a storm of public concern and protest.

Immediately following Steunenberg's death, Idaho Governor Frank Gooding ordered an investigation. A man named Harry Orchard, whose presence in Caldwell was unexplained, was arrested. Orchard's hotel room was searched and bomb-making materials were discovered. Orchard had been a WFM member and had at one time been the bodyguard for WFM President Moyer.

The Idaho governor, mine owners, and other business owners quickly saw an opportunity to implicate Big Bill Haywood and Charles Moyer, both of whom they regarded as a threat to the safety of the citizens of Idaho. Convictions of the two could spell the end of influence for the troublesome WFM.

Orchard confessed, leading to charges being brought against Haywood, Moyer, and George Pettibone. Pettibone was a radical member of the WFM and a former union treasurer who had been arrested at the strike at the Coeur d'Alene mine. Orchard claimed Pettibone was the one who provided him with the bomb-making materials. Under Idaho law, conspirators to a crime are considered to be *legally* present at the scene of the crime even if they were not *physically* present. The three defendants were considered conspirators and, therefore, legally present in Idaho at the scene of the crime even though all three were actually in Colorado at the time the crime was committed.

The actual location of the defendants posed a problem for their prosecution in Idaho. Although they were considered to be legally present at the Idaho crime scene, under the law the three men had to be brought physically to Idaho to stand trial. At the time that Orchard confessed, they were in Colorado. They could only be legally removed from Colorado to Idaho as criminal suspects through a process known as extradition. A request by Idaho to extradite the three accused men could be challenged by their union lawyers in the Colorado courts. The lawyers would argue that the extradition was unlawful in that the three defendants were not present in Idaho at the time the crime was committed.

Idaho Governor Gooding urged Colorado Governor McDonald to extradite Haywood, Moyer, and Pettibone to Idaho. After reading Orchard's 64-page confession, Governor McDonald secretly signed the extradition order. On February 17, 1906, the three men were secretly arrested by Colorado state law enforcement officials in Denver and taken by a special train to Boise under the security of Idaho law enforcement. When news leaked out about the secret arrest and return of the accused men, union lawyers attempted to challenge the legality of the extradition. The Idaho Supreme Court ruled it had no jurisdiction in the case, and the United States Supreme Court held that the extradition was lawful. Union members called the extradition a kidnapping.

The three defendants were tried separately. Big Bill Haywood was first. His trial began on May 9, 1907, following a lengthy jury selection process. The attorneys for the prosecution were a famed Idaho attorney, William Borah, who would go on to serve as a United States senator, and James Hawley, the state's most experienced trial attorney. The defense team consisted primarily of WFM longtime attorney Edmund Richardson and one of the most famous and highly regarded criminal lawyers in the country, Clarence Darrow from Chicago. The trial received nationwide publicity. President Theodore Roosevelt became involved in the case when he called for a conviction, referring to the three defendants as "undesirable citizens."

All three defendants testified at Haywood's trial. Bill Haywood denied the accusations and testified that he opposed violence as part of direct action. During cross-examination by Borah, Haywood fixed his single eye on the prosecutor. Borah later said, "Haywood's glare doubled me up like a jack-knife." Borah tried and failed to crack Haywood's testimony.

Famed defense attorney Clarence Darrow's summation left a powerful emotional impression on the jury. To invoke sympathy for the defendants, Darrow urged jurors to consider themselves as representatives of the poor, the weak, and the weary.

Borah's summation emphasized that the case was a simple murder trial and not an attack on organized labor. He appealed to the courage, intelligence, and duty of the jurors to reach a verdict of guilty. After 9 hours of deliberation, the jury reached its verdict on July 29. Big Bill was found not guilty.

The trial enhanced Haywood's reputation. He became a celebrity, known for outspoken public statements against capitalism as he continued to organize for the IWW. His use of direct action in several labor disputes kept his name in the news. In a 1913 speech in New York, he remarked that he favored the tactics of direct action over the use of the ballot. The Socialist Party of America objected and its membership removed him from their national executive board.

In 1918, Haywood was charged, along with more than 100 others, under the Espionage Act of 1917, enacted during World War I. The charges were conspiring to hinder the draft, encouraging desertion, and intimidating others in connection with labor disputes. Haywood and 101 other defendants were found guilty, all at the same trial, and sentenced to lengthy prison terms. Rather than face a 30-year prison sentence, Haywood skipped his bail and fled to Russia. In Russia, he became a labor advisor to Vladimir Lenin's new revolutionary communist government. Because of his flight to Russia, Haywood was disowned by the IWW.

Big Bill Haywood died in 1926 as an unhappy man who wished he was back in the United States. In accordance with his wishes, half of his ashes were buried in the wall around the Kremlin in Moscow, and half near the Haymarket monument in Chicago.

The major sources for this chapter were:

Dubofsky, M. (1987). *Big Bill Haywood*. New York, NY: St. Martin's Press, Inc.

Johnson, B. (2017). *Assassination: Idaho's trial of the century. Byron Johnson interview.* Idaho Public Television. Available at http://idahoptv.org/productions/specials/trial/commentary/johnson.cfm

Linder, D. O. (2017). Bill Haywood Trial (1907). Available at http://www.famous-trials.com/haywood

Lukas, J. A. (1997). *Big trouble: A murder in a small western town sets off a struggle for the soul of America*. New York, NY: Simon & Schuster.

LEARNING ACTIVITIES FOR "THE WOBBLY GIANT"

Facts of the Case

1. Who were the Wobblies?
2. What early events helped shape the life of Bill Haywood?
3. What is industrial unionism?
4. Why was the Western Federation of Miners (WFM) union formed?
5. Why were William Dudley Haywood, Charles Moyer, and George Pettibone charged with murder?
6. What were the unusual circumstances surrounding the extradition of Haywood, Moyer, and Pettibone?
7. Why did Haywood flee to Russia?

Historical Understanding

1. How are some major differences between Marxism and capitalism?
2. What was the Haymarket Affair?
3. Why were mine owners and state officials in Idaho concerned about the WFM?
4. How did the beliefs of the AFL differ from those of the WFM and the IWW?

Expressing Your Reasoning

Should Colorado Governor McDonald have extradited Bill Haywood and his co-defendants to Idaho? Why or why not?

Key Concepts from History

What do the following have in common?

1. Egypt: In 2011, as part of the Arab Spring in the Middle East and North Afri-
    ca, strikes, sit-ins, and protests by millions of Egyptians led to the resignation
    of President Hosni Mubarak.
2. Ukraine: Beginning in 2013, citizens of the Ukraine began a boycott of Rus-
    sian goods to protest Russian trade embargoes against the Ukraine and the
    Russian military invasion of the Ukraine.
3. Indivisible: Following the November 2016 election of Donald Trump, for-
    mer congressional staff employees organized a nationwide movement of cit-
    izens, called Indivisible, to oppose the policies of President Trump and his
    congressional supporters. Indivisible tactics and strategies included marches,
    picketing, vigils, information gathering and dissemination, and active partici-
    pation at town hall meetings held by Republican senators and members of the
    House of Representatives.

Historical Inquiry

Colorado governor McDonald ordered Bill Haywood and his codefendants to
be extradited to Idaho. If someone accused of a crime flees to another state or
country, must the accused be extradited to the state or country where the crime
was committed?

Using online and other sources, test the hypothesis that someone accused
of a crime who flees to another state or country must be extradited to the state
where the crime was committed. Compose a short essay in which you accept or
reject the hypothesis. To begin your investigation, the following search terms will
be helpful:

- State to state extradition
- Country to country extradition
- Julian Assange, Roman Polanski, and Edward Snowden
- *Ker v. Illinois* (1886) and the Ker Doctrine
- El Chapo extradition claim
- *United States v. Alvarez-Machain* (1992)
- The right of states to extradite

CHAPTER 27

General Manager of the Nation

Nelson W. Aldrich and the Income Tax

Senator Aldrich Depicted as the Evil Power of the United States Senate, 1906

Puck Magazine by John S. Pughe

Americans have a long history of resisting taxes. On December 16, 1773, members of the Sons of Liberty (a secret patriots' society), disguised as Mohawk Indians, threw 92,000 pounds of tea from British ships into the Boston Harbor. The British East India Company owned the tea. The American colonists resisted paying taxes under the Tea Act that the British Parliament had passed. The system was unfair, the colonists argued, because it was "taxation without representation."

They had no representatives in the British Parliament. This event, known as the Boston Tea Party, perhaps best symbolizes Americans' resistance to taxation.

In the United States today, governments at various levels (federal, state, and local) pass laws that tax individuals and corporations. There are many kinds of taxes and many ways to describe them. Direct taxes are taxes imposed on an individual (for example, personal income taxes and inheritance taxes) or on property (for example, real estate taxes). Indirect taxes are taxes imposed on transactions of goods and services (for example, sales taxes and hotel taxes).

Taxes can also be classified as progressive or regressive. For progressive taxes, the rate of tax increases as the taxable amount increases. Another word for progressive taxes is *graduated taxes*. As an example, a person with taxable income of $1,000,000 pays a higher tax rate (that is, a higher percentage) than a person with taxable income of $20,000. For regressive taxes, the rate of tax is the same for everyone (also known as a flat tax). As an example, a wealthy person and a poor person pay the same sales tax rate for concert tickets. Another way to understand the difference between progressive and regressive taxes is that a progressive tax is based on the ability to pay it, and a regressive tax is not based on the ability to pay it.

A national survey conducted in 2016 found that 57% of Americans said they paid "too much" in federal income taxes. It is worth noting that, in a typical year, 45% of Americans do not owe or pay any federal income tax (although they do pay other forms of taxes). Some Americans have called taxation "tyranny" and "legalized larceny." Others say the federal income tax system is motivated by "class hatred," and enforced by an "illegal espionage system." The Internal Revenue Service (IRS), which collects U.S. income taxes, has been nicknamed by its detractors the "Infernal Revenue Service" and the "Income Reduction Service."

The history of federal income taxes in the United States is a long and complex story. The story began with the country's first constitution, the Articles of Confederation—adopted by the Continental Congress on November 15, 1777, and ratified by the 13 states on March 1, 1781. The Articles gave the states, not the U.S. Congress, the power to tax Americans. This posed a problem for the federal government. The only way for the government to raise money was to tax imported goods (with tariffs), to borrow from foreign governments, or to sell federal lands (in the western territories).

The problem was so severe that the U.S. Constitution, which replaced the Articles of Confederation in 1789, gave the U.S. Congress the power of taxation. Three articles in the Constitution address this issue. Article 1, Section 8 states:

> The Congress shall have Power to lay and collect Taxes, Duties, Imposts and Excises, to pay the Debts and provide for the common Defence and general Welfare of the United States; but all Duties, Imposts and Excises shall be uniform throughout the United States.

Article 1, Section 2, Clause 3 states:

> Representatives and direct Taxes shall be apportioned among the several States which may be included within this Union, according to their respective Numbers, which shall be determined by adding to the whole Number of free Persons, including those bound to Service for a Term of Years, and excluding Indians not taxed, three fifths of all other Persons.

Article 1, Section 9 states:

> No Capitation, or other direct, Tax shall be laid, unless in Proportion to the Census or Enumeration herein before directed to be taken.

In summary, the U.S. Constitution gave Congress the power of taxation, directed how such taxes should be allocated among the states, and explained how the population should be counted for purposes of taxation. The apportionment rule meant that direct taxes were imposed on the states in proportion to each state's population relative to the national population. For example, residents of a state with 10% of the country's population would pay 10% of the total direct taxes collected.

The apportionment calculation would cause much controversy in the years ahead (as did the "three fifths of all other Persons" clause). Apportionment of taxes among the states was the law of the land until the ratification of the Sixteenth Amendment to the U.S. Constitution in 1913.

In its earliest years, after the Revolutionary War, the U.S. government needed a great deal of money to pay its expenses and to repay war debts. The war debt alone was around $43 million ($630 million in today's dollars). But, despite Congress's increased power of taxation under the Constitution, it was limited in how it could raise money. The main source of revenue was tariffs—customs duties.

Tariffs, which were payments charged on imported products, accounted for between 80 and 95% of all federal revenue. They were easily collected at the ports. Alexander Hamilton (the first U.S. secretary of the treasury) supported tariffs. In his *Report on Manufactures*, Hamilton argued that tariffs, used in moderation, would raise revenue for the federal government and also encourage domestic manufacturing and economic growth. This foreign trade policy is known as protectionism (protecting a country's domestic industries from foreign competition by taxing imports).

But the tariffs did not raise enough money. In 1791, Congress passed the Excise Whiskey Tax. The Whiskey Tax levied a federal tax on domestic and imported alcohol. Many people (grain farmers, especially) protested the new tax. In 1802, President Jefferson signed into law the repeal of the whiskey tax, passed by Congress.

Resistance to paying taxes takes several forms—opposition to the government that levies the tax, opposition to government policy on taxation, or opposition to the tax itself. Some U.S. citizens have resisted paying taxes as an act of civil disobedience. Others have resisted with violence. Shays' Rebellion (1786–1787) was an armed protest against the Massachusetts state income tax. The 1794 Whiskey Rebellion was a violent protest in western Pennsylvania against the "Whiskey Tax." The John Fries's Rebellion (1799–1800) was an armed revolt in Pennsylvania against taxes on property and slaves. The U.S. government's responses to such uprisings were to send the militia, issue warrants, make arrests, and put rebellion leaders on trial.

In the 19th century, more attempts were made to legislate a federal income tax. During the War of 1812, Secretary of the Treasury Alexander J. Dallas proposed a federal income tax that was never implemented. To help pay for The Civil War, President Lincoln signed the Revenue Act of 1861 into law. As the country's first federal income tax, the Revenue Act of 1861 levied a 3% tax on individual income over $800 (approximately $22,000 in today's dollars). The tax affected very few people in the United States—only about 3% of the population. Under the law, income was defined as "derived from any kind of property, or from any professional trade, employment, or vocation carried on in the United States or elsewhere or from any source whatever." Because the law established a flat rate of tax, it was a regressive tax. The same tax rate applied to everyone (with incomes over $800) with no allowance for tax deductions (tax deductions allow taxpayers to reduce their taxable income).

However, the Revenue Act of 1861 required the states to collect the tax. The federal government had no role in tax collection or in enforcement of the law. Without an enforcement mechanism, the act failed to raise the money needed to finance The Civil War. In the next year, the Revenue Act of 1862 repealed the earlier act and established the office of the Commissioner of Internal Revenue that had the powers of tax collector and tax law enforcer.

Just as important in the history of U.S. income taxes, the Revenue Act of 1862 established as law the tax policy of progressive taxation of income. The act's tax rates progressively increased. The rates were 0%, 3%, and 5%, depending on the individual's taxable income. The federal government still could not raise sufficient funds to pay for the war. With the Internal Revenue Act of 1864, tax rates were increased: 0%, 5%, 7.5%, and 10%. Most of the revenue raised by the law came from New York, Pennsylvania, and Massachusetts. However, the 1864 Act was only a temporary wartime measure. It was allowed to expire in 1873.

Before the Revenue Act of 1864 expired, the U.S. Treasury had collected $376 million ($5.69 billion in today's dollars). Yet the collection system was haphazard, confusing, and inconsistent. People living in northeastern and midwestern states paid the largest share of the taxes collected. Almost every taxpayer complained. Mark Twain, American author and humorist, joked: "I shall never use profanity except in discussing house rent and taxes."

For decades after The Civil War, legislators in Congress, usually from western or southern states, tried and failed—more than 60 times—to pass income tax legislation. It was only in the Progressive Era (about 1890 to 1920) that Americans began to look more favorably on a tax on income. These were years in which laws were passed in an attempt to solve problems resulting from industrialization, urbanization, immigration, and corruption in government. Three presidents in the Progressive Era—Theodore Roosevelt, William Howard Taft, and Woodrow Wilson—supported these politically progressive policies. During this period, four amendments to the Constitution were ratified. The Seventeenth Amendment required that senators be elected directly by the people, rather than appointed by state legislatures; the Eighteenth Amendment (referred to as "Prohibition") declared the production, transportation, and sale of alcohol illegal; and the Nineteenth Amendment guaranteed women the right to vote.

The other constitutional amendment adopted in these years was the Sixteenth Amendment (adopted in 1913). The background to the Sixteenth Amendment is complicated. In 1894, Congress passed a law that reduced tariffs and imposed a 2% income tax on "gains, profits, and incomes" in excess of $4,000 (about $112,000 in today's dollars). A year later, in 1895, the U.S. Supreme Court ruled in *Pollock v. Farmers' Loan & Trust Co.* that income taxes on interest, dividends, and rents were direct taxes, and therefore unconstitutional. Direct taxes had to be levied proportionally among the states by population count.

Nelson W. Aldrich, a very influential Republican senator from Rhode Island, eventually helped pass the Sixteenth Amendment. He was born on November 6, 1841, in Foster, Rhode Island. He began his career as a wholesale grocer. In 1866, he married Abigail Pearce Truman Chapman. They had 11 children, one of whom, Abby, married John D. Rockefeller, Jr., whose father was cofounder of Standard Oil. After holding various political positions, Aldrich was elected to the U.S. Senate in 1881, where he served for 30 years.

Aldrich was a powerful senator. He was 6 feet tall with penetrating, icy eyes, and excellent political skills. By the 1890s, along with Orville H. Platt, William B. Allison, and John Coit Spooner, he was one of the "Big Four" key Republicans who wielded great power. He was nicknamed the "General Manager of the Nation" because of his control over tariff and monetary policies. He used his position as chairman of the Senate Finance Committee to expand his investments in the banking, sugar, rubber, gas, and electricity industries. His stance on tariffs, and the protectionism they offered, benefited these industries. He pushed through tariff bills in 1890, 1894, and 1897. The 1890 bill was the McKinley Tariff, which raised tariff rates to 48%, the highest level in U.S. history to date. For pushing through legislation favorable to industry, he was rewarded with generous campaign contributions.

Aldrich did not speak frequently on the Senate floor; instead, he preferred to do his negotiating in the more informal settings of the congressional committee rooms. As one historian wrote, Aldrich "did not bother with oratorical display but relied upon his charm, his commanding appearance, his superior mind, his ability to speak forthrightly, and his exceptional memory for details." During this period, he was a fierce opponent of the income tax, calling it "communistic."

Aldrich was viewed by progressives as an opponent of reform. Nothing captures that sentiment better than the carton of Aldrich at the introduction of this chapter. The cartoon appeared in a 1906 issue of *Puck Magazine*, a political humor magazine that exposed political corruption. The cartoon depicted Aldrich as a large spider in a cobweb labeled "Senate Committee Room," that was spread between the U.S. Capitol and a Standard Oil tower. Flies were caught in the web: "Anti-Trust Bill," "Free Alcohol Bill," "House Bill," "Philippine Tariff Bill," and "Legislation Needed."

Public opinion in favor of progressive policies, including the income tax, continued to grow. One reason was the Panic of 1907 that caused an economic recession (a period of slow economic growth including decreased consumer spending, generally lasting several months or more). The New York Stock Exchange fell nearly 50%. People rushed to their banks to withdraw their funds. This is called a bank run. Industries laid off a third of their employees. Cities and states established public works projects to employ men who were out of work.

The government was under pressure to respond to the Panic. With Edward Vreeland, a Republican from New York, Aldrich wrote the Aldrich-Vreeland Act in 1908. The act allowed banks to issue emergency currency, putting more money into circulation. It also established the Federal Reserve system (nicknamed the Fed), which is the central banking system for the United States, charged with promoting a sound banking system and a healthy economy. Yet the prohibition on income taxes, as unconstitutional direct taxes, remained.

At the beginning of the recession, President Theodore Roosevelt had only 1 year left in his term in office, and he did not plan to seek a third term. He avoided the income tax issue by declaring that a decision about it should be delayed until the next administration. Roosevelt had declared support for a progressive income tax, but his support was tempered: He acknowledged that the Supreme Court's 1895 rejection of the income tax in *Pollock v. Farmers' Loan & Trust Co.* concerned him.

The income tax issue was left unresolved until the administration of Roosevelt's successor, Ohio lawyer and judge, and Roosevelt's secretary of war, William Howard Taft. Taft had inherited a $100 million budget deficit—the largest since The Civil War. In his inaugural address in 1909, he promised to press for some tariff reductions (as well as a graduated inheritance tax to compensate for the lost revenues. He was also supportive of the income tax but, like Roosevelt, was wary of challenging the Supreme Court ruling against the income tax. Unlike his predecessor, Taft had neither the will nor the skill to intervene in the legislative process. He called Congress into a special session shortly after his inauguration to charge them with tariff reform. He then waited to see what Congress would come up with.

Congress presented five separate proposals on taxes and tariffs. Taft had to decide which of them to support. Representative Sereno Payne from upstate New York had authored and helped pass a bill, the Payne tariff bill, through the House.

It increased tariffs on some goods (cotton, gloves, hosiery, plate glass, and fruit) and imposed new duties on others. It also included an inheritance tax (between 1 and 5%) but no taxes on corporations. Senator Nelson Aldrich offered his own version of the Payne tariff bill, adding 847 amendments to it. It did not include an income tax, corporation tax, or the inheritance tax from the Payne tariff bill.

Aldrich was optimistic about the success of the bill. Senate opposition, however, was strong and loud. Several bills were drafted as alternatives to the tariff bills. One of them called for a constitutional amendment for an income tax.

With the introduction of these bills, Aldrich was fighting against lower tariffs and the income tax. Taft did not know how to respond. He was also distracted from politics by his wife's health problems.

As Senate support for the income tax grew, Aldrich became deeply concerned. On May 24, 1909, he and two other senators went to the White House to meet with Taft. President Taft had been eager to forge a relationship with Aldrich. Taft had said about Aldrich: "A man with whom I don't always agree, but whose effectiveness, straightforwardness and clearheadedness, and whose command of men everybody . . . must recognize."

Together, Aldrich and Taft decided their tactic would be to persuade the Republicans to agree to a corporation tax, and convince supporters of an income tax to push for a constitutional amendment instead of legislation that would be vulnerable to being ruled unconstitutional by the Supreme Court. One historian called their compromise, known as the Payne-Aldrich Tariff Act, "genius." Aldrich did not like the corporation tax, but believed it was less objectionable than other possibilities. One senator remarked, "This is the very distressing and embarrassing alternative and there is no other." Aldrich responded, "Yes, that is exactly it."

Taft and Aldrich each began wooing senators to support the act. Taft invited them to golf games and dinners on the White House terrace; Aldrich took senators on evening rides in Rock Creek Park, a beautiful national park in Washington, D.C. Aldrich was able to get the Aldrich tariff bill passed in the Senate, 45 to 34, on July 7, 1909. After some adjustments were made to the bill (the corporation tax was reduced from 2% to 1% and some tariffs were reduced), the House narrowly approved the final bill by a vote of 195 to 183 on July 31. Taft then signed it. Corporations with $5,000 and more in income would be taxed at 1%. The bill also included the constitutional amendment on the income tax; however, it still had to be ratified.

The two-step process for amending the Constitution is contained in Article 5 of the U.S. Constitution. There are two ways for amendments to be proposed: either by Congress with a two-thirds vote in both the Senate and the House of Representatives, or by a national convention, called by Congress, on the matter and approved by two-thirds of the state legislatures. There are also two ways for proposed amendments to be ratified: through approval either by three-fourths of the state legislatures or by state ratifying conventions. Proposed amendments state the manner of ratification to be followed. The state ratifying conventions approach has been used once, for the Twenty-first Amendment, repealing Prohibition. All other amendments, including the Sixteenth, followed the route of approval by state legislatures. Thus, after congressional approval of the income tax, three-fourths of the states would have to approve it; 36 of the then 48 state legislatures had to ratify the Amendment or it would die.

The Sixteenth Amendment states: The Congress shall have power to lay and collect taxes on incomes, from whatever source derived, without apportionment among the several states, and without regard to any census or enumeration.

Aldrich hoped ratification of the Sixteenth Amendment would fail. He feared the amendment gave the federal government too much power. He also knew his donors would not support the income tax. No amendment had been ratified for more than 40 years. Nevertheless, Aldrich was taking a gamble on its failure.

The ratification process among the state legislatures lasted 4 years: 1909 to 1913. Supporters argued income taxes were a fair and predictable way to raise funds to operate the government. Opponents argued "income" should not apply to wages, that progressive tax rates violate equal protection rights (guaranteed by the Fourteenth Amendment), and that a direct income tax was opposed by the nation's founders.

State legislatures had mixed views on the amendment. In the South, income tax was generally favored over tariffs. Southerners had the lowest per capita income tax burden because, on average, their incomes were lower than those of people living in the Northeast and Midwest. The North had about 90% of the country's income. There was some opposition in the South to the amendment: Southerners thought it could dangerously strengthen the federal government and might infringe on their oppression of African Americans. They also claimed they would receive fewer benefits from the income tax than others. However, the South ended up supporting the Amendment because southerners believed northerners had lost interest in protecting the rights of African Americans and, as one historian argued, the southern and western states thought they were "colonies" of the northeastern states. Many westerners also believed they were being exploited by eastern railroad industrialists.

Many people and businesses in the northeastern and midwestern states opposed the amendment. William Bourne Cockran, a U.S. representative from New York, said that forcing a small number of people to support the federal government through a direct tax would create a "class distinction." New York lawyers from the banking and business sectors charged that, if the amendment passed, 10 or 12 states would pay 90% of the tax bill. They complained the money would be spent on wasteful projects in the West and South.

The Republican Party split over the income tax issue. A new political party formed that was called the Progressive Party. With this split in the Republican Party, combined with Taft's support of the 1909 Payne-Aldrich Tariff Act, the

Republicans did poorly in the 1910 midterm elections. They lost the presidency in the election of 1912 when Woodrow Wilson, a Democrat, defeated the incumbent, President Taft. On February 25, 1913, Secretary of State Philander Knox announced that three-fourths of the states had ratified the Sixteenth Amendment. Four states rejected the amendment: Utah, Connecticut, New Hampshire, and Rhode Island (Nelson Aldrich's home state). President Wilson signed the Revenue Act of 1913 that imposed the federal income tax after the ratification of the Sixteenth Amendment.

The Revenue Act of 1913 levied a 1% tax on single individuals with taxable income over $3,000 and on couples with taxable income over $4,000. ($1,000 in 1913 is the equivalent of about $25,000 today.) There was also a 6% tax on taxable income over $500,000. It was a graduated (progressive) tax. That is the system that exists today. At the time of this writing, the highest individual marginal tax rate is 37%.

People will always argue about the need for taxes and on the use of tax revenues. Benjamin Franklin wrote in 1789: "Our new Constitution is now established, and has an appearance that promises permanency; but in this world nothing can be said to be certain, except death and taxes."

The major sources for this chapter were:

Buenker, J. D. (1981). The ratification of the federal income tax amendment. *Cato Journal, 1*(1), 183–223.

Einhorn, R. L. (2014). Look away Dixieland: The south and the federal income tax. *Northwestern University Law Review 108*(3), 773–798.

Huret, R. D. (2014). *American tax resisters*. Cambridge, MA: Harvard University Press.

Merrill, H. S., & Merrill, M. G. (2015). *The republican command, 1897–1913*. Lexington, KY: University Press of Kentucky.

Weisman, S. R. (2002). *The great tax wars*. New York, NY: Simon & Schuster.

LEARNING ACTIVITIES FOR "GENERAL MANAGER OF THE NATION"

Facts of the Case

1. What role did the income tax play during The Civil War?
2. Describe apportionment in relation to taxes.
3. What is the difference between direct and indirect taxes?
4. What is the difference between progressive and regressive taxes?
5. What were Senator Aldrich's personal motives for supporting tariffs and opposing an income tax?
6. What was the ruling in *Pollock v. Farmers' Loan & Trust Company*?

Historical Understanding

1. Describe several of the ways Americans protested taxes during the early years of the Republic.
2. Why did Alexander Hamilton support tariffs?
3. Describe the nature of political and social reforms in the Progressive Era.
4. How does the U.S. Constitution (excluding the Sixteenth Amendment) address taxation?
5. How can the U.S. Constitution be amended (using the Sixteenth Amendment as an example)?

Expressing Your Reasoning

Should Senator Nelson Aldrich have supported the 1909 Payne-Aldrich Tariff Act that proposed an income tax amendment to the U.S. Constitution? Why or why not?

Key Concepts from History

What do the following have in common?

1. The billionaire investor Warren Buffett said he pays a lower tax rate than the people employed in his office. In 2011, his average federal income tax rate was 17.4%. His employees paid an average tax rate of 36%. The explanation is that most of Buffett's taxable income is from investments (taxed at a top rate of 15%) whereas the top rate for other income (e.g., salaries and wages) at the time was 39.6%.
2. A 1959 reform to Florida's property tax code reduced the rates for "agricultural" land. The aim was to encourage more farmers to work within the state. However, people could legally qualify for this special rate so long as they had livestock on their property. For example, the Walt Disney Company and other landowners hired "Rent-a-Cow" ranchers who grazed their animals on the properties. The reduction in tax revenue to the state of Florida is estimated in millions of dollars annually.
3. Oil companies in the United States have tax advantages that other companies do not. Large oil companies are able to defer their tax payments and are also able to reduce their taxable income by special deductions called "depletion allowances." This system is justified on the basis that the tax incentives encourage investment in exploration. Opponents argue that oil companies have huge profits and do not need the tax incentives.

Historical Inquiry

States in the South and West tended to support the income tax, whereas states in the North and East tended to oppose it. Using online and other resources, test the hypothesis that in 2016, states in the South and West, on average, received a disproportionately larger share of federal dollars returned to their states from federal programs than states in the Midwest and Northeast. Compose a short essay in which you accept or reject the hypothesis. Use evidence to support your conclusion. To begin your investigation, the following search terms will be helpful:

- 2016 most federally dependent states
- 2016 least federally dependent states
- Givers and takers in the federal budget

CHAPTER 28

A War to End All Wars

American Entry Into World War I

Woodrow Wilson, 1912

National Portrait Gallery, Smithsonian Institution

It was April 6, 1917. In Europe, two massive military forces were divided by a 475-mile line (known as the Western Front). In rows of fortified trenches, the forces of Germany and its allies, and Britain and France with theirs, had been battling and bloodying each other for 3 years in what came to be called the Great War. (Other major theaters of the war included the Eastern Front, where Russia was engaged against Germany and its allies until late 1917.) The carnage of the war was unprecedented. Casualties were not in thousands, or tens of thousands, or even hundreds of thousands. They were in the millions.

Fighting was stalemated along the Western Front, but not for much longer. On April 7, 1917, the United States entered the Great War, which we more commonly call World War I. America decisively brought its vast industrial and manpower resources to fight the war alongside Britain and France and against Germany. President Woodrow Wilson led his nation into war.

Woodrow Wilson was born in 1856 in Staunton, Virginia. He was the third of four children born to Scotch-Irish parents, the Reverend Joseph Wilson and his wife, Jessie. When Woodrow was not yet 2 years old, his family moved to Augusta, Georgia.

Woodrow Wilson spent the formative years of his youth, during The Civil War and its aftermath, in Augusta. As an 8-year-old, Wilson watched as captured Confederate president Jefferson Davis was led through town in chains. Memories of the chaos and destruction of that war had a lasting influence on Wilson.

After The Civil War, during Reconstruction (1865–1876), Wilson's father moved the family first to Columbia, South Carolina, and then to Wilmington, North Carolina. Woodrow had a comfortable childhood. He attended a small school in Augusta and was also schooled at home by his parents. Later, he studied at Davidson College in North Carolina from where he transferred to Princeton University. He studied political philosophy and history and excelled at oratory and debate. After graduating from Princeton, Wilson attended the University of Virginia Law School and practiced law in Georgia before giving up law to pursue study of political science and history. In 1886, he received his PhD in political science from Johns Hopkins University.

In 1883, Wilson had gone to Rome, Georgia, to assist in the settlement of an uncle's estate. While in Georgia he met Ellen Axson, a talented art student and the daughter of a minister from Savannah. The two fell in love and were married in 1885. The Wilsons had three daughters: Margaret, born in 1886, Jessie in 1887, and Eleanor in 1889.

Wilson pursued a rich academic career. He taught at Cornell University in New York and at Bryn Mawr College in Pennsylvania. In 1888, he left Bryn Mawr to teach at Wesleyan University in Connecticut, where he also coached the football team and founded the debate team. In 1890, Wilson was chosen by the Princeton University board to be a professor of jurisprudence and political economy. He relished the intellectual life of teaching and writing, and he became a widely respected scholar, author, and a popular lecturer. In 1902, university trustees unanimously elected Wilson, popular among faculty, students, and townspeople, to be president of Princeton.

Wilson was drawn to public life. He felt an ambition for an active political career and his public speeches began to reflect his ideas about social reform. He spoke out against great wealth, claiming that those who possess it are cut off from sympathy with the mass of the population. In his writings, Wilson proposed that the federal government be given more power to control the excesses of big business.

As one who thought the power of wealth was corrupting, Wilson was placing himself within the emerging tide of the Progressive Era (a social and political movement [1890–1920] in the United States that sought reforms to solve problems caused by industrialization, urbanization, immigration, and corruption in government).

Wilson's progressive ideas met resistance among conservative Princeton trustees, but they were popular in New Jersey. His name was soon mentioned as a leading Democratic candidate for governor.

Elected governor of New Jersey in 1910 at age 54 in a sweeping victory, Wilson pushed a progressive agenda. Under his leadership reform legislation was passed for worker's compensation (insurance providing wage replacement and medical benefits to employees injured in the course of employment), a public service commission to set fair rates for electricity and other utilities, primary elections for state officials, and prosecution of corrupt practices.

Wilson's reputation as a popular progressive governor increased calls for him to run for the presidency. He arrived on the national scene when there were growing calls for reform. The industrial growth of the late 19th century had empowered businessmen. They had produced economic growth and prosperity, but whole classes of people and regions of the country had been left out and left behind. Workers, farmers, and the poor swarming in the cities were looking for reforms to put them within reach of political power and a share of the national wealth.

In 1912, Woodrow Wilson was nominated as the Democratic Party's candidate for president. He was elected in November, in large part because of the third-party candidacy of former Republican president Theodore Roosevelt. Roosevelt split from the Republican Party and as head of the Progressive Party appeared on the ballot; incumbent president William Howard Taft was the Republican candidate.

With two opponents, one conservative (Taft) and the other progressive (Roosevelt), splitting a majority of the popular vote (51% between them), Democrat Wilson won the election. He received a huge majority in the Electoral College (435 of 524), but only 42% of the popular vote. The Democrats remained a minority party, although they gained control of both houses of Congress.

Wilson ran on a progressive platform. One of its major planks opposed monopoly (exclusive control of an industry by a single company). Wilson's position, and that of the Democratic Party, was that competition be maintained in all branches of private industry. The president favored a free market by deliberate government action, including the breakup of trusts (large companies with monopolistic control of a market).

The progressive domestic program of Wilson's presidency is known as the New Freedom. That term refers to three types of progressive legislation supported by the president and enacted by Congress: tariff reform, business reform, and banking reform.

Tariff (import tax) reform consisted of lowering tariffs. Businesses that wanted to protect their markets against foreign products opposed the tariff reforms of the New Freedom.

Major business reform included creation of the Federal Trade Commission. The commission was authorized to investigate and halt unfair and illegal business practices.

Two major banking reform laws were passed under the Wilson administration. In 1913, the Federal Reserve Act put the U.S. government in charge of issuing money and regulating the banks. The act created the central bank of the United States to provide the nation with a safer, more flexible, and more stable monetary and financial system.

Wilson had bold plans for extending his progressive agenda. He hoped to abolish child labor, set an 8-hour day for railroad workers, slash tariffs further, introduce an inheritance tax, and create a bank loan program for farmers.

Three amendments to the U.S. Constitution also contributed to Wilson's progressive legacy. The Sixteenth Amendment, ratified in February 1913 and supported by the president, after his election but before his inauguration, established the federal income tax.

The Seventeenth Amendment, ratified while Wilson was president, provided for direct election of senators. Previously, each state legislature had elected a state's two U.S. senators. With ratification of the Seventeenth Amendment, senators were elected directly by vote of the people.

Wilson supported adoption of the Nineteenth Amendment, ratified in 1920, which established the right of women to vote.

A fourth constitutional amendment, the Eighteenth Amendment (commonly called Prohibition), was ratified by the states in 1919 while Wilson was president. It banned the manufacture, sale, and transportation of alcoholic beverages in the United States and its possessions. The Volstead Act, created by Congress to enforce Prohibition, was enacted over the president's veto. Wilson correctly thought that the law would be unenforceable. (Prohibition was repealed by the Twenty-first Amendment, ratified in 1933.)

Wilson was also progressive on matters of organized labor. He made it clear that he supported collective bargaining (negotiation of wages and other conditions of employment between management and employee unions) and mediation (intervention between conflicting parties to promote settlement or compromise of labor disputes). Later in his term, Wilson intervened, with support from Congress, to help settle a railroad strike. He insisted upon the 8-hour workday, a progressive measure that pleased the unions.

On matters of race, Wilson backed away from progressive calls for racial justice. While campaigning for president, he had promised justice for Black people, and he received a larger share of their vote than any previous Democratic candidate. When Wilson acted to appoint Blacks to federal offices, southern Democratic senators threatened rejection of his appointments or reprisals against his legislative program.

With economic reform as his priority, Wilson faced a dilemma. He was torn between losing the support of African Americans and progressive forces that had elected him, and losing the support of racist southern senators and congressmen whose votes he needed in support of New Freedom economic reforms. He yielded to pressures from his party's segregationists (those who believed that the races should be kept separate). During his administration federal civil service employees were segregated, and limits were placed on federal government employment of African Americans. Of the segregation of federal employees, Wilson said: "I do approve of the segregation that is being attempted in several of the departments." To a friend he wrote: "We are trying—and by degrees succeeding—a plan of concentration which will put them all together and will not in any one bureau mix the two races." Progressives were bitterly disappointed.

Wilson was determined to transform American foreign policy as much as the country's domestic policies. He aimed for a foreign policy that favored democracy and opposed imperialism (extending the rule or authority of an empire or nation over foreign countries). Most of all, the new president sought a peaceful resolution of international disputes, and he was resolved not to be drawn into war. Conflict with Mexico, however, undermined his resolve to seek peaceful resolution of conflicts. In 1915, Wilson sent troops to Mexico to support the constitutional president and the next year to pursue the Mexican bandit Pancho Villa.

On August 4, 1914, Ellen Wilson died of kidney disease at age 54. The death of his wife was a shattering blow for the president. Two days later, the First World War broke out in Europe. The great powers of Europe faced off against one another in a bloody, protracted, and devastating conflict. The Triple Entente (France, Britain, and Russia, later, along with other countries, called the Allies or Allied Powers) fought bitterly against the Triple Alliance (Germany, Austria-Hungary, and Italy, later, along with other countries, called the Central Powers).

The U.S. had a strong tradition of distancing itself from European political entanglements. Most Americans were united about not being drawn into a European war. At the time of the war's outbreak, Wilson regarded the European war as an outgrowth of imperialistic rivalries (competition among countries to extend their power by acquiring territories for economic and/or political gain). The president called for a policy of strict and impartial neutrality for the United States. In a popular official proclamation of August 4, 1914, he announced that the United States "must be neutral in fact as well as in name" and "impartial in thought as well as in action."

Though Americans were committed to a policy of neutrality, their sentiments toward the European war were divided. In the 1910 census, 8,262,618 Americans, nearly 9% of the United States population, claimed Germany as their country of origin. Another 15 million people were of German ancestry. One-quarter of the total population could trace their background to Germany.

Second only to German Americans in number were Irish Americans, totaling 4,504,000 in the 2010 census, 5% of the total U.S. population. Most Irish Americans favored independence of Ireland from British control, and were therefore not sympathetic to Britain when the Great War began. Anti-Russian Poles, Jews, and Finns had come to America to escape tsarist oppression. (The tsar, now commonly spelled *czar*, was the Russian monarch.) Most of them favored the Central Powers against Russia.

On the other side, pro-British and therefore pro-Allied sentiment in the U.S. at the outbreak of the war was formidable. An American cultural, economic, WASP (White Anglo-Saxon Protestant) elite, including former president Theodore Roosevelt and Wilson himself, were Anglophiles (people who viewed Britain favorably). Wall Street financiers were closely tied to London financial markets. Polls showed pro-Allied sentiment among college professors, teachers, and clergymen.

Wilson was outraged by the German invasion of Belgium, a violation of international law, and by reports of atrocities committed by the invading armies. Still, despite his personal feelings and lifelong affinity for Britain, he insisted that the United States remain neutral.

Two moves of the belligerents (parties at war) in 1915, however, jeopardized American neutrality. The German imperial government declared that the waters around Great Britain would be considered a war zone. Enemy ships, including merchant ships, in the zone would be subject to attack by its fleet of submarines (called "U-boats"), leaving crew and passengers to drown. In response, the British declared a total naval blockade of Germany and its neighbors, cutting off the enemy from war materials and desperately needed food imports.

Both moves imperiled American vessels. The president warned that he would hold Germany to "strict accountability" in recognizing the neutral rights of American shipping. He did not, however, protest the British blockade. The Royal Navy's refusal to allow ships of neutral countries to trade with Germany was a violation of international law. One observer wryly commented: "Britain rules the waves and waives the rules."

Wilson clung to his neutrality policy, insisting upon the rights of neutral nations under international law. The president's resolve was tested when a British ship was sunk off the coast of Africa, killing 111 people, including one American. Secretary of State William Jennings Bryan, strongly favoring neutrality, argued that Americans traveling on belligerent ships did so at their own risk. He urged restraint. Robert Lansing, a State Department counselor, argued that Germany had crossed a line and that the United States should retaliate. For the moment, Wilson sided with Bryan.

And then, on May 2, 1915, the British luxury passenger liner *Lusitania* set sail from New York with 1,257 passengers aboard. The previous day, the German embassy in the United States had placed a newspaper advertisement warning people of the dangers of sailing on the *Lusitania*.

Five days later, the captain of a German submarine, *U-20*, spotted through his periscope a ship with four smokestacks in the declared "zone of war" off the Irish coast. He fired a single torpedo. A great explosion occurred, sending the ship to the bottom in 18 minutes. As the ship rolled over, it dumped more than a thousand people to their deaths, including 128 Americans. No effort was made by the U-boat to rescue the survivors in the water. The name *Lusitania* could be seen on the side of the ship as it sank.

A second explosion aboard the sinking ship was caused by millions of rounds of American Remington bullets, artillery shells with explosive fuses, and tons of aluminum powder used in explosives, all contraband (goods forbidden to be supplied by neutrals to those engaged in war) bound for the Allies. The British denied, in the face of the evidence, that there was contraband aboard.

Newspapers devoted their pages to heart-rending details such as the corpses of drowned mothers with babies clinging to their breasts. The sinking of the *Lusitania* caused a storm of protest in the United States and raised the possibility of rapid American entry into the European war.

On May 14, after deliberating with his cabinet, Wilson sent two notes to the German government. The notes condemned the sinking of the *Lusitania* and demanded that Germany cease its submarine warfare on all commercial ships. The strong language of Wilson's second message to the Germans prompted Secretary of State Bryan to resign. Bryan thought the president's message tilted the United States toward war. The secretary of state complained about the president's criticism of Germany's submarine warfare but his refusal to criticize, in turn, Britain's naval embargo (an official ban on trade or other commercial activity).

The German response to Wilson's notes was an apology that averted war: "Liners will not be sunk by our submarines without warning and without safety of the lives of noncombatants, provided that the liners do not try to escape or offer resistance." There were no further attacks on merchant ships in 1915.

More mildly, Wilson protested the British policy of seizing merchant ships at sea. Though they did not pose the direct threat to human life of German submarine warfare, the British were seizing merchant ship cargoes. Ships sailing in British waters and those bound for Germany were seized. Cargo confiscated included food and hospital supplies for civilians. American shipping companies protested these seizures of their property. The seizures also drew criticism on humanitarian grounds.

Wilson attempted to mediate a peace between the warring nations; he failed. The president's closest advisor, friend, and trusted envoy, Colonel Edward House, received an icy reception from belligerents on both sides. Notes from the president himself to German and British leaders offering to mediate a peace agreement personally were rebuffed. The vast armies continued the stalemated bloodletting along the front in France, with troops being mowed down daily in fighting from their trenches.

Amid the diplomatic frustrations in 1916, Wilson began his election campaign for a second term. A major slogan on campaign banners, leaflets, and buttons was "He kept us out of war!" Wilson won re-election, narrowly defeating Republican candidate Charles Evans Hughes of New York. Wilson's progressive reforms and strict neutrality in the Great War were popular. They gave him his slim margin of victory. Soon after the election, in a note to a close advisor, the president declared, "There will be no war. . . . It would be a crime against civilization for us to go in."

By early 1917, any hopes of advancing toward peace were undermined by two events. On January 31, the German ambassador to the United States handed then American secretary of state, Robert Lansing, an official note. It formally notified the United States that on the following day U-boats would begin operating in the war zone without restriction, attacking all ships, including American ships, suspected of carrying goods to any of Germany's adversaries.

The German government believed that submarine attacks were the only possible way to break the crippling British blockade. The German chancellor, Theobald von Bethmann-Hollweg, acknowledged that renewed U-boat attacks ran the risk of war with the United States. In a cable to his ambassador in Washington, he wrote, "We are determined to take this risk."

The second shock came when the British intercepted and decoded a highly secret message from the German foreign minister, Arthur Zimmerman, to the German ambassador in Mexico. The message has come to be known as the Zimmerman Telegram. It proposed a military alliance between Mexico and Germany if the United States entered the war. At the peace table following a German victory, Mexico would receive territories lost to the United States, including the states of Texas, New Mexico, and Arizona. The Zimmerman Telegram fueled propaganda that demonized all things German and emblazoned in the public mind an image of Germans as treacherous.

The resumption of unrestricted submarine warfare nullified previous pledges by Germany not to attack merchant or passenger ships. Wilson severed diplomatic relations between the United States and Germany; but he still hoped to avoid a declaration of war.

German violations of international law applied to neutral nations during wartime disturbed the president. He also harbored a wider concern. He envisioned a regime of liberty in the world, and he thought that an Allied victory would enable the United States to prosper and thrive in a new world order. Further, he came to think that American entry into the war would bestow on the United States global leadership in making peace and preventing future catastrophes. This Wilsonian ideal of making a world "safe for democracy," along with resentment of submarine attacks, a wartime manufacturing boom in the United States, and growing sympathy for Britain, all contributed to a national mood increasingly in favor of America's entry into the war.

In March 1917, news reached Washington of revolution in Russia. The Russian tsar had been deposed. A newly elected Russian government, democratic but

fragile, was promptly recognized by the United States. (When the Bolsheviks—
Russian communist revolutionaries—came to power in November, they withdrew
Russia from the war.) Russian withdrawal enabled Germany to move troops from
the Eastern Front to fight the Allies on the Western Front.

The president called upon Congress to see the Great War as "a war to end all
wars." On April 2, 1917, he appeared before Congress. Abandoning neutrality,
he eloquently called for a declaration of war against the German Empire. The
Senate voted for war 82–6; in the House of Representatives, the vote was 373–50.
The president promptly signed the joint resolution of Congress. America was at
war, and nearly 3 million of its young men would be drafted to fight.

The lopsided votes in Congress did not reflect how divided public opinion
was in the country. There were prominent antiwar leaders in both houses of
Congress—for example, the House majority leader, Democratic Representative
Claude Kitchen of North Carolina, and progressive Republican Senator Robert
("Fighting Bob") La Follette of Wisconsin. A popular new protest song was being played on Victrolas (early record players) and sung in music halls across the
country. Its chorus:

> I didn't raise my boy to be a soldier,
> I brought him up to be my pride and joy.
> Who dares to place a musket on his shoulder
> To shoot some other mother's darling boy?
> Let nations arbitrate their future conflicts.
> It's time to lay the sword and gun away.
> There'd be no war today
> If mothers all would say,
> "I didn't raise my boy to be a soldier!"

The prowar side also had widespread support, including that of former president Theodore Roosevelt and national organizations such as the National Security League, the Navy League, and the American Rights Committee.

Why did the president forsake neutrality and decide to enter a war he dreaded
and had sought to avoid? Several major factors were operating:

- Skilled propaganda in America, mostly by the British, depicted Germany
  as a militaristic aggressor led by the kaiser (the German monarch), and as
  bloodthirsty, "barbaric Huns" perpetrating atrocities.
- Growing reliance on sales of war material, food, and other goods to Britain,
  France, and Russia raised fear that an Allied defeat would crush the nation's
  economic boom and jeopardize repayment of huge bank loans to the Allies.
- German submarine attacks on American shipping, in violation of international law protecting freedom of the seas, enraged the public and angered
  the president.

- The Russian Revolution of March 1917 overthrew the tsar and introduced some democracy in Russia, eliminating opposition from Americans who had been unwilling to support the Allies when they included a repressive autocracy.
- The growing "Preparedness Movement" to bolster military training of citizens and spending for expanding the army and navy gained converts leaning toward America's joining the war.
- The Zimmerman Telegram emboldened those who favored American intervention.

Beginning in the fall of 1917, an American Expeditionary Force (AEF) was sent across the Atlantic. These American reinforcements broke the deadlock on the Western Front and ensured Germany's defeat. By the summer of 1918, about one million American troops (nicknamed "Doughboys," a term whose origin is unclear) had arrived on the Western Front. They played a decisive role in the war's final battles, including Château-Thierry, Belleau Wood, and the Battle of the Argonne Forest. The AEF sustained about 320,000 casualties: 53,402 battle deaths, 63,114 noncombat deaths, and 204,000 wounded. At sea, the U.S. Navy put an end to the German submarine menace.

Americans paid $31.3 billion (equal to $452 billion in today's dollars) to fund the conflict, including $9.5 billion ($137 billion today) loaned to the Allies. Income tax rates were raised to fund the war, and the income tax became for the first time, and remains, the main federal source of revenue. War expenditures increased the U.S. national debt fivefold to $27.4 billion by 1919 ($402 billion in today's dollars).

A war hysteria beset the country when America entered the War. The Espionage Act passed by Congress in 1917 led to restriction of expression deemed subversive to the war effort. Mail, radio, news reports, and other communications with foreign countries were censored by the Trading with the Enemy Act of 1917. What officials considered "disloyal, profane, scurrilous or abusive language" about the United States, its constitution or flag, or uniforms of the army or navy was prohibited by the Sedition Act of 1919. More than 1,000 ordinary Americans were convicted and imprisoned for criticizing the president or the war.

Discrimination against German Americans spread during wartime. In the public schools of Nebraska, the teaching of the German language was banned. German books were banned from libraries. Symphony orchestras and opera companies in major American cities canceled performances of German works. The anti-Germanism conditioned Americans to believe that Germany should be severely punished for the Great War.

In the wake of the transfusion of American troops, an armistice silencing the guns on all the battlefields took effect at "the eleventh hour of the eleventh day of the eleventh month" (11:00 a.m., November 11, 1918). It marked a victory for the Allies and a complete defeat for Germany. Fifteen million soldiers and civilians had died in the war, 9,450,000 killed in battle or dead as a result of battle injuries.

Casualty statistics present only part of the grim toll of the war. For Britain, France, Germany, and Russia, a whole generation was decimated. The best educated and many of the most promising young men of an entire generation tended to be junior officers who were most exposed on the battlefield. They were nearly wiped out, leaving a leadership vacuum after the war. During Europe's postwar years, there were legions of limping, blind, or wheelchair-bound victims. Masses of widows had little chance of finding a husband. Amid the agony and devastation, optimism was shattered.

America's decision to go to war was a rare pivot point in history. Had the United States remained neutral, the history of the 20th century would probably have been much different. By ending the stalemate, the U.S. guaranteed an overwhelming British-French victory. That victory ensured that there would be no mediated end to the conflict and no compromises, but rather a harsh peace that turned out to sow the seeds of future conflict.

Without American intervention, the warring countries would likely have been forced to negotiate a settlement. Their circumstances would have left them little other choice. They faced severe shortages of food and other necessities, looming economic bankruptcies, plunging morale and rising restlessness of their populations, frustrated despair of their leaders, depletion of their weapons, and a fast dwindling supply of manpower for their armies.

If the warring powers had negotiated a "peace without victory," which Wilson had called for in 1916 but was unable to bring about, might subsequent developments have been different? Might Germany have pursued its prewar movement toward democratic government rather than a Nazi dictatorship that triggered an even more destructive and horrific second world war followed by Soviet occupation of Eastern Europe? Might the Austro-Hungarian Empire have devolved peacefully rather than becoming a smoldering tinderbox of extreme nationalities? Might turmoil and violence have been averted in the Middle East if unstable nation states had not been carved from the Ottoman (Turkish) Empire? Might there have been a more manageable arrangement of international debts without the severely punitive reparations that were imposed? Could the crippling economic burdens that stymied economic growth and fostered resentments have been avoided? Might those economic burdens that contributed to the cascading events of the stock market, currency, and bank crashes and, ultimately, to the Great Depression have been averted? Hypothetical, counter-factual results of American nonintervention are not certain. What is certain is that American intervention in the war changed the course of history.

In January 1918, with victory in sight, it fell upon Woodrow Wilson to set forth terms for a just peace. He did that with his Fourteen Points, principles for peace that he proposed for peace negotiations. The first six of the Fourteen Points dealt with principles of diplomacy—for example, freedom of navigation on the seas, and self-determination (the term used to describe the right of peoples, including those colonized, to vote to determine who would govern them and how they would be governed). Others of Wilson's Fourteen Points addressed territorial issues—for example, evacuation of all Russian territory, restoration of Belgium, adjustment of Italian frontiers, and evacuation of French territory.

The final point of the Fourteen Points was a hopeful expression of Wilson's idealism. It presented a vision for a new international order after the World War. It called for creation of a League of Nations, an association of nations to guarantee the independence and territorial integrity of all states.

Although the Fourteen Points were the agreed-upon basis for peace, they did not include specific provisions. Those were to be negotiated at a peace conference in Versailles, a Paris suburb where French kings had earlier lived in splendor at the Versailles Palace.

Wilson left Washington for Versailles in December 1918 to represent the United States personally at the Paris peace conference. He was hailed as a triumphal hero in Europe. His motorcade was greeted in the streets of three countries he visited by vast, cheering crowds throwing flowers in his path and with hands outstretched to touch him.

Back home, however, there was a challenge to Wilson's acclaim. Republicans had won a majority in both houses of Congress in the election of 1918. Some who had voted for Democrats in 1916 cast their ballots for Republicans because they opposed either the president's decision to enter the war, his peace plans, or both. The president's loss of a Democratic majority in the Senate would prove disastrous for his policies.

Leading the Versailles conference, as the Council of Four, were the leaders of France, the United States, Great Britain, and Italy (Georges Clemenceau, Wilson, Lloyd George, and Vittorio Orlando, respectively). (Despite its membership in the Triple Alliance with Germany and Austria-Hungary, Italy had joined the Allied side in the war.)

Guided by, but often compromising, the principles of the Fourteen Points, the four leaders struggled to reach agreements on a wide variety of peace terms. In the end, the Treaty of Versailles imposed punishing territorial concessions and humiliating reparation payments on Germany. Article 231 of the treaty (the "war guilt clause") blamed Germany solely for the war, tainting the fragile German democratic government that had emerged at war's end and signed the treaty.

These crippling peace terms left a sting of resentment in Germany, a bitter reservoir tapped by Hitler and the Nazis for revenge when they came to power in the 1930s. During their rise to power, they claimed that Germany had been betrayed at Versailles, "stabbed in the back" by the "November Criminals." The charge brought wild cheers from German audiences.

For Wilson, however, the keystone of the peace conference was creation of the League of Nations, which he regarded as a "political and moral principle." To the American president, the League was crucial for the future peace of the world. To gain acceptance of it, he reluctantly abandoned his vow of "peace without victory" and made concessions to the vengeful victors at Versailles.

The negotiators at Versailles finally agreed upon creation of the League of Nations. Now Wilson would have to persuade two-thirds of the United States Senate to approve the treaty.

There was a mounting desire to get back to prewar business as usual in the United States, and Republican senators resisted a new foreign entanglement. Article X of the League of Nations treaty required all members of the League to protect one another from external aggression. This requirement for mutual defense was a major point of conflict between supporters of the treaty and its opponents in the Senate. Led by Henry Cabot Lodge, Massachusetts senator, majority leader, and chair of the Committee on Foreign Relations, Republicans aimed to defeat the League and to discredit its champion, the president. In February 1919, Wilson's archenemy, Lodge, opened a full-scale attack on the League of Nations.

Realizing that he faced possible defeat in the struggle for ratification of the League treaty in the Senate, Wilson appealed directly to the people. On September 2, 1919, he boarded a train in Washington, D.C., that would take him for the next 27 days on a whirlwind tour across the country, leading to the Pacific Coast. Stopping for more than 30 major speeches, the president was cheered by supportive, enthusiastic crowds. The tour was exhilarating, but exhausting.

In Pueblo, Colorado, on September 25, 1919, the president spoke his last words before a public audience. He fell ill after that speech, and his next speech in Wichita had to be canceled. Six days later, back in Washington, Edith Wilson, the president's second wife, found him on the floor in the bathroom of the White House. He was unconscious, and his face and head were bloodstained. He had suffered a massive stroke.

In the days ahead, the president's wife and physician concealed the true nature of the president's illness, describing it as simple exhaustion from overwork. It was, however, clear to the doctors attending him that his symptoms would not clear up. One of those symptoms was paralysis of his left side. The president's attention span and emotional control were also adversely affected by his stroke.

In the meanwhile, the League treaty was the chief issue before the country. The president, now a very sick man, refused all compromises offered by Senator Lodge. Most of the compromises were reservations to Article X stipulating that no military action be taken under the League without authorization by Congress.

On March 19, 1920, the Senate rejected the Versailles Treaty and the League of Nations by a vote of 49 to 35, seven votes shy of the two-thirds required for ratification. The disabled president, who had obstinately refused any compromise, was devastated. On November 15, 1920, the League of Nations held its first meeting in Geneva, Switzerland, without the United States as a member. In the years that followed, the League proved to be ineffective.

Incapacitated, Wilson finished the remaining months of his term as president. A new president, Warren Harding, had campaigned against Wilson's policies and was elected by a landslide in 1920. During the campaign, Harding, responding to the isolationist (favoring a policy of remaining apart from the affairs or interests of other countries) mood of the country, called for a return to "normalcy."

Wilson received the Nobel Peace Prize in 1920. Embittered by his defeats, however, the ex-president lived with his wife, Edith, in seclusion in a house on S Street in Washington, D.C., until his death in 1924.

The major sources for this chapter were:

Heckscher, A. (1991). *Woodrow Wilson.* New York, NY: Charles Scribner's Sons.

Kazin, M. (2017). *War against war: The American fight for peace 1914–1918.* New York, NY: Simon & Schuster.

Pines, B. Y. (2013). *America's greatest blunder: The fateful decision to enter World War One.* New York, NY: Hillcrest Publishing.

LEARNING ACTIVITIES FOR "A WAR TO END ALL WARS"

Facts of the Case

1. What reforms did Woodrow Wilson support as governor of New Jersey and then as president?
2. Why did President Wilson fail to keep his promise to African Americans?
3. What resulted from the sinking of the *Lusitania*?
4. Why did President Wilson abandon his vow of neutrality in the Great War?
5. What did Wilson mean by "a peace without victory?"
6. Why did President Wilson place great importance on the League of Nations?

Historical Understanding

1. What was the Progressive Era?
2. Why did Germany pursue unrestricted submarine warfare?
3. Why did the United States enter the Great War and what were the effects of its entry?
4. What were the Fourteen Points?
5. What were the human and economic costs of the Great War to the belligerents?
6. Why did Germans resent the Versailles Treaty?
7. Why did the U.S. Senate reject the League of Nations?

Expressing Your Reasoning

Should President Woodrow Wilson have asked Congress to declare war against Germany? Why or why not?

Key Concepts from History

What do the following have in common?

1. The League of Nations was an intergovernmental organization founded in 1920 as a result of the peace conference that ended the First World War. It was the first international organization whose principal mission was to maintain world peace. Its primary goals, as stated in its Covenant, included preventing and settling international disputes. Article X of the League Covenant required members "to preserve as against external aggression the territorial integrity and existing political independence" of any League member.
2. The United Nations (UN) is an intergovernmental organization to promote international cooperation. A replacement for the ineffective League of Nations, the UN was established in 1945 after World War II in order to prevent another such conflict. There are now 193 member nations of the UN. Chapter VII of the United Nations Charter sets out the UN Security Council's powers to maintain peace. It allows the council to "determine the existence of any threat to the peace, breach of the peace, or act of aggression" and to take military and nonmilitary action to "restore international peace and security."
3. The North Atlantic Treaty Organization (NATO) is an intergovernmental military alliance based on the North Atlantic Treaty signed in 1949 among European and North American countries. The 28 independent member states of NATO agree to mutual defense in response to an attack by any external party. Article 5 of the NATO treaty states that an armed attack against one or more treaty members in Europe or North America shall be considered an attack against them all.

Historical Inquiry

Woodrow Wilson was elected president in 1912 with 42%, a plurality, of the popular vote. Although he had the largest popular vote total among the presidential candidates on the ballot, he did not receive a majority of the popular vote. Is it possible for a candidate to win the popular vote and lose a presidential election?

Using online and other sources, test the hypothesis that a candidate for president of the United States can receive a plurality of the popular vote and lose the election. Compose a short essay in which you accept or reject the truth of the claim. Use evidence to support your conclusion.

To begin your investigation, the following search terms will be helpful:

- Presidential election of 1824
- Presidential election of 1876
- Presidential election of 1888
- Presidential election of 2000
- Presidential election of 2016
- U.S. Constitution, Article II, Section 1, Clause 3
- Twelfth Amendment to the U.S. Constitution

Part VIII

BETWEEN THE WARS
1919–1940

CHAPTER 29

Stealing North

The Jim Crow South and Richard Wright

Movie Theater in Leland, Mississippi, 1939

Courtesy of the Library of Congress

Before The Civil War, race relations in the United States were shaped by the enslavement of African Americans. Black slaves, most of whom were in the South, were considered property and treated as inferiors by Whites. Many northern Whites opposed slavery, but believed Blacks should be confined to a lower class and kept separate from Whites. Although his ideas would later change, Abraham Lincoln, while a candidate for the U.S. Senate in 1858, expressed such a view during a debate with his opponent, Stephen Douglas:

> I will say then that I am not, nor ever have been in favor of bringing about in any way the social and political equality of the white and black races—that I

am not nor ever have been in favor of making voters or jurors of negroes, nor of qualifying them to hold office, nor to intermarry with white people; and I will say in addition to this that there is a physical difference between the white and black races which I believe will forever forbid the two races living together on terms of social and political equality. And inasmuch as they cannot so live, while they do remain together there must be the position of superior and inferior, and I as much as any other man am in favor of having the superior position assigned to the white race.

The experiences of The Civil War, including his Emancipation Proclamation, changed President Lincoln's views about African Americans. For example, in his final public statement shortly before his assassination in April 1865, the president supported suffrage for those Blacks who had served in the army.

After The Civil War, during Reconstruction (1865–1876), the Constitution was amended to prohibit slavery (Thirteenth Amendment); provide citizenship and rights of citizenship, including equal protection of the law and due process of law, to former slaves (Fourteenth Amendment); and to guarantee Black men the right to vote (Fifteenth Amendment).

Black Americans benefited further from opportunities afforded by Reconstruction policies. During this period, there was increased mixing of the races in southern states. The presence of federal soldiers in the South and changes in the law brought expanded contact between Blacks and Whites. Black people began to appear where they had been absent: in the jury box, on the judge's bench, in legislatures, at the polls, in the marketplace, and even in the best staterooms of steamships. These contacts were not to endure.

After the contested presidential election of 1876, Republicans agreed to withdraw federal troops from the South, and that brought an end to Reconstruction. Power in the southern states went to the "Democratic Redeemers," who went on to pursue their agenda of returning the South to its prewar condition, including denial of the vote to African Americans (disenfranchisement). After 1877, White southern Democrats reversed the gains that Blacks had made during Reconstruction

Toward the end of the 19th century, legislation was adopted to again segregate, impoverish, and humiliate an African American population who, many Whites believed, had gained too much during Reconstruction. Gradually, a pattern of complete racial segregation (separation of the races) emerged in the old Confederacy. Though not as pervasive, racism was also evident in the North. For example, Blacks and Whites were segregated, including in their government workplaces, and some federal jobs were denied to Black people. This period marks the beginning of what has come to be called the "Jim Crow Era." (The name Jim Crow came from a White actor who ridiculed Blacks in a song-and-dance act.)

At the dawn of the 20th century, a wave of Jim Crow laws swelled in the South, where 90% of the nation's African Americans lived. These state laws were intended to segregate the races and keep Black people in an inferior social position. Disenfranchisement took several forms. In some southern states, only those who owned a considerable amount of property were allowed to vote; this qualification excluded most Blacks. The literacy test was also used to keep African Americans out of voting booths. It pretended to limit the vote to people who could read. Blacks usually failed the tests because those given to them were intentionally made much more difficult that those given to Whites. Another obstacle to Black voting was the poll tax. Even if a Black person paid the tax, the election judge would usually find some mistake in the receipt to keep that person from voting.

These devices were enormously effective. For example, in Louisiana in 1896, there were 130,334 registered Black voters. By 1904, there were 1,342 (a decrease of 99% in 8 years). Between the two dates, literacy, property, and poll tax qualifications were widely adopted. Blacks soon disappeared from legislatures. Juries also became all White because jurors were selected from lists of eligible voters.

Jim Crow laws drew the color line almost everywhere. Along the avenues and byways of southern life, signs appeared that read "Whites Only" or "Colored." These signs could be seen posted at theaters, boarding houses, toilets, drinking fountains, waiting rooms, and ticket windows.

In South Carolina, a 1915 law prohibited workers of different races from working together in the same room. A Mississippi law segregated patients in hospitals. Alabama prohibited White female nurses from attending Black male patients. Prisoners were separated by race in 10 states. Blacks were barred from White public parks by a 1905 Georgia law. Local ordinances in Virginia excluded Blacks from living in White neighborhoods. In North Carolina and Florida, the law required that textbooks used by public school children of one race be kept separate from those used by the other. In all southern states, the law required separate schools for Black and White children. In Atlanta, baseball teams of different races were prohibited from playing each other. It was unlawful for a Black person and a White person to play checkers in Birmingham, Alabama. And so it was across the South at soda fountains, bars, waiting rooms, libraries, streetcars— even in cemeteries.

Jim Crow cars rattled across the tracks of southern railways. By law, railroads kept separate cars for Black and White passengers. On June 7, 1892, Louisiana native Homer Plessy walked into a New Orleans station and bought a first-class ticket. He boarded the train and took a seat. Suddenly, the conductor informed him that he had to move to the next coach: The car Plessy occupied was for White passengers only, and Plessy, who was one-eighth Black, was not allowed to ride in it. When told to leave, however, he refused. The conductor called a police officer who forcibly removed Plessy from the car and took him to jail. Plessy was charged with violating the Louisiana law that required "separate accommodations for the white and colored races."

Plessy's case became a stormy landmark. His lawyers argued in a Louisiana court that railway segregation ran contrary to the U.S. Constitution's guarantee of equal protection of the laws. The judge denied their arguments and found Plessy guilty. A final appeal was made to the U.S. Supreme Court. In *Plessy v. Ferguson* (1896), the highest court in the land ruled against Homer Plessy. The justices decided that "separate but equal" facilities for White and Black people were constitutional. This decision placed racial segregation under the protection of the federal government. Jim Crow laws that enforced segregation, but not equality, were to thrive for more than a half century following the *Plessy* decision.

Jim Crow era racism appeared in forms other than segregation laws. During the first year following World War I, for example, 70 African Americans were lynched, several of them veterans still in uniform. During these years, the Ku Klux Klan (KKK) flourished in both the North and South. The Klan, a White supremacist organization, inflamed race prejudice and encouraged racial violence.

What was it like to be Black in the Jim Crow South? In his memoir, African American author Richard Wright describes his experiences as a youth in Jackson, Mississippi, during the 1920s.

He lived with his mother, grandmother, and brother. They were very poor. Richard had shabby clothes and little to eat. In school he wrote a story that was published by the local Black paper. Encouraged by this recognition of his talent, Richard began dreaming of a career as a writer. He believed that it would be impossible to succeed in the South. The North symbolized opportunity for him. To get there, he had to raise money for the train fare.

At school Richard inquired about jobs and heard of a White family who wanted a boy to do chores. He went to the address after school and was hired. He was put to work mornings, evenings, and all day Saturday for $2 (about $22 in today's currency) a week, plus breakfast and dinner.

The first morning on the job Richard chopped wood, lugged coal, washed the front porch, swept the kitchen and back porch, helped wait on the table, washed the breakfast dishes, and went to the store to shop. In his autobiography, Richard recalls his discussion with the woman of the house upon his return from the store one day:

"Your breakfast is in the kitchen."

"Thank you, ma'am."

I saw a plate of thick, black molasses and a hunk of white bread on the table. Would I get no more than this? They had had eggs, bacon, coffee. . . . I picked up the bread and tried to break it; it was stale and hard. Well, I would drink the molasses. I lifted the plate and brought it to my lips and saw floating on the surface of the black liquid green and white bits of mold. . . . I can't eat this, I told myself. The food was not even clean. The woman came into the kitchen as I was putting on my coat.

"You didn't eat," she said.

"No, ma'am," I said. "I'm not hungry."

"You'll eat at home?" she asked hopefully.

"Well, I just wasn't hungry this morning, ma'am," I lied. "You don't like molasses and bread," she said dramatically.

"Oh yes, ma'am, I do," I defended myself quickly, not wanting her to think that I dared criticize what she had given me.

"I don't know what's happening to you niggers nowadays." She sighed, wagging her head. She looked closely at the molasses. "It's a sin to throw out molasses like that. I'll put it up for you this evening."

"Yes, ma'am," I said heartily.

Neatly she covered the plate of molasses with another plate, then felt the bread and dumped it into the garbage. She turned to me, her face lit with an idea.

"What grade are you in school?"

"Seventh, ma'am."

"Then why are you going to school?" she asked in surprise.

"Well, I want to be a writer," I mumbled, unsure of myself; I had not planned to tell her that, but she had made me feel so utterly wrong and of no account that I needed to bolster myself.

"A what?" she demanded.

"A writer," I mumbled.

"For what?"

"To write stories," I mumbled defensively.

"You'll never be a writer," she said. "Who on earth put such ideas into your nigger head?"

"Nobody," I said.

"I didn't think anybody ever would," she declared indignantly.

As I walked around her house to the street, I knew that I would not go back. The woman had assaulted my ego; she had assumed that she knew my place in life, what I felt, what I ought to be, and I resented it with all my heart. Perhaps she was right; perhaps I never would be a writer; but I did not want her to say so.

In 1924, when Richard was 15, he took a summer job as a water boy in a brickyard. For a dollar a day, he carried a pail of water from one laboring gang of Black men to another. The owner's dog went about the brickyard snapping and growling at the workers. Richard was afraid that the dog would bite him. One afternoon, while getting water from the pond, he felt something sharp sink into his thigh. He had been bitten; the teeth marks showed deep and red. Afraid of infection, Richard reported the bite to the office and returned to work. As described in Wright's autobiography, later in the afternoon, the boss, a tall White man, came toward him:

"Is this the nigger?" he asked a black boy as he pointed at me.

"Yes sir," the black boy answered.

"Come here, nigger," he called me.

I went to him.

"They tell me my dog bit you," he said.

"Yes, sir."

I pulled down my trousers and he looked.

"Humnnn," he grunted, then laughed. "A dog bite can't hurt a nigger."

"It's swelling and it hurts," I said.

"If it bothers you, let me know," he said. "But I never saw a dog yet that could really hurt a nigger."

He turned and walked away and the black boys gathered to watch his tall form disappear down the aisles of wet bricks.

Soon afterward, the brickyard went out of business, and Richard was again out of work. He graduated from junior high school first in his class. Now he would look for a full-time job. Richard found employment as a porter and delivery boy in a clothing store operated by a White man. The store sold cheap goods on credit. Richard watched several times, frightened but tight-lipped, as his employer beat Black customers who had not paid their bills. As Wright reports in his autobiography, the boss's son cornered him one morning:

"Say, nigger, look here," he began.

"Yes, sir."

"What's on your mind?"

"Nothing, sir," I said, trying to look amazed, trying to fool him.

"Why don't you laugh and talk like the other niggers?" he asked.

"Well, sir, there's nothing much to say or smile about," I said, smiling.

His face was hard, baffled; I knew that I had not convinced him. He whirled from me and went to the front of the store; he came back a moment later, his face red. He tossed a few green bills at me.

"I don't like your looks, nigger. Now, get!" he snapped.

I picked up the money and did not count it. I grabbed my hat and left.

Wright held a series of petty jobs for short periods after leaving the clothing store. He was usually driven off because Whites did not like his attitude. Most of the money he earned went to support his family. Nearing his 17th birthday, he was no closer than ever to his goal of saving enough money to head northward. One night a friend told him about a job at the local Black movie theater. "The girl who sells tickets is using a system," he explained. "If you get the job, you can make some good gravy."

In his autobiography, Wright describes what happened at his last job in Mississippi:

My chances for getting a job were good; I had no past record of stealing or violating the laws. When I presented myself to the Jewish proprietor of the movie house I was immediately accepted. The next day I reported for duty and began taking tickets. The boss man warned me:

"Now look, I'll be honest with you if you'll be honest with me. I don't know who's honest around this joint and who isn't. But if *you* are honest, then the rest are bound to be. All tickets will pass through your hands. There can be no stealing unless you steal."

I gave him a pledge of my honesty, feeling absolutely no qualms about what I intended to do. He was white, and I could never do to him what he and his kind had done to me. Therefore, I reasoned, stealing was not a violation of my ethics, but of his; I felt that things were rigged in his favor and any action I took to circumvent his scheme of life was justified. Yet I had not convinced myself.

During the first afternoon the Negro girl in the ticket office watched me closely and I knew that she was sizing me up, trying to determine when it would be sage to break me into her graft. I waited, leaving it to her to make the first move.

I was supposed to drop each ticket that I took from a customer into a metal receptacle. Occasionally the boss would go to the ticket window and look at the serial number on the roll of unsold tickets and then compare that number with the number on the last ticket I had dropped into the receptacle. The boss continued his watchfulness for a few days, then began to observe me from across the street; finally he absented himself for long intervals . . .

While I was eating supper in a near-by café one night, a strange Negro man walked in and sat beside me.

"Hello, Richard," he said.

"Hello," I said. "I don't think I know you."

"But I know *you*," he said, smiling.

"How do you know me?" I asked.

"I'm Tel's friend," he said, naming the girl who sold the tickets at the movie.

I looked at him searchingly. Was he telling me the truth? Or was he trying to trap me for the boss? I was already thinking and feeling like a criminal, distrusting everybody.

"We start tonight," he said.

"What?" I asked, still not admitting that I knew what he was talking about.

"Don't be scared. The boss trusts you. He's gone to see some friends. Somebody's watching him and if he starts back to the movie, they'll phone us," he said.

I could not eat my food. It lay cold upon the plate and sweat ran down my armpits.

"It'll work this way," he explained in a low, smooth tone. "A guy'll come to you and ask for a match. You give him five tickets that you'll hold out of the box, see? We'll give you the signal when to start holding them out. The guy'll give the tickets to Tel; she'll re-sell them all at once, when the crowd is buying at the rush hour. You get it?"

I did not answer. I knew that if I were caught I would go to the chain gang. But was not my life not already a kind of chain gang? What really did I have to lose?

"Are you with us?" he asked.

I still did not answer. He rose and clapped me on the shoulder and left. I trembled as I went back to the theater. . . . I took the tickets with my sweaty fingers. I waited. I was gambling; freedom or the chain gang. There were times when I felt that I could not breathe. I looked up and down the street; the boss was not in sight. Was this a trap? If it were, I would disgrace my family.

The man I had met in the café came through the door and put a ticket in my hand.

"There's a crowd at the box office," he whispered. "Save ten, not five. Start with this one."

Well, here goes, I thought. He gave me the ticket and sat looking at the moving shadows upon the screen. I held onto the ticket and my body grew tense, hot as fire; but I was used to that too. Time crawled through the cells of my brain. My muscles ached. I discovered that crime means suffering. The crowd came in and gave me more tickets. I kept ten of them tucked into my moist palm. No sooner had the crowd thinned than a black boy with a cigarette jutting from his mouth came up to me.

"Gotta match?"

With a slow movement I gave him the tickets. He went out and I kept the door cracked and watched. He went to the ticket office and laid down a coin and I saw him slip the tickets to the girl. Yes, the boy was honest. The girl shot me a quick smile and I went back inside. A few moments later the same tickets were handed to me by other customers.

We worked it for a week and after the money was split four ways, I had 50 dollars. Freedom was almost within my grasp. Ought I risk any more? I dropped the hint to Tel's friend that maybe I would quit; it was a casual hint to test him out. He grew violently angry and I quickly consented to stay, fearing that someone might turn me in for revenge, or to get me out of the way so that another more pliable boy could have my place. I was dealing with cagey people and I could be cagey.

I went through another week. Late one night I resolved to make that week the last. . . . Saturday night came and I sent word to the boss that I was sick. . . . My mother sat in her rocking chair, humming to herself. I packed my suitcase and went to her.

"Mama, I'm going away," I whispered.

"Oh, no," she protested.

"I've got to, mama. I can't live this way."

"You're running away from something you've done?"

"I'll send for you, mama. I'll be alright."

"Take care of yourself. And send for me quickly. I'm not happy here," she said.

"I'm sorry for all these long years, mama. But I could not have helped it." I kissed her and she cried.

"Be quiet, mama. I'm all right."

I went out the back way and walked a quarter of a mile to the railroad tracks. It began to rain as I tramped down the crossties toward town. I reached the station soaked to the skin. I bought my ticket, then went hurriedly to the corner of the block in which the movie house stood. Yes, the boss was there, taking the tickets himself. I returned to the station and waited for my train, my eyes watching the crowd.

An hour later I was sitting in a Jim Crow coach speeding northward, making the first lap of my journey to a land where I could live with a little less fear. Slowly the burden I had carried for many months lifted somewhat. My cheeks itched and when I scratched them I found tears. In that moment I understood the pain that accompanied crime and I hoped that I would never have to feel it again. I never did feel it again, for I never stole again; and what kept me from it was the knowledge that, for me, crime carried its own punishment.

The major sources for this chapter were:

Bader, K., & Lehr, D. (Writers), Gray, S., & Cram, B. (Directors) (2017). Birth of a movement. (Television film.) In series *Independent Lens.* Arlington, VA: Public Broadcasting System.

Woodward, C. V. (1974). *The strange career of Jim Crow* (3rd ed.) New York, NY: Oxford University Press.

Wright, R. (1945). *Black boy.* New York, NY: Harper & Brothers.

LEARNING ACTIVITIES FOR "STEALING NORTH"

Facts of the Case

1. Why did Richard quit his job doing chores for a White family?
2. For what purpose was Richard trying to save money?
3. How was Richard treated by the owner of the brickyard?
4. Why was Richard fired from the clothing store?
5. What agreement did Richard reach with the theater owner?
6. Describe how the ticket scheme worked.

Historical Understanding

1. What was Abraham Lincoln's position on racial equality before The Civil War?
2. What were some benefits of Reconstruction to African Americans?
3. What were the two major purposes of Jim Crow laws?
4. Give three specific examples of Jim Crow laws.
5. What precedent was set by the case of *Plessy v. Ferguson*?

Expressing Your Reasoning

Should Richard have participated in the ticket scheme? Why or why not?

Key Concepts from History

What do the following have in common?

1. Immigration of Chinese people to California began in 1850 at the beginning of the Gold Rush. As the Chinese became successful, tensions grew. Some White Californians were wary of the cultural and ethnic differences. The government of California worked to prevent Chinese immigration and restricted work they were permitted to do. Many Chinese turned to the laundry business, and in San Francisco about 89% of the laundry workers were of Chinese descent. In 1880, the elected officials of the city of San Francisco passed an ordinance making it illegal to operate a laundry in a wooden building without a permit from the board of supervisors. At the time, about 95% of the city's 320 laundries were operated in wooden buildings. Approximately two-thirds of those laundries were owned by Chinese people. Although most of the city's wooden-building laundry owners applied for a permit, only one permit was granted of the 200 applications from any Chinese owner, while virtually all non-Chinese applicants were granted a permit.
2. In 1946, an African American man, Herman Sweatt, applied for admission to the University of Texas School of Law. He was refused admission. The university president met with Sweatt and informed him that he possessed every essential qualification for admission, except that of race, upon which ground alone his application was denied. The Texas state constitution prohibited racially integrated education. At the time, no law school in Texas would admit Black students.
3. In 1958, Mildred Jeter and Richard Loving traveled from their home in Virginia to Washington, D.C., to get married. Mildred was African American and also had Native American ancestry. Richard was White. They traveled to Washington to evade Virginia's Racial Integrity Act that made marriage between people classified as "Whites" and people classified as "Colored"

a crime. After marrying, the couple returned to the small town of Central Point, Virginia. Local police raided their home in the early morning hours of July 11, 1958. When the officers found the Lovings sleeping in their bed, Mildred pointed out their marriage certificate on the bedroom wall. They were told the certificate was not valid in Virginia. The Lovings were charged with violating state law, punishable by a prison sentence of between 1 and 5 years. They pled guilty and were sentenced to 1 year in prison. The sentence was suspended on condition that the couple leave Virginia and not return together for at least 25 years.

Historical Inquiry

In 1954, in a landmark decision, *Brown v. Board of Education*, the Supreme Court of the United States overturned the precedent of "separate but equal" set by the case of *Plessy v. Ferguson* more than half a century earlier. In the opinion for the *Brown* decision, the chief justice of the Supreme Court stated that "separate educational facilities are inherently unequal." The decision made racially segregated schools in the United States an unconstitutional violation of the Equal Protection Clause of the Fourteenth Amendment. Segregated schools were ordered to integrate.

Using online and other sources, test the hypothesis that American schools have desegregated since 1954. Compose a short essay in which you accept or reject the hypothesis. Use evidence to support your conclusion.

To begin your investigation, the following search terms will be helpful:

* *Brown v. Board of Education*
* All deliberate speed
* Racial segregation of schools
* School segregation facts
* De facto segregation
* De jure segregation

CHAPTER 30

Dust Can't Kill Me

Bank Foreclosures in the Great Depression

Farmer and Sons in a Dust Storm. Cimarron County, Oklahoma (Arthur Rothstein, 1936)

In the 1910s, Fred and Katherine Folkers moved from Missouri to the Oklahoma Panhandle. They settled near Boise City, a small town founded in 1908 and later the county seat of Cimarron County.

The Oklahoma Panhandle, with its three counties (Cimarron, Texas, and Beaver), is a strip of land 166 miles long and 34 miles wide at the northwest corner of the state of Oklahoma. The Panhandle is bordered by Colorado and Kansas to the north, New Mexico to the west, Texas to the south, and the rest of Oklahoma to the east. It is called the Panhandle because its shape resembles a frying pan handle. The name *Oklahoma* is a compound of two Choctaw Indian words: *okla* ("person") and *humma* ("red"). The Choctaws were the first Native

Americans forced to relocate from their homes in the southeastern United States under the Indian Removal Act of 1830.

The Folkerses acquired their land in the Oklahoma Panhandle under the Homestead Acts. Under the acts, the U.S. government offered heads of families free public land if they cultivated the land for 5 years. With thousands of other families, the Folkerses took a chance at earning a living by farming. It was fiercely hot in the Panhandle, with little rainfall. High winds whipped the fields. Prairie fires often swept through the crops and the dry grass. Yet, for some years, farmers in the Panhandle made a good living growing wheat.

This period of relative prosperity in the Oklahoma Panhandle ended in the 1930s. Massive dust storms followed a period of severe drought that began in 1932 and lasted nearly 10 years. The drought and dust storms caused the largest human-made and natural ecological disaster in U.S. history. The area that included the panhandles of Oklahoma and Texas and southeastern Colorado and southwest Kansas came to be known as the Dust Bowl. Many farmers lost their farms when they could not repay their bank loans after their crops failed. In the Panhandle, these were years of hardship, poverty, despair, and mass migration.

In his 1878 *Report on Lands of the Arid Region of the United States,* John Wesley Powell, a famous explorer of the American West, warned about farming in the American West: "All of the country west of the 100th or 99th meridian, except a little in California, Oregon, and Washington Territory, is arid, and no part of it can be redeemed for agriculture except by irrigation." Irrigation is a controlled watering system, using pipes, sprinklers, and ditches, that substitutes for rainfall when there is little natural precipitation. Irrigation is essential in many parts of the world where rain is scarce and unpredictable.

However, the farmers in the Oklahoma Panhandle either had no knowledge of or ignored Powell's warning. Lured by the government's provision of free land and speculators' promises, and encouraged by their belief that rain would come, they went on farming. They were then deceived—first, by nature; second, by humans. It was unusually wet in the early 1900s on the Great Plains (the flat lands west of the Mississippi River and east of the Rocky Mountains). People thought the rain would continue, providing enough moisture to grow wheat and other crops. Various speculators and promoters promised future settlers that "rain follows the plow." The policy of free land was too tempting to resist.

Boise City, the small town near the Folkerses' property, was one of the first towns settled in the Oklahoma Panhandle. The Southwestern Immigration and Development Company of Guthrie, Oklahoma, owned by J. E. Stanley and A. J. Kline, prepared brochures that advertised Boise City as an elegant, tree-lined town with paved streets, many houses and businesses, railroad service, and a river. Buyers from Missouri, Illinois, and Indiana purchased 3,000 lots, "sight unseen."

The Boise City scheme was a hoax. There were no paved streets, no river, and no homes or businesses; there was one concrete building; a block-long, concrete sidewalk; and a windmill. In fact, Stanley and Kline did not even own the lots. Eventually, when the hoax was revealed, the two promoters were jailed for 2 years.

Each with their own motives, railroads, banks, politicians, and newspaper editors also lured settlers to this undeveloped land with their false promises. With its program of free public land legislated by the various Homestead Acts, the U.S. government, however, made a true promise. The Kinkaid Act of 1904 offered 640 acres (a "section" of 1 square mile) to homesteaders in western Nebraska. The Enlarged Homestead Act of 1909 offered 320 acres elsewhere in the Great Plains. The Stock-Raising Homestead Act of 1916 offered 640 acres for ranching activities. The U.S. government also offered free train rides to prospective homesteaders so they could see the land. The slogan was "Health, Wealth, and Opportunity."

By 1910, homesteaders had claimed nearly 200 million acres throughout the nation. The U.S. government encouraged the homesteaders to work the land. In 1909, the Federal Bureau of Soils proclaimed: "The soil is the one indestructible, immutable asset that the nation possesses. It is the one resource that cannot be exhausted, that cannot be used up." The land was free and forever.

Timothy Egan's *The Worst Hard Time: The Untold Story of Those Who Survived the Great American Dust Bowl*, which draws on interviews with Fred and Katherine Folkerses' children: Faye Folkers Gardner and Gordon Folkers, as well as Faye Folkers Gardner's self-published family history, *So Long, Old Timer!*, describe the experiences of the Folkerses. When the Folkerses homesteaded in Cimarron County in the Oklahoma Panhandle, they had a few mules, a horse, a plow, and a lot of hope. Fred planted cherry, peach, apple, and plum trees, and huckleberry, gooseberry, and currant bushes. He carried water to his crops in buckets and plowed the land with a horse-drawn plow.

The Folkerses lived in a small shack built of wood planks with wallpaper on the inside and tarpaper on the outside. They pasted newspapers to the walls for insulation. When centipedes scratched and clawed in the walls, Katherine Folkers crushed them with her flat iron.

Farmers needed loans to buy tools, livestock, and seed. Many months passed between planting crops, when cash was spent, and selling crops, when cash was collected. Banks often refused to make loans to farmers in the American West. These loans were just too risky. After a few years of heavy rain and good crops, in the early 20th century, however, bank managers were more willing to lend money to farmers.

In 1916, the U.S. Congress passed the Federal Farm Loan Act. Among other things, the act created 12 regional farm loan banks. Farmers could borrow amounts from $100 to $10,000, for 5 to 40 years, by mortgages on their land and land improvements. If a borrower could not pay the interest on a mortgage loan or repay the mortgage loan itself, the lender (for example, a bank) could foreclose on the property. In foreclosure, the lender had the legal right to the property. Farm mortgages in the United States doubled between 1910 and 1920—from $3.3 billion to $6.7 billion (about $85 billion in today's dollars).

What could go wrong? Homesteaders in the Oklahoma Panhandle had free land, easy access to loans, and a favorable climate with plenty of rain. And when the gasoline-powered, mass-produced tractor was developed in the early 20th century, farming improved dramatically. Farmers could plant and harvest faster and better with tractors than with horses and mules. Author Timothy Egan writes:

> no group of people took a more dramatic leap in lifestyle or prosperity, in such a short time, than wheat farmers on the Great Plains. In less than ten years, they went from subsistence living to small business-class wealth.

In 1910, wheat sold for only 80¢ a bushel. As the global supply of wheat decreased during World War I (1914–1918), wheat prices rose. The U.S. government encouraged wheat production and even guaranteed the price of wheat at $2 a bushel. Woodrow Wilson, the U.S. president, said: "Plant more wheat, wheat will win the war." When World War I ended, wheat sold for $2.45 a bushel. When wheat prices dropped after the war, wheat farming was still profitable. With new farming methods and tools, farmers could produce more bushels of wheat per acre. Few people imagined that the price of wheat would drop to 32¢ a bushel, as it did in the 1930s.

As wheat prices began to fall, wheat farmers turned to deep plowing of their fields using heavy tractors. They thought that the ideal ground for raising crops was fine soil. With these tractors, farmers could plow their land to a depth of 20 inches. In ordinary plowing, the depth is about 8 inches. The benefit of deep plowing is that it loosens the soil and makes it easier to plant seeds. It also produces higher grain yields than regular plowing. Yet deep plowing destroys the deep-rooted prairie grasses that hold topsoil and retain moisture, even during periods of high winds. In the Great Plains, including the Oklahoma Panhandle, farmers were changing the land. Wheat stalks were replacing the prairie grasses in what was called the "Great Plow-Up." No one at the time seemed worried.

Egan comments: "If the farmers of the High Plains were laying the foundation for a time bomb that would shatter the natural world, any voices that implied such a thing were muted."

By the late 1920s, the Folkerses' annual harvest was 10,000 bushels of wheat. They could send their wheat to Chicago and New York by the new railroads. With their profits, they built a house when their shack collapsed in a hailstorm. They made purchases from the mail-order Sears and Roebuck catalog that advertised everything needed for the home and farm, delivered by railroad boxcar—plows, cultivators, cast-iron wood stoves, clothesline ropes, buckets, cabinets, even a complete kitchen. The Folkerses also bought a car—a 1928 Dodge—new clothes, and a piano (with lessons) for Faye, their daughter.

Others also benefited from the new wealth that wheat produced. The population of Boise City increased to 1,200 people. The town had a railroad station, a new courthouse, some restaurants, a bookstore, a newspaper, and a tractor dealership.

Paul and Dora Arnett moved to Beaver County in the Oklahoma Panhandle in 1921. Although they missed the opportunity to acquire free public land under the Homestead Acts, they were able to purchase a quarter section (160 acres) with a mortgage loan. Like the Folkerses, the Arnetts did well. In the 1920s, Great Plains wheat farmers harvested high numbers of bushels per acre.

In 1929, the Arnetts had a daughter, Pauline. Years later, she described her family's life on the farm. Her comments were published in Dayton Duncan's *The Dust Bowl,* which was the basis for a documentary film directed by Ken Burns:

> Wheat was just a bonanza, and everybody had good crops. Like a lot of folks, I think [my parents] thought it would last forever. They plowed up every piece of land they could get ahold of. And the more wheat they raised, the more land they plowed up. . . . They were able to acquire more land probably than they should have.

On October 29, 1929 (forever remembered as "Black Tuesday"), the U.S. stock market crashed. Stock market assets lost $14 billion (nearly $200 billion in today's dollars) in a single day. The stocks of companies plummeted. It was the worst stock market crash in U.S. history, and it marked the beginning of the Great Depression that lasted for 10 years (1929 to 1939).

However, on the Great Plains, life continued as usual—for a while.

Because of the good harvests in the 1920s, more than 250 million bushels of wheat had been stockpiled by the early 1930s. Wheat prices fell because of the oversupply. President Herbert Hoover pleaded with farmers to reduce wheat production, but the farmers did not listen. The Great Plains farmers simply grew more wheat. In 1931, wheat farmers harvested a record-breaking wheat crop. But events caught up with the wheat farmers. The price of wheat had gone from over $1.50 per bushel in 1925 to about $1 per bushel in 1930; it reached a low of 32¢ per bushel in 1932. At the same time, a drought that had begun in the eastern United States moved westward to the Great Plains; it would last through the 1930s. With drought came the dust storms. Duncan described them as "a catastrophe of biblical proportions."

Because of the deep plowing and its removal of the prairie grasses, the topsoil in the Great Plains had dried, becoming a powdery substance, like sand. Without rain, wheat planted in the fall months could not develop roots that could protect the land from the wind. The powerful winds blew away the topsoil.

In January 1932, the dust storms began on the Great Plains. The southern states were the hardest hit as the wind, blowing at 60 miles per hour, swept across the land. The wind covered farms in drifts of dust like snow. Thick dust clouds reached as high as 10,000 feet above the earth. Ships 300 miles offshore in the Gulf of Mexico reported dust on their decks. Visibility on the ground was often

3 feet or less. Billows of dust choked cows and horses. People's lungs filled with dust, causing "dust pneumonia." So began the Dust Bowl that lasted almost a decade.

Fourteen dust storms in the Great Plains were reported in 1932; 28 in 1933. On April 14, 1935, one of the nation's worst dust storms began in the Oklahoma Panhandle and blew south. That day is known as Black Sunday. For 2 days, high winds blew away 350 million tons of topsoil, some of which even reached New York City. Dust and dirt in the air was so thick that the days seemed as black as nights.

These were terrifying years for farm families. Along with the rich topsoil, the wind blew away people's livelihood. Some farmers clung to the hope that rain would fall and the wheat would grow. For many farmers, it was a false hope as the drought and the dust storms continued, and the wheat harvests failed. As they struggled to feed and clothe their families, the farmers fell behind on their farm and equipment mortgages. Banks began to foreclose on people's farms.

By 1933, the average farm foreclosure rate had jumped to 38.8% from 17.4% in 1926. More than 200,000 farms were foreclosed on in 1933. By 1934, when farm property values in Boise City had declined by 90%, farmers owed the banks far more than their farms were worth. They also owed property taxes.

The banks held public auctions after they foreclosed on the farms. Farm families watched in humiliation and grief as their land, their livestock, their plows and tools, and even their furniture were sold at very low prices. Sometimes farmers resisted the sale of their neighbors' property. They bid pennies for the property and made clear that outsiders, seeking to grab farmland and equipment cheaply, were unwelcome. T. K. Watkins describes these "penny auctions":

> When the bidding commenced, someone in the crowd would start it off at fifteen cents or so, and it rarely got beyond a few dollars before the bidding stopped and the auctioneer would close the sale. If anyone in the farmyard might be so ignorant of what was going on as to put in a serious bid, a suitably burly man would be likely to step up and put a hand on his shoulder with the words, "That bid's a little high, ain't it?"

After the crowd purchased the land cheaply, they offered to sell it to the original owners "for a penny." These sales were often successful, but banks soon figured out ways to get around them.

Paul and Dora Arnett were among the families in financial trouble. They still had a large mortgage on their farm. Pauline Arnett Hodges remembered her father's words to her mother:

> Oh Dora, it's going to get better. It'll get better. Mr. Igo [their banker] is going to let us continue for a little while longer. If we just had a crop we could pay off that mortgage.

But Paul was mistaken. The bank foreclosed on the Arnett's farm in the winter of 1934–1935, when Pauline was 6 years old. The Arnetts moved to a rented house in town that had no electricity and no running water. Dora then had a nervous breakdown. As Pauline recalled, her self-confident, hard working father was severely depressed with no work and no income. He began drinking heavily.

Thousands of other farm families were just as desperate. And so began the "Migration of Despair" as millions of people migrated from Oklahoma and other states to California, where they lived in migrant camps and sought work picking fruit. John Steinbeck, in his famous novel *The Grapes of Wrath*, vividly described the hardship and despair of life in California for farm families who had migrated because of the drought, the dust, and the foreclosures.

In the U.S. presidential election of 1932, nearly 3 years into the Great Depression, voters expressed their anger at the ballot box. They overwhelmingly voted against the incumbent Republican president, Herbert Hoover, and voted for the Democratic candidate, Franklin Delano Roosevelt. Voters were furious over Hoover's handling of the economy. They thought he treated the 1929 stock market crash as a temporary event that would soon pass. Hoover's efforts to support the failing economy at home were too few and too late. Voters called Hoover the "do-nothing president."

Roosevelt, or "FDR" as he was (and still is) called, campaigned on a promise of recovery for Americans. Roosevelt's promise, the "New Deal," called for federal public works projects and assistance programs for farmers, the poor, the unemployed, and the elderly, as well as financial reforms that placed safeguards between lenders and borrowers. The New Deal focused on the "3 Rs": relief, recovery, and reform. With the support of the Democrats in Congress, Roosevelt signed these programs into law.

Roosevelt was deeply concerned about the poor and the unemployed, especially the nation's farmers. He thought the country could not recover from the Great Depression unless farming was once again a prosperous activity. The New Deal provided more federal dollars to the states affected by the Dust Bowl than to any other region. One of the first acts under the New Deal, the Agricultural Adjustment Act (AAA) of 1933, was designed to boost agricultural prices by reducing surpluses: The government bought livestock for slaughter and paid farmers not to plant. Taxes on companies that processed farm products paid for this aid to farmers.

The New Deal helped many farm families in the Oklahoma Panhandle. In 1934, the U.S. government bought thousands of cattle and sheep and provided loans to more than 300 farmers in Cimarron County. An estimated 4,000 to 5,500 families in six counties of the Panhandle received some form of federal relief: government scarcity payments (money for not planting crops) or government jobs. The largest federal agency, the Work Projects Administration (WPA), gave millions of mainly unskilled men and former farmers jobs in these public projects. They built roads, constructed hydro-electric dams, and worked on conservation projects.

The Arnetts were eligible for such assistance through the New Deal. Paul finally found work in road construction. He was paid $3 a day and then, as foreman, $5 a day (the equivalent of approximately $90 in today's dollars). Pauline described this desperate time:

> We would have starved to death because we had no other way to make any money. The New Deal for us—the farm programs, but the WPA in particular—was just a lifesaver for us.

Some farmers endured these hard times on their farms. The Folkerses were one of these families. They lost all their savings when their local bank failed in the Great Depression. They still had a debt of $10,000 (the equivalent of about $150,000 in today's dollars) as the U.S. entered World War II. However, as the price of wheat per bushel steadily increased during the War, the Folkerses were able to repay their loans. Fred farmed in the Oklahoma Panhandle until his death in 1965.

The land in the Great Plains, especially in the southern Plains that include the Oklahoma Panhandle, permanently changed during the Dust Bowl years. The U.S. government tried to protect the land: The Soil Conservation and Domestic Allotment Act of 1936 paid farmers to reduce their production. The goal of the act was to prevent further soil erosion. The U.S. government also purchased 11.3 million acres of farmland to restore as national grasslands.

The Dust Bowl also made radical changes in the American population. Although some families like the Folkerses and the Arnetts stayed in Oklahoma, by 1940 approximately 2.5 million people, disparagingly referred to as "Okies," had left. This was the largest internal migration in U.S. history.

In 1940, Woody Guthrie, the American folk singer, recorded an album called *Dust Bowl Ballads*. His songs were based on his life and travels when he left the Great Plains for California. One song in the album, "Dust Can't Kill Me," described how the dust killed everything in a farmer's life—his wheat, his barn, his homestead, his family, his baby, his tractor—but it couldn't kill him.

The major sources for this chapter were:

Alston, L. J. (1983). Farm foreclosures in the United States during the interwar period. *Journal of Economic History, 43*, 885–903.

Egan, T. (2006). *The worst hard time: The untold story of those who survived the great American dust bowl.* Boston, MA: Houghton Mifflin.

Galbraith, J. K. (1972). *The great crash, 1929* (3rd ed.). Boston, MA: Houghton Mifflin.

Hamilton, D. E. (1991). *From new day to new deal: American farm policy from Hoover to Roosevelt.* Chapel Hill, NC: University of North Carolina Press.

Henderson, C. (1936, May). Letters from the Dust Bowl. *The Atlantic Monthly.* Available at https://www.theatlantic.com/magazine/archive/1936/05/letters-from-the-dust-bowl/308897/

Painter, B. (2015, April 12). Of character: 80 years have not clouded Pauline Arnett
     Hodges' memories of Black Sunday. *The Oklahoman*. Available at http://newsok.
     com/article/5409409
Perkins, V. L. (1969). *Crisis in agriculture: The agricultural adjustment administration
     and the New Deal, 1933*. Berkeley, CA: University of California Press.
Watkins, T. H. (2009). *The Great Depression: America in the 1930s*. Boston, MA: Back
     Bay Books.

LEARNING ACTIVITIES FOR "DUST CAN'T KILL ME"

Facts of the Case

1. How was Boise City settled?
2. What was life like for wheat farmers like the Folkerses and Arnetts during the 1920s?
3. How did the price of wheat change from the 1910s to the 1930s?
4. How did the farm tractor change farming practices in the United States?
5. What happened to the Arnetts during the Great Depression?

Historical Understanding

1. What were the requirements and the purpose of the Homestead Acts?
2. What was the New Deal and how did it help farmers in the Great Plains?
3. What were the causes of the dust storms? What were they like?
4. During and after the Dust Bowl, how did the U.S. government try to improve the land in the Great Plains?

Expressing Your Reasoning

Should the bank have foreclosed on Paul and Dora Arnett during the time of the Dust Bowl? Why or why not?

Key Concepts from History

What do the following have in common?

1. The 2010 Affordable Care Act provides financial assistance in the form of health-care insurance premium payments for low-income and middle-income people. The amount of the aid depends on income and family size. Payments are made directly to insurance companies that offer health care insurance.
2. Amtrak is a public-private passenger railroad service founded in 1971 by 20 railroad companies. The service was designed to provide a network of train transportation throughout the United States. Amtrak receives federal money

annually. In 1971, Amtrak received $40 million in direct federal aid. This aid reached a peak of $1.25 billion in 1981. Amtrak continues to receive federal aid to help pay for salaries and projects.

3. In 2016, the city of Boston and the commonwealth of Massachusetts offered General Electric (a shareholder-owned, multinational corporation) $145 million in business incentives (property tax reductions and various government grants) to move its corporate headquarters from suburban Fairfield in Connecticut to Boston in Massachusetts. "Project Plum" (the project code name), which created 800 jobs in Boston, is intended to contribute to the redevelopment of the city's waterfront.

Historical Inquiry

The Dust Bowl caused an enormous amount of destruction to the environment. Do scientists predict the United States will experience a second Dust Bowl? Using online and other resources, test the hypothesis that scientists predict the United States will experience a second Dust Bowl. Compose a short essay in which you accept or reject the hypothesis. Use evidence to support your conclusion. To begin your investigation, the following search terms will be helpful:

- Second Dust Bowl
- Dust Bowl Recurrence
- 21st-century Dust Bowl

CHAPTER 31

Deportees

Deportation and Repatriation to Mexico, 1929–1939

Mexican Repatriation Cartoon

Wall Street stock markets crashed on October 29, 1929, a day known as Black Tuesday. In just one day, the stock market traded 16 million shares and billions of dollars were lost. On October 28, the Dow Jones Industrial Average (Dow), a price-weighted average of significant stocks traded on the New York Stock Exchange, closed at 260 points, a drop of 13%. On October 29, the Dow closed at 230 points, an additional drop of 12%. Over the next several months the Dow made several brief recoveries. But, by 1932, the value of the stock market was only 20% of what it had been in the summer of 1929. On July 8, 1932, the Dow average reached its lowest point, closing at 41 points. The stock market crash marked the beginning of the Great Depression and the start of a desperate time for many Americans, including people of Mexican ancestry living in the United States.

A depression is a severe economic downturn that lasts at least several years. Depressions result in very high unemployment, business failures, and a large number of bankruptcies. The Great Depression lasted from 1929 to 1939. The bottom fell out of the economy in the United States and much of the world, especially in Europe. It was the worst economic disaster in the history of the industrialized world.

The expansion of the U.S. economy during the 1920s had resulted in a doubling of the nation's wealth. Investors of various income levels bought stock. Hoping that the economic boom would continue, investors made reckless investments that resulted in stock prices rising higher than their actual value. When panic set in, investors began selling their stocks. Many stocks became worthless. By 1932, the value of General Motors stock was $8 a share. It had been $73 a share in September 1929.

Life savings were lost. Factories and other businesses dramatically cut production. Workers were fired and wages fell. Buying power decreased. Many Americans were forced to buy essentials on credit, leaving them with debt. Although the stock market crash marked the beginning of the Great Depression, economists disagree about the relation between the crash and the Depression. Some argue that the crash caused the Depression. Others maintain that it was a symptom, not a cause, and that the Depression resulted from other economic weaknesses within the banking and currency systems in the United States and elsewhere in the world. Investors were buying stocks on margin (purchasing stocks on credit while paying only 10–20% of the actual price), and when stocks crashed, many of those who bought on margin were overwhelmed with debt and wiped out financially.

The Great Depression also hit Europe and other industrialized areas. After World War I, the United States aided the economies of European countries recovering from war with investments and loans. When the Great Depression first struck the United States, these loans and investments ended. In addition, countries trying to protect their own industries imposed new tariffs (taxes on imported goods) and raised others, which greatly reduced international trade. By 1932, the volume of international trade had declined by 50%. The worldwide depression made the recovery of war-ravaged Europe more difficult.

President Hoover tried to reassure people that the Depression would be short-lived, but the situation worsened. Industrial production dropped by 50% between 1929 and 1930. During this same time, farmers were forced to sell their crops at very low prices. Hoping to earn enough money to pay their loans, many farmers continued to plant large acreage, causing an oversupply that further reduced prices. Many farmers could not pay their mortgage payments and lost their farms to foreclosure of their mortgage loans by banks. Between 1929 and 1932, one-third of all farmers lost their farms. Other farmers had farm equipment repossessed because they had purchased it on credit and could not make the payments.

In many cities, churches and private charities, and later state governments and the federal government, opened soup kitchens and breadlines to feed hungry people. Homeowners lost their homes through foreclosures on mortgages, because they had no money to make the payments. Possessions bought on credit were repossessed by stores when consumers could not make payment.

Unemployment went from 4 million in 1930, to 6 million in 1931, and then to 15 million in 1932. That year the unemployment rate reached its peak high at 25%. Depositors, hoping to hold on to their savings, withdrew their money from banks, leading to a series of bank failures. Many banks did not have enough in deposits to cover the withdrawals. By 1933, half of the banks in the nation had gone out of business.

President Hoover did not believe it was the responsibility of government to enact large programs to create jobs or provide economic relief to citizens. The government instead provided loans to businesses, including banks, but this strategy did not end the crisis. In the presidential election of 1932, Americans rejected Hoover with the overwhelming victory of Democrat Franklin Delano Roosevelt (FDR). Roosevelt won 472 electoral votes to Hoover's 59, and he won the popular vote 57% to Hoover's 40%. FDR carried 42 of the then 48 states.

In a program called the New Deal, FDR's administration took executive actions and proposed legislation to stabilize industrial and agricultural production, stimulate the economy, and create jobs. FDR's New Deal measures made things better for Americans, but it was World War II, in the next decade, that led to a full economic recovery. The war economy provided countless jobs resulting from businesses and factories being at full production levels. The value of the stock market, however, as measured by the Dow, did not reach the pre-crash levels until 1955. An additional outcome of the Great Depression was a national consensus that the federal government should play a greater role in assuring economic stability.

During the decade-long depression, hundreds of thousands of people of Mexican ancestry living in the U.S. left for Mexico. Were they deported? Were they repatriated? Were they coerced? Did they leave voluntarily? The answer to each question is yes. Were some Mexican citizens? Were some U.S. citizens? Were some legally in the U.S.? Were some illegally in the U.S.? The answer to each of these questions is also yes. People of Mexican ancestry in the U.S. faced both repatriation and deportation. To be repatriated means to return, or be returned, to one's country of origin. To be deported means to be lawfully expelled from a country.

The number of people of Mexican ancestry who left the United States during the Great Depression is difficult to determine. Estimates range from 350,000 to over 1,500,000. Records of those leaving were poorly kept by the governments of the United States and Mexico. Many crossed the border into Mexico at places where there were no checkpoints and therefore no records of entry. The 1930 census lists 1,422,533 people of Mexican ancestry living in the United States. This number included those who were Mexican nationals (citizens of Mexico) and Mexican Americans (citizens or lawful residents of the United States). The numbers did not include those residing in the United States who had entered the country unofficially.

It is estimated that 40 to 60% of those who went to Mexico during the Great Depression were American citizens. Many of these were young children who had been born in the United States and were citizens by birth. They were neither deported nor repatriated. Most had never lived in Mexico and were taken there so parents could keep their families intact. Older children, being more independent, were more likely to remain in the United States if they were able.

Following the victory of the United States in the Mexican-American War (1846–1848), Mexico ceded all or parts of the present-day states of California, Arizona, New Mexico, Nevada, Utah, Wyoming, and Texas to the United States. The thousands of Mexicans living in these areas had 1 year to decide to become American citizens or to return to Mexico and retain their Mexican citizenship. Ninety percent chose to become American citizens. The remainder went to Mexico, where they received grants of land. Those who lived in what became the U.S. territory of New Mexico who did not seek U.S. citizenship were allowed to remain in the territory and retain their Mexican citizenship.

During a surge of immigration from 1899 to 1928, between half a million and a million Mexicans entered the United States, many of them after the Mexican Revolution of 1910. Mexicans came to the United States to obtain better employment and a better life for their families. Some left Mexico because of the poor economic conditions following the revolution; others left because they were on the losing side and were escaping persecution following the revolution. Some planned to stay, others hoped to earn enough to return to Mexico and buy a farm or start a business.

During this period, life was difficult in Mexico. Matters were made worse by land owners who decided to switch from growing the food staple, corn, to producing more profitable coffee, cotton, or sugar, and to raising cattle. These products could be exported. The price of corn increased by 50%. Foreign investment in railroad expansion and in the mining and textile industries did little to help the people who had lost their farms.

Emigration from Mexico was easy (to emigrate is to leave one country for another; to immigrate is to enter or settle in a foreign country). Immigration by Mexicans into the United States over a 2,000-mile border could be done legally through checkpoints, or illegally by walking across an unmarked border or wading across a river. Mexicans wishing to immigrate were also aided by *coyotes*, a term for those who illegally smuggle migrants into the country. Strict border enforcement and harsh punishments for illegal entry did not come until 1929.

Many Mexicans had traditionally entered the United States as migrant workers to obtain seasonal agricultural employment in the American Southwest. Once the work was completed, they would return home. Opportunities for steady employment and good pay, however, caused many to stay. In the early 1900s, labor shortages led to opportunities in other parts of the United States as well: laying railroad tracks in many states, packing meat in Chicago factories, assembling automobiles in Detroit, canning fish in Alaska, harvesting sugar beets in Minnesota, and sharecropping in Louisiana.

During this time, modern irrigation methods had transformed deserts in California (the Imperial Valley), Texas (the Rio Grande Valley), and Arizona (the Salt River Valley) into fertile farmlands. The development of refrigerated railroad cars and better methods of packaging farm goods allowed the goods to be shipped anywhere in the country. Agricultural production tripled as a result of these innovations. These factors all contributed to increased employment opportunities in the United States for Mexicans in both agriculture and industry.

Emigration northward by Mexican workers was boosted by the expansion of railroads in Mexico. Families were able to move from central and southern Mexico more easily by rail toward the American border. Pressure from agricultural and other industries in the United States resulted in the waiving of literacy tests for Mexicans entering the U.S. who could not speak or write in English. Workers were needed, and Mexicans were viewed as reliable and hardworking.

Like many immigrant groups coming to America, Mexicans tended to live in their own communities where they shared a common language and culture. Many workers came first to establish themselves before sending for their families to follow. Mexican workers with job skills had to accept nonskilled employment. Many employers seeking cheap and plentiful workers did not see beyond a stereotype of Mexicans as suited only for manual labor. In industrial employment, Mexican workers were usually given the hardest and most dangerous jobs. Despite the obstacles, many Mexicans became employed in manufacturing, and as bakers, painters, mechanics, machinists, and upholsterers.

The so-called "cycle of migration" made temporary immigration of Mexicans acceptable to those who would not otherwise welcome them. They expected that Mexican migrant workers would engage in seasonal work, return to Mexico with their earnings, and that both countries would benefit from this arrangement. This expectation overlooked reality. Many Mexicans found life in the U.S. too good to return to Mexico. Instead, they migrated to other parts of the U.S. seeking agricultural employment and often accepting nonagricultural types of work.

The Mexicans' hopes of finding a better life in the U.S. crashed with the American stock market in October 1929. Agricultural and manufacturing production slowed and unemployment dramatically increased during the Depression that followed the crash. A public outcry erupted for Mexicans to leave the country. The prevailing view was that the departure of Mexican workers would open employment for Anglos (White Americans of non-Hispanic descent). The pressure of public opinion forced public officials and private businesses to find ways to rid the nation of Mexicans, whether they were citizens or not.

Because of the economic effects of the Great Depression, feeling unwanted, or fearing hostility, some Mexicans returned to Mexico on their own initiative. Mexican workers were pressured to leave at federal, state, and local levels. President Hoover faced pressure to act from Congress and from both state and local governments. Labor unions also exerted pressure on Hoover and other public figures to find ways to remove Mexicans from the country in the hope of increasing employment opportunities for Anglos. Cities and counties with large numbers of Mexicans, such as Los Angeles, were under great stress to provide aid to needy families.

President Hoover did not endorse legislation by Congress, nor did he issue any executive orders that specifically called for the deportation or repatriation of Mexicans residing in the United States. He did, however, through an executive order, greatly reduce, almost to zero, the number of visas granted to Mexicans wishing to enter the country. Hoover also supported Secretary of Labor William Doak's proposals to increase the number of Bureau of Immigration agents. Those agents assisted local officials in conducting raids in Mexican communities to identify undocumented Mexicans and have them deported to Mexico. Thousands of undocumented Mexicans (those in the United States illegally because they are without documents indicating U.S. citizenship, or resident status) were deported during the Great Depression.

The most famous raid in Los Angeles took place at La Placita, a city park frequented by Mexicans. Hundreds of Mexicans were rounded up and faced deportation if they could not show documents indicating they were in the country legally or were citizens. Many of those without the necessary papers were deported by federal agents. The well-publicized raid caused fear and panic in Mexican communities across the country.

Many Mexicans who had immigrated to the United States never sought citizenship. For some, immigration was only for the short term until they made enough money to return to the country they loved, Mexico. In some Mexican communities, there was social pressure not to seek citizenship. Some believed they would always be seen as Mexicans and not fully welcome in American society. In the meantime, while maintaining their Mexican identity, many developed a stronger affection for and appreciation of America. Their children born in the United States were citizens and knew no other country.

Under Department of Labor secretary Doak's leadership, authorities began to monitor Mexicans who were active in labor strikes or protests. Once identified, they would be labeled as communists, subversives, or political radicals and arrested. Deportation without any judicial proceeding often followed for those who were not citizens. Doak's policies helped fuel public support for the removal of Mexicans.

As the Depression worsened, states passed laws that required public employees to be U.S. citizens. Mexicans, even those who were citizens or had legal resident status, were the first to be fired by companies reducing their workforce as the economy continued to decline.

To facilitate quick removal, some local governments hired buses and trains to remove Mexicans. To discourage an easy return to the United States by Mexicans, officials often took to shipping them by rail to central or southern Mexico, from where a return was more difficult.

Mexicans had difficulties challenging deportation proceedings. Many did not understand the deportation process or their legal rights, and it was expensive to hire an attorney. The language barrier added to their problems. The Bureau of Immigration deportation hearings were not judicial proceedings. The bureau's hearing officer simply heard the case against the person and then made a ruling. Once deported, it was difficult to reenter the country legally. Some families with a husband and father in jail awaiting deportation agreed to leave the country voluntarily on the condition that the man would be released from jail.

Those taken into custody who requested an immigration hearing ran the risk of losing at the hearing, which meant they would be prevented from ever returning. Those who chose to leave voluntarily might be able to return to the U.S. sometime in the future if they had no criminal record and were not receiving public assistance. Returning illegally became a punishable offense by an act of Congress during the Great Depression.

The U.S. Constitution's Fourth Amendment protection from unlawful search and seizure and the Fifth and Fourteenth Amendments protections against denial of due process of law could have been called on to protest the roundups. There were, however, no constitutional challenges to the anti-Mexican discrimination in either federal or state courts.

Deportation is a federal prerogative: City and county officials could not deport immigrants. Local government authorities could, however, detain immigrants on behalf of federal immigration agents. More often, local officials used the strategy of persuading and coercing immigrants to repatriate. Repatriation was used as a gentler and more acceptable removal strategy than deportation. Even for Mexicans who were citizens of the United States, the threat of going through a deportation process was often enough to make them want to leave their country. Natural-born U.S. citizens (those born in the United States or to a parent who was a U.S. citizen at the time of the birth) could not (and cannot) legally be deported. But if Mexican Americans were caught in a raid without documents proving their citizenship, they might face a deportation hearing with no access to the birth certificates, citizenship documents, visas, and residency papers required. Mexican diplomats in the United States attempted to assist Mexicans in understanding the deportation process and their legal rights. Mexicans reported harassment, beatings, intimidation, and verbal abuse to Mexican consulates (local diplomatic offices maintained by foreign governments in large cities across the country). In the end, however, there was little the diplomats could do to stop coercion or the immigration raids on Mexicans, or to assist them in deportation hearings.

At various times during the 1930s, the Mexican government attempted to encourage repatriation with offers of land and employment to those who returned. These efforts to assist Mexican workers in the United States were undertaken to help Mexican nationals who were struggling in the United States and to stimulate Mexican agricultural development. The programs lacked consistency and sufficient financial resources to make them useful or effective.

In various places in the United States, especially in California, there were people who opposed the treatment those of Mexican ancestry were receiving. Many large agricultural businesses depended on Mexicans as a reliable labor force even during the Depression. Sympathy and assistance came from the relatives, friends, and, in many cases, employers who valued their employees of Mexican ancestry.

A federal criminal justice commission, known as the Wickersham Commission, investigated the anti-Mexican policies of Secretary of Labor Doak. In 1931, the commission issued a denunciation of his methods that caused the Hoover administration to tell the secretary to "tone down" his actions. Doak continued his policies but moderated his anti-Mexican rhetoric.

For many of the tens of thousands who returned to Mexico, life was difficult. There were a great number who had never been to Mexico, or to the particular part of Mexico where they were deposited. Mexico was a nation of various peoples, cultures, and languages, depending on the region. Mexicans who were brought to Mexico often felt that they had been left in a place they did not recognize or understand. A poor Mexican economy did not offer employment opportunities. Many young family members had to adjust to a culture, including an educational system, that was foreign to their experience in the United States. Mexicans returning home were often looked down upon as traitors who had left their native land.

In spite of the obstacles against returning to America, many Mexicans did return as economic conditions improved during the 1930s, especially in response to the federal government's employment initiatives under the leadership of President Roosevelt. Employers again began to seek Mexicans to work in both agriculture and in industry. Under the administration of FDR, there were fewer Mexican deportations and attempts to persuade, coerce, intimidate, or force people to leave the country than there had been during Hoover administration.

The story of Mexican deportation during the 1930s was not widely reported or discussed following the end of the Great Depression. The story took on new life as the result of the 2006 publication of the work of Professors Francisco Balderrama and Raymond Rodriquez, *Decade of Betrayal: Mexican Repatriation in the 1930s*. The authors described how Mexicans were treated in the United States during the Great Depression:

> Americans, reeling from the economic disorientation of the depression, sought a convenient scapegoat. They found it in the Mexican community. In a frenzy of anti-Mexican hysteria, wholesale punitive measures were proposed and undertaken by government officials at the federal, state, and local levels. Laws were passed depriving Mexicans of jobs in the public and private sectors. Immigration and deportation laws were enacted to restrict emigration and hasten the departure of those already here. Contributing to the brutalizing

experience were the mass deportation roundups and repatriation drives. Violence and "scare-head" tactics were utilized to get rid of the burdensome and unwanted horde. An incessant cry of "get rid of the Mexicans" swept the country.

As a result of the efforts of the two professors, a new interest in the story took hold in California. After reading *Decade of Betrayal*, former California state senator Joseph Dunn called for a state investigation. The investigation led to the state of California issuing a formal apology in 2005, the Apology Act, to those individuals and families who were mistreated as the result of state action in the 1930s. The county of Los Angeles issued its own apology in 2012.

The United States government has not apologized. Proposed apology legislation was introduced in Congress but never enacted into law. The federal, state, and local officials who advocated for, and engaged in, policies of Mexican deportation and repatriation believed they were acting in the best interest of the country during a time of severe crisis.

The major sources for this chapter were:

Balderrama, F., & Rodriquez, R. (2006). *Decade of betrayal: Mexican repatriation in the 1930s*. Albuquerque, NM: University of New Mexico Press.

Grattan, B., & Merchant, E. (2013). Immigration, repatriation, and deportation: The Mexican-Origin population in the United States, 1920–1950. *International Migration Review, 47*(4), 944–975.

Hoffman, A. (1974). *Unwanted Mexican Americans in the Great Depression: Repatriation pressures 1929–1939*. Tucson, AZ: The University of Arizona Press.

Wagner, A. (2017, March 6). America's forgotten history of illegal deportations. *The Atlantic*. Available at https://www.theatlantic.com/politics/archive/2017/03/americas-brutal-forgotten-history-of-illegal-deportations/517971/

LEARNING ACTIVITIES FOR "DEPORTEES"

Facts of the Case

1. Why had many Mexicans immigrated to the United States prior to the Great Depression?
2. Why were people of Mexican ancestry targeted for removal from the United States?
3. What is the difference between deportation and repatriation?
4. Why did many people of Mexican ancestry voluntarily leave the United States during the 1930s?

Historical Understanding

1. What was the Great Depression?
2. What role did government play in the deportation and repatriation of people of Mexican ancestry during the 1930s?
3. Why were Mexican deportation and repatriation gradually reduced following the presidential election of Franklin Roosevelt (FDR)?

Express Your Reasoning

Were federal, state, and local authorities justified in deporting and repatriating people of Mexican ancestry during the Great Depression? Why or why not?

Key Concepts from History

What do the following have in common?

1. Not long after the Libyan dictator Muammar Gaddafi gained power in 1969, he retaliated against Italian residents for what he termed the taking of Libyan wealth by Italians during the colonization of Libya by Italy in 1911. In Libya, Jews faced anti-Semitic laws after they were granted citizenship. Their passports were labeled "Libyan Jews" and carried restrictions because of their culture and religion. Gaddafi justified the action by claiming that Jews living in Libya had aligned with Israel. In October 1970, Gaddafi expelled thousands of Italians and Jews living in the country. Fearing discrimination, many Jews and Italians had emigrated from Libya before Gaddafi's order. The expulsion is known as the Day of Vengeance.
2. Following the Gulf War in 1991, the government of Kuwait expelled over 200,000 Palestinians living in the country. The expelled Palestinians settled in Jordan, where they were granted citizenship. The Palestinians were pressured to leave by the use of terror, violence, and economic discrimination. Two hundred thousand Palestinians had already fled Kuwait before the end of the war and were banned from returning. The expulsion policy was a reaction by Kuwait to the alignment of the Palestinian Liberation Organization (PLO) leader, Yassar Arafat, with the dictator of Iraq, Saddam Hussein.
3. Bhutan is a small and remote Asian kingdom that is located between China and India. In 1990, tensions between the Hindus and Buddhists resulted in the removal of over 100,000 ethnic Nepalis from Bhutan to Nepal. The expulsion of the Nepalis (a minority largely of the Hindu religion) was carried out by the Bhutanese military in an effort to preserve its Buddhist culture and identity.

Historical Inquiry

Was the deportation and repatriation of people of Mexican ancestry residing in the United States during the 1930s repeated during the presidency of Donald Trump?

Using online and other sources, test the hypothesis that Mexican deportation and repatriation of people of Mexican ancestry residing in the United States during the 1930s was repeated during the presidency of Donald Trump. Compose a short essay in which you accept or reject the hypothesis. To begin your investigation, the following search terms will be helpful:

- The history of U.S. deportation and repatriation
- Deportations under Presidents Obama and Trump
- Illegal immigration
- Children of the undocumented
- DACA—Deferred Action for Childhood Arrivals
- Dreamers

CHAPTER 32

United We Sit

Flint Sit-Down Strike

Sit-Down Strikers in a Fisher Body Plant, 1937

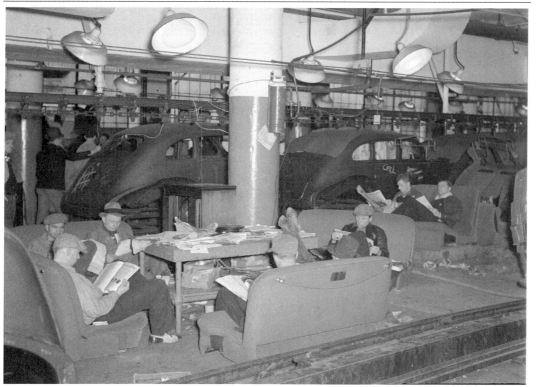

Photograph by Sheldon Dick. Courtesy of the Library of Congress.

It was early evening of a bitterly cold winter day, December 30, 1936. The place was General Motors' auto assembly plant in Flint, Michigan. The event was an attempt by the autoworkers employed in the giant automobile factory to shut it down. When the starting whistle blew to begin the evening shift, there was no roar of machinery. There was only silence. Then a third-floor window swung open. A worker leaned out and shouted, "She's ours!"

Thus began the great General Motors sit-down strike at the Fisher Body Plant. For 6 weeks, Americans' attention was riveted on Flint. The sit-down strike was a lead story in newspapers, newsreels, and radio newscasts. One historian called this strike the most significant conflict between U.S. labor and management in the 20th century. What prompted the small and weak United Automobile Workers union (UAW) to challenge the giant and powerful General Motors Corporation (GM)?

The Great Depression (1929–1939) was still under way when the sit-down strike began. As the spring of 1937 approached, however, economic conditions had improved. Production, profits, and wages had regained their 1929 levels. The unemployment rate remained high at 14.3%, but it was lower than the 25% rate seen in 1933.

Automobile manufacturing was the number one industry in the United States, and GM was the number one automaker. GM's 1936 sales of 1.5 million Chevrolets, Pontiacs, Oldsmobiles, Buicks, LaSalles, and Cadillacs made it the largest manufacturer in the world. It was also the most profitable—$284 million (almost $5 billion in today's currency) in pre-tax profits for 1936.

These profits were widely distributed to GM's stockholders (those who own shares of the company's stock). There were hundreds of thousands of them across the country. They were pleased with the performance of the company they owned. They opposed any changes that might threaten the production of so many golden eggs.

At GM, unions were considered a disruptive new influence. Plant managers were allowed to meet with employee representatives to discuss wages, hours, and working conditions at local plants. The company refused, however, to recognize a labor union formally or to enter into a written contract with one. To prevent the union from gaining worker support, GM hired private detectives to spy on union workers in its factories.

Although auto workers received relatively high hourly wages and other benefits, their work schedule was irregular. Automobile production was seasonal. During periods of low production fewer workers were needed. The fear of being laid off during these periods hung over the head of every worker. The plant foreman usually decided who would be kept and who would lose their jobs during downtimes. He often showed favoritism. Length of service did not protect a worker against layoff. The company could fire anyone it wished.

In 1936, 15% of GM's hourly workers had been laid off for part of the year. For those who were laid off, high hourly wages did not translate to high annual incomes. A study by the federal government in 1936 estimated that a family of four needed an annual income of $1,435 (about $25,000 in today's currency) to live comfortably. Average earnings for those laid off that year were below $1,150 (about $20,000 in today's dollars).

Workers not only felt insecure about keeping their jobs. They were also dissatisfied about the nature of their work. The major complaint was that the work schedule was exhausting: 9 hours a day, 5 days a week. The wife of a Chevrolet plant worker put it this way: "My husband, he's a torch solderer. . . . You should see him come home at night, him and the rest of the men in the buses. So tired like they was dead and irritable. . . . And then at night in bed, he shakes, his whole body, he shakes."

One cause of fatigue was the speed-up (increasing the pace set on an assembly line). As the workers stood in their places, tools in hand, the line monotonously moved one car after another past them. A foreman holding a stopwatch would sometimes yell at the workers to hurry. A Buick worker complained, "We didn't have time to go to the toilet. . . . You have to run to the toilet and run back." The faster the line moved, the higher the output. GM workers believed that the company was always trying to increase profits by getting more production with fewer workers. A Fisher Body Plant worker protested bitterly: "You might call yourself a man if you was on the street, but as soon as you went through the door and punched your card, you was nothing more or less than a robot. . . . It takes your guts out, that line."

During the Great Depression, some workers began to turn to unionism as the best hope for improving their lot. Through unions they hoped to increase wages and benefits, improve job security, and slow down the pace of their work.

The auto workers' union was not well established during the early 1930s. By 1935, only 5.4% of the wage earners employed in the auto industry had joined the UAW.

Union leaders recognized that if the automobile workers were to be organized, the UAW would have to penetrate GM's Flint stronghold. If the union could prove its strength in Flint, auto workers everywhere would be more willing to join the UAW. By the summer of 1936, the UAW had only 150 members out of 45,000 auto workers in Flint. That drab industrial city was the home of GM's Fisher Body Number One, the largest automobile body plant in the world. Chevrolet, Buick, AC Spark Plug, and other Fisher body factories were also located there. More than one-half of the city's labor force was made up of GM auto workers. Eighty percent of Flint's families were dependent, directly or indirectly, upon the GM payroll.

In November 1936, the UAW leadership announced its goals for the auto workers. These goals included elimination of speed-up, seniority based on length of service alone (last hired, first fired, when layoffs were necessary), an 8-hour day and 40-hour week, time-and-a-half pay for overtime, and improved safety measures. One goal, however, stood high above the others: recognition by GM of the UAW as the only labor union with which the company would bargain. As 1936 drew to a close, GM leaders remained as opposed as ever to unions.

The hopes of UAW leaders were raised by the landslide re-election of Franklin Roosevelt in 1936. The president was considered a friend of organized labor. "You voted New Deal at the polls and defeated the Auto Barons—now get a New Deal in the shop," a UAW official told the auto workers.

Recent changes in federal law further increased the optimism of labor leaders. In 1935, Congress passed, and President Roosevelt signed into law, the National Labor Relations Act (NLRA), sometimes referred to as the Wagner Act after its chief sponsor Senator Robert Wagner of New York. The Wagner Act required employers to bargain with their workers. It also prohibited employers from using "unfair labor practices," including firing union members and interfering with union organizing efforts. The new law also set up the National Labor Relations Board. Among other things, it held elections among the workers of a company to find out whether they wished to be represented by a particular union.

Renewed efforts in the last months of 1936 to organize the auto workers of Flint were unsuccessful. By late December, only 10% of the city's GM workers had joined the UAW. Union leaders were convinced that if an election under the NLRA were held, the UAW would lose it. Even if the UAW had won an election under the NLRA, GM would not have accepted the results. The company expected the Supreme Court to declare the Wagner Act unconstitutional and had decided not to obey it in the meantime.

It seemed that a dramatic display of union strength would be required to get the majority of workers to embrace the UAW. The workers were not necessarily opposed to the UAW, but they were waiting to see how the union would fare in a struggle with the giants of the industry. The stage was set for a strike. But what kind of strike? Normally, when workers went on strike, they walked off their jobs. Carrying signs, they usually marched in picket lines around the outside of the building where they worked. In the past, this kind of strike had often been smashed by police breaking through the line of pickets.

UAW leaders decided upon a special kind of strike in Flint—a sit-down strike. Instead of walking off their jobs, strikers would remain at their machines overnight and refuse to operate them. An attempt by police to break the strike might prompt the strikers to damage expensive company machinery. Also, in a sit-down strike, it would be very difficult for strikebreakers to replace the strikers at their jobs.

A union leader at Flint's Fisher One was asked if his workers were ready for a sit-down strike. "Ready? They're like a pregnant woman in her 10th month!" On December 30, 1936, it began. Workers at Fisher Body One and nearby Fisher Two sat down inside the plants. David was trying out a new weapon against Goliath. The fate of the UAW rested upon the outcome of the contest.

A strike in one key automobile plant could paralyze other factories that depended on its product. During the first few weeks of the sit-down strike in Flint, parts shortages caused closings of 50 other plants. Production of Chevrolets and Buicks was grinding to a halt just as the new year began. Across the country the total number of idled GM workers soon reached 136,000. Non-strikers complained about being deprived of work by the striking minority.

The strike spread to other places, but the spotlight remained on Flint, the principal seat of GM's power. A proud GM worker wrote to his wife: "We have the key plant of the General Motors and the eyes of the world are looking at us. We shure done a thing that GM said never could be done."

Sit-down strikers conducted themselves with military discipline inside the struck plants. Strike committees drafted and enforced strict rules of conduct. Dining halls were established in the plant cafeterias. Sleeping quarters were improvised from car seats. For recreation there were lectures and games of ping-pong and volleyball. Some strikers went roller-skating between the long lines of idle machinery. A feeling of solidarity grew among the strikers inside the plants. Morale was high.

Critical support for the strike was provided by the Women's Emergency Brigade. Formed on January 20, 1937, it was an expression of the UAW Women's Auxiliary movement. Reporting on the formation of the brigade, its founder, Genora Johnson said, "We will form a line around the men, and if the police want to fire then they'll just have to fire into us." Starting with 50 members who were wives, mothers, and sisters of strikers, the Flint Brigade grew to 350. The Women's Emergency Brigade fed the strikers; staffed picket lines; and ran a first aid station, a speaker's bureau, and a day care center.

General Motors officials and many Flint residents were horrified at the sit-down tactic employed by the strikers. They saw it as an offense to the American tradition of property rights. Some assigned the blame for its introduction in Flint to "outside agitators," "radicals," and "reds" (communists). In Washington, Vice President John Garner called for the strikers to be removed by force, but President Roosevelt declined.

GM insisted that the sit-downers were illegally trespassing on company property. The company refused to bargain with the strikers until the plants were evacuated. General Motors president Alfred Sloan said the UAW was seeking a labor dictatorship. His company would not accept any union as the sole bargaining agent for its employees.

Tension mounted in Flint. On January 11, 1937, it exploded into violence. General Motors cut off heat to the Fisher Two plant. The temperature outside was 16 degrees. At dinnertime, company guards refused to let the dinner meal be delivered to the strikers. In response, UAW leaders decided to bring in union members from other cities to take over the main gate of the plant. At 8:30 P.M., a squad of men, armed with billy clubs, approached the company guards blocking the gate. The guards fled. Their commander telephoned Flint police headquarters for help. Riot-equipped police officers were dispatched to the scene.

The police stormed the plant entrance. Tear gas wafted inside. Members of the Women's Emergency Brigade used long clubs to break factory windows so the workers inside would not suffocate. The strikers fought back with bottles, bolts, steel car-door hinges, and torrents of water from the plant's fire hoses. The police were turned away. By the end of the battle, 13 strikers suffered gunshot wounds. Eleven policemen were also injured. Most of them had gashed heads. Heat and food were restored after the violent incident.

The outbreak of violence brought Michigan's new governor, Frank Murphy, to Flint. Throughout his career, Murphy had demonstrated a genuine sympathy for the afflicted and the unfortunate. Born and raised in Michigan, Murphy had graduated from the University of Michigan with a law degree. In a paper for a course he took at the university Murphy had written: "If I can only feel, when my day is done, that I have accomplished something toward uplifting the poor, uneducated, unfortunate, 10-hour-a-day-laborer from the political chaos he now exists in, I will be satisfied that I have been worthwhile."

Frank Murphy's secret ambition was to become president of the United States. During the early 1930s, he had been mayor of Detroit and then appointed by President Roosevelt to be governor-general of the Philippine Islands. When he won the 1936 race for governor of Michigan, one newspaper noted that Murphy would be a presidential possibility in 1940. The thought had already occurred to the newly elected governor.

Unlike many public officials of his time, Murphy sympathized with workers. He believed that workers had the right to join unions and to strike. He favored arbitration (settlement of conflicts by an impartial third party) rather than force to settle labor disputes. He was determined to avoid violence during strikes. The government, he believed, must not take sides during a strike. According to Murphy, police ought to keep peace without favoring either strikers or their employers.

Murphy received strong support for his election from labor unions. While campaigning he declared, "I am heart and soul in the labor movement." Upon his election, he received a congratulatory message from the president of the American Federation of Labor. Murphy responded, "My administration in Lansing will mark a new day for labor in Michigan."

The new governor arrived in Flint the day after violence had broken out. Murphy ordered National Guard troops and state police into the city. "Peace and order will prevail," the governor vowed. By the end of the day, 1,289 guardsmen, most of them in their late 20s, had arrived. Their number would double by the end of the month. The troops blockaded the area near the struck plants. They made no attempt to eject the strikers or deny them access to food.

In the past, strikers throughout the United States had reason to fear the arrival of troops. They had been used to break strikes, often violently. In Flint, however, strikers cheered the arrival of soldiers because they trusted the man who sent them. "Under no circumstances," Murphy declared, "would the troops take sides."

Critics of the governor charged that it was his obligation to take sides. The governor, they claimed, ought to employ the power of the state to restore GM property to its rightful owners. Some said Murphy's neutrality was really a pro-strike policy.

Murphy wanted to break the stalemate by negotiation between the UAW and GM. His first efforts to bring about a negotiated settlement broke down. A major obstacle was the position of GM's President Sloan. He refused to bargain with "a group that holds our plants for ransom without regard to law or justice."

The strikers were unlawfully occupying GM property. Governor Murphy was urged to enforce the law and eject the strikers by force. An attempt by troops to drive out the sit-downers would produce certain bloodshed. On February 2, the pressure mounted on Murphy to evict the strikers forcibly. A Flint judge issued an injunction (court order) requiring evacuation of the Fisher Body plants within 24 hours.

After the judge's order was read to the strikers at Fisher Two, they sent the following telegram to the governor:

> We have decided to stay in the plant. We have no illusions about the sacrifices which this decision will entail. We fully expect that if a violent effort is made to oust us many of us will be killed and we take this means of making it known to our wives, our children, and to the people of the state of Michigan and of the country that if this result follows from the attempt to eject us you are the one who must be held responsible for our deaths.

The legal responsibility to act was thrust upon Governor Murphy by the injunction. Would he order an assault on the occupied plants? "I'm not going down in history as Bloody Murphy," the governor declared. "It would be inconsistent with everything I have ever stood for in my entire life." Murphy refused to use bullets and bayonets to drive strikers from the plants.

Instead, the governor brought GM and UAW leaders to Detroit for negotiations. Murphy personally served as mediator. He jumped back and forth between the two parties carrying proposals and counterproposals. After a final, grueling 16-hour session, the deadlock was broken. The 40-day sit-down strike came to an end. GM had lost production of 280,000 cars, valued at $175 million (more than $3 billion in today's currency).

As part of the settlement, the UAW agreed to evacuate the plants. In exchange, GM recognized the UAW and agreed to bargain exclusively with it. The union had won a major victory. The settlement opened the floodgates of union membership. UAW membership swelled rapidly. In the wake of the sit-down strike, the UAW was recognized by Chrysler, Ford, and the smaller automobile manufacturers.

Governor Murphy, more than anyone else, affected the outcome of the strike. He had insisted that welfare payments be made to the strikers' families. He had dispatched troops to Flint, not to break the strike, but to prevent violence. He had delayed enforcement of a court order that could have broken the strike. He had personally kept the strike talks going day and night until a settlement was reached.

When the dispute finally ended, reactions were mixed. Labor leaders applauded Murphy for his handling of the strike. "A great achievement of a great American," was the praise offered by President Roosevelt.

Many others were sharply critical of the governor for failure to enforce the law and protect GM property. Critics emphasized that the sit-downers had broken the law by committing criminal trespass. A member of Congress accused Murphy of having "sowed the seeds of armed rebellion and anarchy."

Soon after the settlement of the GM sit-down strike, a rash of sit-down strikes spread across the country, especially in Michigan. Workers of every stripe—garbage collectors, waitresses, hospital workers, dime store clerks—sat down on their jobs. There were 477 sit-down strikes during 1937. A group of civic leaders in Boston wired the U.S. Senate in March 1937:

> It is rapidly growing beyond control . . . if minority groups can seize premises illegally, hold them indefinitely, refuse admittance to owners and managers, resist by violence and threaten bloodshed all attempts to dislodge them, and intimidate properly constituted authority to the point of impotence, then freedom and liberty are at an end, government becomes a mockery, suspended by anarchy, mob rule, and ruthless dictatorship.

In 1939, the U.S. Supreme Court outlawed the sit-down strike as a violation of property rights. The citizens of Michigan rendered a verdict of their own a year earlier. Frank Murphy was defeated for re-election as governor. The sit-downs had been a major cause for his defeat. According to one newspaper, the voters carried "pictures of 1937 in the back of their heads when they went to the polls." Frank Murphy's hopes of becoming president had been dealt a shattering blow. He was never to hold elective office again. President Roosevelt, however, appointed Murphy attorney general of the United States and later justice of the U.S. Supreme Court.

The major sources for this chapter were:

Fine, S. (1969). *Sit-down: The General Motors strike of 1936–37.* Ann Arbor, MI: University of Michigan Press.

Fine, S. (1979). *Frank Murphy: The New Deal years.* Chicago, IL: University of Chicago Press.

Sear, S. W. (1982) Shut the goddam plant! *American Heritage, 33*(3), 49–64.

LEARNING ACTIVITIES FOR "UNITED WE SIT"

Facts of the Case

1. What was GM's policy toward labor unions during the 1930s?

2. Identify at least two complaints auto workers had about their jobs.
3. Why did the United Auto Workers (UAW) choose Flint as the location for the sit-down strike?
4. Why was the sit-down type of strike chosen as a tactic by the UAW?
5. In what ways did Governor Murphy influence the outcome of the GM sit-down strike?
6. What effect did the GM sit-down strike have upon Frank Murphy's political career?

Historical Understanding

1. During the 1930s what was the leading industry in the United States and which corporation was the largest manufacturer in that industry?
2. How are mediation and arbitration different as means to settle a labor dispute?
3. What did the UAW gain from the Flint sit-down strike?
4. What were the major provisions of the National Labor Relations Act (NLRA) of 1935/Wagner Act?

Expressing Your Reasoning

Should Governor Murphy have ejected the sit-down strikers from the Fisher Body Plant in Flint? Why or why not?

Key Concepts from History

What do the following have in common?

1. The Detroit Federation of Teachers (DFT), a union of teachers employed by the Detroit Board of Education, negotiated a collective-bargaining agreement. According to the terms of the agreement, all teachers who declined to join the union were required to pay the union a fee that was equivalent to membership dues. In 1969, a group of nonunion teachers sued the Board of Education claiming that being forced to support union activities that they would not otherwise support violated their right to freedom of association under the First Amendment. In 1977, the case was appealed to the U.S. Supreme Court. In a unanimous decision, the Court affirmed that an employees' union, elected by a majority of employees, has the exclusive right to represent workers in contract negotiations (collective bargaining). Further, such collective bargaining agreements were legal for public employees, as they are also for employees working in the private sector. The Court found that nonmembers of the union may be assessed fees to recover the costs of "collective bargaining, contract administration, and grievance adjustment purposes." In its decision the Court also insisted that objectors to union

membership or policy may not have their dues used for other ideological or
political purposes.

2. The certified union for more than 4,500 employees of the public schools of
    Madison, Wisconsin, is called Madison Teachers Incorporated (MTI). The
    union negotiated a collective bargaining agreement, effective until 2015,
    with the Board of Education of the Madison Metropolitan School District
    (the Board). That agreement recognized that some employees of the Board
    chose not to be members of MTI. Under terms of the agreement, however,
    nonunion employees were required to pay a proportionate share of the cost of
    the collective bargaining process and the administration of the collective bar-
    gaining agreement. That cost, called a "fair share," was equal to the amount
    of dues uniformly required of all members of MTI.

3. In 1968, the Communications Workers of America (CWA) used union mem-
    bers' dues, in part, to support Vice President Hubert Humphrey's campaign
    for president of the United States and Senator Joseph Tydings' re-election
    campaign. Harry Beck was a maintenance worker with the Chesapeake & Po-
    tomac Telephone Co. in Maryland and a member of the CWA. He protested
    the use of his union dues for a political cause in which he did not believe,
    and he asked for a refund. The CWA refused, arguing that using union dues
    for political expenditures was appropriate and legal. Beck resigned from the
    union but continued as an employee of the telephone company. In 1976, he
    and 19 other nonunion members of the CWA's bargaining unit at the tele-
    phone company sued the union for a refund. The National Labor Relations
    Act permits an employer and a union to enter into an agreement requiring
    all employees in the bargaining unit to pay union dues as a condition of con-
    tinued employment, whether or not the employees become union members.
    The collective bargaining agreement between CWA and the telephone com-
    pany contained a clause under which all represented employees who do not
    become union members must pay the union fees in amounts equal to the dues
    paid by union members. The employees who chose not to become union
    members filed their suit in federal district court, challenging CWA's use of
    their fees for purposes other than collective-bargaining activities. They alleged
    that expenditure of their fees on activities such as organizing the employees
    of other employers, lobbying for labor legislation, and participating in so-
    cial, charitable, and political events violated CWA's duty of fair representation
    and the First Amendment to the Constitution. The court agreed with the
    plaintiffs that collection of nonunion members' fees for purposes unrelated to
    collective bargaining violated CWA's duty of fair representation and ordered
    reimbursement of excess fees.

Historical Inquiry

The Flint sit-down strike strengthened the United Auto Workers union (UAW). Has the union continued to gain strength since 1937? Using online and other sources, test the hypothesis that the UAW has continued to become stronger since 1937. Compose a short essay in which you accept or reject the hypothesis. Use evidence to support your decision.

To begin your investigation, the following search terms will be helpful:

- How the UAW grew
- History of the UAW
- GM and the UAW in historical perspective
- The United Auto Workers

Part IX

HOT AND COLD WAR
1941–1989

CHAPTER 33

Yearning to Breathe Free

Jewish Refugees and the Voyage of the *St. Louis*

Jewish Refugees Aboard the *St. Louis* in Havana Harbor

On May 13, 1939, 937 passengers—men, women, and children—boarded the German Hamburg-America Line (HAPAG) luxury liner *St. Louis* for a voyage from Hamburg, Germany, to Cuba. Some of those boarding had been in prison camps; some had been waiting to be imprisoned. Almost all were Jews seeking escape.

At the dock, a band played and flags flew. Friends and family members on the pier waved good-bye to the ship's passengers. There was celebration, but also sadness, as the *St. Louis* prepared to steam out to the calm waters of the

North Atlantic. The passengers realized that they were leaving—probably forever—Germany, the country that had been their homeland all their lives.

One of the passengers, Babette Spanier, aboard with her husband, Fritz, and their twin girls, had been reluctant to leave Berlin. As Jews, she and her family had endured the insults, the taunts, the jostling on the streets, and the bans from shops, theaters, schools, and public facilities such as parks or swimming pools. German Jews had been stripped of their citizenship in 1935. Yet Babette wished she could stay in her home country. As she explained later, her family had prospered in Germany for more than 400 years: "We regarded ourselves as German through and through. We spoke German, we thought in German, we *were* German. The very idea of leaving the country where our roots were was heartbreaking."

The reluctance to flee their homeland had vanished for German Jews aboard the *St. Louis*, including Babette Spanier, after *Kristallnacht* (Night of Broken Glass). On that night, November 9–10, 1938, the Nazi government of Germany orchestrated a national attack against all Jews. Throughout the country, Jews were beaten in the streets. Synagogues were desecrated and burned; Jewish-owned apartment buildings were set on fire; Jewish shop windows were smashed and the stores vandalized; black-booted men with guns took 20,000 Jews into "protective custody." Half of the Jews arrested were sent to concentration camps at Buchenwald, Sachsenhausen, and Dachau. (Concentration camps are places where large numbers of people, especially political prisoners or members of persecuted minorities, are deliberately imprisoned in a relatively small area with inadequate facilities, sometimes to provide forced labor or to await mass execution.)

The police arrested only a small number of the attackers, none of whom was brought to trial. Following *Kristallnacht*, even the most patriotic German Jews began to realize that Germany was no place for Jews.

U.S. President Franklin Roosevelt was shocked by the events of *Kristallnacht*. He said he "could scarcely believe that such things occur in a 20th century civilization." In reaction, the president extended the time limit on visitors' visas for about 15,000 German Jews then visiting the United States. By his action, the German Jews could remain in the United States for an additional 6 months. He doubted that "we have a right to put them on a ship and send them back to Germany under the present conditions."

Anti-Semitism (prejudice and/or hostility toward Jews) had its origins long before Nazi Germany. Jews were scattered throughout Europe. At first, anti-Jewish feeling was a religious matter. Although Christianity was a child of Judaism, and Jesus was a Jew, early Christians resented the refusal of other Jews to accept Jesus as the messiah. In the third century A.D., Christianity became the official religion of the Roman Empire. Europe gradually became Christian.

Throughout the Middle Ages (roughly 500–1500 A.D.), local governments and populations discriminated against Jews, denying them rights to own land or hold public office, expelling them from cities, forcing them to live in restricted areas, and often attacking them.

The 19th century saw the beginnings of an anti-Semitism not based on religion, but on a belief that Jews were a separate "race." At the time, "race" meant a group of people set apart because of inherited traits such as skin color. Nineteenth-century racists labeled Jews as "wanderers" whose "rootlessness" was inherited through their blood. These racists, pretending to be scientific, depicted Jews as dangerous criminals whose traditions were wrapped in mystery and evil and were inherited from one generation to the next. Jews became scapegoats for ills that befell Europe. Anti-Semites in the 19th and 20th centuries inflamed fear and hatred of Jews. Pogroms (organized massacre and pillaging) regularly targeted Jews in eastern European villages.

Historian Raul Hilberg characterized the progression of anti-Semitism over time in his book *The Destruction of the European Jews*. He wrote:

> The missionaries of Christianity had said in effect: You have no right to live among us as Jews. The secular rulers who followed had proclaimed: You have no right to live among us. The German Nazis at last decreed: You have no right to live.

It had not yet reached that point on the morning that the *St. Louis* set sail from Hamburg, but the threat was looming. The National Socialist German Workers Party (Nazis) had taken total control of Germany. Its *fuehrer* (leader), Adolf Hitler, had total power. He proclaimed the myth that those with "pure Aryan blood" were racially superior. The term *Aryan* was applied to those of Nordic or Germanic ancestry who were fair-skinned, light-haired, and light-eyed.

Trumpeting hatred for the Jews, the Nazis treated them as an inferior race, denying them all civil rights. Under Nazi rule, conditions for Jews became increasingly harsh. They could not vote; had no police protection; could not appeal to the law courts; were excluded from schools, the professions, and business; and they were increasingly harassed and beaten in public. Jewish property and businesses were seized by the government. Some Jews were imprisoned in concentration camps. Others were simply dumped over the border into neighboring countries.

In November 1918, Germany had been defeated in World War I. Its *kaiser* (emperor) fled to the Netherlands. A democracy, the Weimar Republic, was installed in Germany, but from its inception was associated with defeat in the Great War. The new government's first official act was the signing of the Versailles Treaty that ended the war. That treaty took away German territory and imposed $33 billion (more than $2 trillion in present-day dollars) in reparations to be paid to the victorious Allies. Many Germans were humiliated by the treaty. They felt betrayed by those who signed it and claimed that Germany had been "stabbed in the back."

Extremist political parties exploited the discontent and vied for power. There was violence in the streets, especially between the Communists and the Nazis.

The Nazis talked of restoring national pride, rejecting the Versailles Treaty, regaining lost territory, and rearming and restoring the army. They blamed the Jews for Germany's problems.

The German president appointed Hitler chancellor of Germany. In March 1933, he was empowered by the legislature (*Reichstag*) to enact laws without its approval. Four months later, the Nazi Party was proclaimed by law to be the only legal party in Germany. The power of the *fuehrer* was now absolute.

The passengers departing Germany on the *St. Louis* that fine day in 1939 were not looking back at the specter of the Nazis. That was behind them. They had escaped. As the ship set sail, they looked forward to luxurious enjoyment of the voyage and, optimistically, to their safety in Cuba. Most expected that, after a while, they would emigrate from Cuba to the United States.

A crew of 231 cleaned, polished, entertained, cooked, and served sumptuous meals to the passengers seated at linen-covered tables. They tended to every whim of the passengers aboard the *St. Louis*.

The experienced captain of the *St. Louis*, Gustav Schroeder, instructed the crew, some of whom were Nazis, to attend courteously to these paying passengers. They were, he directed, to be treated as any other passengers on the ship's voyages. Personally, Schroeder loathed the Nazi ideology and opposed Hitler's policies. For years, he had resisted requests to join the Nazi Party.

What neither Captain Schroeder nor the passengers realized was that the voyage of the *St. Louis* had been encouraged by Nazi Minister of Propaganda Joseph Goebbels. Some of the passengers had booked passage at their own initiative. Others, some of whom were imprisoned in Nazi concentration camps, were offered passage on the ship if they pledged never to return to Germany. Goebbels's intent was to lull Jews into booking passage on the voyage and to arrange for Cuba to refuse to accept them. He expected that Cuba and other nearby countries would refuse to admit the Jewish passengers. In response, he planned a propaganda campaign to publicize that the rest of the world, like Germany, did not want Jews.

Of the 937 passengers aboard the *St. Louis*, 734 were on the waiting list for American visas. They expected to remain in Cuba until they could immigrate to America. They would, however, have to wait for their names to come to the top of a long list.

The U.S. National Origins Immigration Act of 1924 set strict limits on immigration. Each nation received a quota specifying the number of immigrants who could come to the United States each year. Under the law, people approved to immigrate were placed on a waiting list numbered in the order they had been approved—first come, first served. Those with lower numbers were admitted until the quota for the year had been filled. After a quota had been filled for a year, people waiting for the next year's quota kept their places on the waiting list.

The 1939 quota for Germany had been filled well before the *St. Louis* set sail. There were many Germans, some already in Cuba, on the waiting list to immigrate from Germany to the United States. Many aboard the *St. Louis* were on that waiting list, but many of them had higher numbers than those on the list but not aboard the *St. Louis*. Many of the *St. Louis* passengers were not on the waiting list at all.

News that the *St. Louis* would be sailing to Havana did not please Cuban President Frederico Bru. Cubans had been influenced by the Nazis' anti-Semitic propaganda. President Bru, aware of the clamor against the Jewish refugees, and concerned about rising unemployment in his country, was determined to prevent the ship's passengers from landing. He issued a decree denying entry to passengers on the *St. Louis*.

Midway through the voyage, word of the Cuban president's decree reached the ship. The passengers were alarmed. If Cuba would not accept them, they wondered, where would they go? Most of all, they dreaded being returned to Germany.

At the suggestion of Captain Schroeder, a *St. Louis* passenger committee was formed to work with the captain and with outside agencies to address the situation. For the time being, the captain assured committee members that he would keep the ship on course to Havana in hope that President Bru's decree would be rescinded. On May 23, he told the committee, "We will sail to Havana. But I cannot say what will happen when we get there."

When the *St. Louis* arrived in Cuba during the predawn hours of May 27, it was forced to dock in the middle of Havana Harbor rather than at the HAPAG pier as it would normally have done. The passengers placed their packed luggage outside their cabin doors and prepared to go ashore.

They were denied permission to disembark. Cuban police guards blocked the gangways, and police boats circled the ship sweeping it at night with searchlights. Stranded in the bay, the ship was ordered to depart Cuban waters "on this day, Thursday, June 1." The order warned that the Cuban navy would "conduct" the *St. Louis* out of territorial waters if it refused to go. Of the 937 passengers, only 28 were allowed to disembark in Havana, including those with valid visas and one passenger hospitalized after slashing his wrists and jumping overboard in a suicide attempt.

With tens of thousands of onlookers watching from the shore, the *St. Louis* glided slowly out of Havana Harbor toward the open sea. The mood aboard ship was grim. Captain Schroeder, however, had not abandoned hope. He steered the ship northward toward nearby Florida. The captain hoped the United States would take in the refugees. As the ship sailed along the Florida coast, the anguished passengers could see Miami's palm trees and beaches from the deck of the ship.

The passengers' committee twice cabled President Franklin Roosevelt, pleading with him to intercede. At the behest of various organizations, eminent Americans were sending pleas to the U.S. Department of State and to the White House seeking intervention by the American government. The story of the *St. Louis* attracted a great deal of media attention across the world. Newspapers in the

United States and in other countries reported it on their front pages. *The New York Times* headline for Friday, June 2, was: "CUBA ORDERS LINER AND REFUGEES TO GO."

President Roosevelt was not indifferent to the plight of Jews persecuted by the Nazis. In 1938, he had called an international conference at Evian, France, to consider what could be done about the Jewish refugee problem. Thirty-two countries attended. Many statements of sympathy for the refugees were made, but no significant way of dealing with them came from the conference.

Although it had been an internal German matter and not an international incident, as already mentioned, FDR had publicly condemned *Kristallnacht* and temporarily extended the visas of 15,000 German Jews then visiting the United States so that they would not have to return to such conditions. When Germany annexed Austria in 1938, Roosevelt combined the immigration quotas of Germany and Austria to provide more opportunity for Austrian Jews to flee the Nazis by immigrating to the United States. In April 1939, the president claimed to a member of his cabinet that, at a private lunch, he had personally persuaded the president-elect of Paraguay to admit 5,000 refugees. FDR publicly supported a Jewish homeland in Palestine and pressured the British, who governed Palestine at the time, to keep it open to Jewish immigrants.

Two of the most influential members of the president's cabinet discussed the situation of the *St. Louis* after the ship had been sent away from Cuba. Secretary of the Treasury Henry Morgenthau, Jr., seeking a safe harbor for the refugees, contacted Secretary of State Cordell Hull. The two had a series of three telephone conversations on June 5 and 6. Morgenthau asked whether the State Department could do anything to help provide sanctuary for the passengers, and he offered possible courses of action. Hull offered no support and told Morgenthau that it was a matter "primarily between these people and the Cuban government." He explicitly said that it was not a matter for the U.S. government.

When Morgenthau asked whether the *St. Louis* passengers might be accepted in the U.S. Virgin Islands, Hull replied that "under the law we're helpless in that respect," because tourist visas could not be issued to them unless they had a definite home from which they were coming and to which they could return. This was a cruel irony: They were not admitted to the Virgin Islands because they could not return to Germany where they no longer had a home, so they were ordered to return to Germany.

President Roosevelt had many considerations in mind when the *St. Louis* was sent away from Cuba. His policies for economic recovery from the Great Depression were stalled. Unemployment had risen to 30 million. Labor leaders, who supported the president's *New Deal* economic policies, complained that the jobs available were being taken by foreigners willing to accept minimal wages. Some workers said that every job taken by an immigrant was one less job for an American citizen. One U.S. senator said, "Let Europe take care of its own people. We cannot take care of our own, to say nothing of importing more to care for." The Democratic Party had lost seats in Congress in the 1938 election, and President Roosevelt wanted to regain them in 1940. He also sought election to an unprecedented third term in 1940. Admitting refugees jeopardized his political goals.

The president knew that with another war brewing in Europe, a majority of Americans supported a strict isolationist (non-involvement) policy. Support for admitting European refugees might be regarded as entanglement in the affairs of European countries. Such a perception by isolationists could increase opposition to the president's intention of revising the strict U.S. Neutrality Act. The president aimed to amend the act in order to provide aid to Great Britain in the event of war in Europe.

Immigrants with close relatives in the country were given preferential status under U.S. immigration law. Many Americans, especially those with family and friends on the immigration quota waiting list, would resent moving Jewish refugees to the front of the line. There were also other ships at sea with Jewish refugees aboard whose quota numbers on the waiting list were ahead of some of those on the *St. Louis.*

Although most Americans decried Nazi policies, they opposed offering a home to its victims. A July 1938 poll by *Fortune* magazine indicated that 83% of Americans opposed relaxing restrictions on immigration. Two-thirds of the respondents agreed with the proposition that "we should try to keep them out."

Some Americans actually supported the Nazis. The German-American Bund was an organization consisting only of American citizens of German descent. Its main goal was to promote a favorable view of Nazi Germany in the United States. During a Bund rally of 20,000 people in February 1939, at Madison Square Garden in New York City, the Bund leader attacked President Roosevelt in anti-Semitic terms, repeatedly referring to him as "Frank D. Rosenfeld" and calling his New Deal the "Jew Deal."

In 1939, a bill was proposed in Congress to admit, over 2 years, 20,000 refugee children beyond the immigration quota from Germany. First Lady Eleanor Roosevelt supported the bill, and many religious leaders expressed support. Organizations favoring restrictive immigration strongly opposed the bill, as did anti-Semitic members of Congress. Two-thirds of the respondents to a March 1939 national Gallup poll opposed admitting additional refugee children. The bill never came to a vote. FDR declined to support it because he did not want to antagonize members of Congress whose support he needed for other legislation.

Nativists were people who endorsed slogans like "America for Americans," or spoke of the need for citizens to be "100%" American. Some nativist and racist organizations—for example, the notorious Ku Klux Klan (KKK) that claimed a membership of 4.5 million at the time—openly expressed the belief that refugees from Europe posed the greatest of threats to the United States. In 1939, the Imperial Wizard (leader) of the KKK said: "The Negro is not a menace to Americanism in the sense that the Jew or Roman Catholic is a menace." Popular radio priest and anti-Semitic demagogue Father Charles Coughlin of Royal Oak, Michigan, found sympathy among his millions of listeners across the country when he proclaimed a nativist message over the airwaves: Refugees, like those on the *St. Louis*, he thundered, were a threat to the "purity" of the United States.

Some worried that there might be German spies among the Jewish refugees aboard the *St. Louis*. Evidence to support that possibility surfaced later in Europe when the U.S. ambassador to France claimed that many Nazi agents had entered France as Jewish refugees. In 1940, the president reported during a news conference that American authorities had uncovered involuntary refugees recruited as spies by Nazi officials who threatened to harm their relatives still in Germany. Adding credence to this fear, retrospectively, was the fact that there were indeed Nazi spies secreted among the crew of the *St. Louis* who smuggled documents from Cuba back to Germany.

In June 1939, then, the U.S. Department of State, with its share of anti-Semitic staff, refused to alter the strict quotas and denied entry of the passengers aboard the *St. Louis*. President Roosevelt could have issued an emergency executive order overruling that decision, but did not. The official view of the U.S. government was expressed by the immigration inspector in Miami: "The *St. Louis* will not be allowed to dock here or at *any* U.S. port." The ship turned and headed east across the Atlantic, back toward Europe. Captain Schroeder was determined that his passengers should never have to face Nazi horrors again. He considered crashing the huge liner into the rocky shoreline of southern England, or setting fire to the ship, with the hope that the passengers could be evacuated to safety in England.

On June 13, news of relief arrived on ship. After lengthy negotiations with the American Jewish Joint Distribution Committee and American diplomats, four European governments had agreed to accept the *St. Louis's* passengers. Great Britain accepted 288; France, 224; Belgium, 214; and the Netherlands, 181. After precisely 40 days and 40 nights of wandering on the high seas, the refugees appeared to be safe. But they returned to a Europe about to be overrun by Hitler.

Beginning in September 1939, the German Army swept through Europe. Along with conquering the continent, Germany planned to provide a "final solution" to the "problem" of the Jews—that is, their existence. Nazis were no longer forcing Jews to emigrate. They were now transporting them to labor camps and killing centers. Six million Jews were murdered in Germany and countries occupied by Germany during World War II. This slaughter is known as the Holocaust.

Most of the 288 *St. Louis* refugees fortunate enough to be sent to Britain survived the war. Of the 620 refugees forced to return to the European mainland, 254 perished during the Holocaust, including entire families and children as young as 6, mostly in death camps and other killing centers.

About half of the original 937 *St. Louis* passengers eventually immigrated to the United States. Other survivors went to Israel or remained in Europe. Attitudes vary among survivors, as captured in interviews of them by scholars from the U.S. Holocaust Memorial Center Sarah Oglivie and Scott Miller and reported in their book *Refuge Denied*. Some were bitter: for example, Michael Barak who, at age 3, had been a passenger on the *St. Louis* with his mother and father. When the Germans occupied the Netherlands, the three were sent to a Nazi concentration camp. His father died en route to Auschwitz in Poland, the largest Nazi concentration camp. Michael and his mother survived. They immigrated to Israel after the war. In 1999, Michael Barak told an interviewer from the U.S. Holocaust Memorial Museum: "I hold the United States responsible for the death of my father. My father, like the other 900 passengers on the *St. Louis*, was off the coast of Miami, and he ended up in Auschwitz."

Ilse Marcus spoke to researchers from the U.S. Holocaust Memorial Museum in 2004, at age 90. She had lived in an apartment overlooking Central Park in Manhattan since 1949, 4 years after her liberation from Auschwitz. The pictures in her apartment were of her husband, her parents, and her brother, who were with her on the *St. Louis*. Waving in the direction of the trees, she said:

> Don't be deceived by the pleasant view. When I sit in my chair by the window, this is not what I see, these pretty green things. I only see the faces of my family. I have been in this apartment more than 50 years, and every single night, I have sat in that chair and gone over and over again in my mind the events of the past.

Ilse grew up in Breslau, Germany (now Wrocław, Poland). Her father owned a hardware store, and the family lived prosperously above the store. During *Kristallnacht*, her father's store was looted. Soon afterward, her husband, father, and brother were arrested and sent to the Buchenwald concentration camp. Three weeks later, they were returned, contingent on a promise to leave Germany. They applied for visas to the United States and were given number 52,327 on the quota waiting list. It was clear they would not get into the United States for a long time.

The German government had seized all of the family's assets and property. Using their last remaining cash, they purchased tickets to Cuba on the *St. Louis*. Ilse (then 25), her husband, parents, and brother, like many aboard the *St. Louis*, hoped to wait there until their quota number came up for entry to United States. Ilse vividly remembers the desperate cruise from Havana to Miami along the coast of Florida after the *St. Louis* had been expelled from Cuba. She said, "At that moment, we met the cruel face of America."

Her family was among those accepted by Belgium after the *St. Louis* was forced to return to Europe. When the Nazis occupied Belgium, Ilse and her mother were separated from the men of their family. The two women were ordered by the Nazis, as all other Jews were, to wear a badge with a yellow Star of David on their chests. Instead, Ilse purchased false identity papers. She and her mother were betrayed by other Belgians, arrested by the *Gestapo* (Nazi secret police), and deported in a cattle car by train to the Auschwitz concentration camp. On the train with Ilse and her mother were 662 Jews, 62 of whom were children. The trip took 2 days. There was no food or water, temperatures were below freezing, and everyone stood the entire time for lack of room. Five passengers did not survive the journey.

When the train arrived at Auschwitz, beneath glaring lights, armed guards with dogs brutally pulled the passengers from the railroad cars, and shouted orders to line up into separate lines of men and women. Young children remained with their mothers. About 140 men and 98 women were selected as prisoners and had permanent identification numbers tattooed on their arms. Their heads were shaved; they were issued striped lightweight uniforms; and they slept in overcrowded, vermin-infested, unheated barracks with no running water or sanitary facilities. More than 700 prisoners in each barrack, they slept several to a wooden bunk in three-tiered bunks with wooden planks and a thin layer of straw as mattresses. Ilse was among the women selected as a prisoner to do forced labor.

Separated into lines of men or women, the other passengers who got off the train, including the children, were taken to what appeared to be shower rooms. They were told to strip naked. When they entered large rooms with fake showerheads overhead, poison gas was dropped from an opening in the roof into the "shower room." Their dead bodies were removed from the gas chambers and burned in ovens by Auschwitz prisoners. Ilse's mother was among those gassed and cremated.

As a slave laborer at Auschwitz, Ilse rose in her squalid barrack at 4:00 A.M.; stood outside for roll call, with no protection from bad weather; and ate a near-starvation breakfast. Then she would work from 6:00 A.M. until 6:00 P.M. carrying stones from one side of a field to another. While laboring during the long days, Ilse caught glimpses of skeletons piled high and whiffed burning flesh. She also saw lines of men, women, and children, walking grimly toward the gas chambers.

Sometimes Ilse was relieved from carrying rocks in the fields to work in a nearby factory that made weapons for the German war effort. She took great pride in jimmying the timing devices on grenades so that they would blow up in the hands of German soldiers when they pulled the pins. Ilse and the other enslaved workers also sabotaged rifles on the assembly line. They removed vital screws from the firing mechanisms, making them unusable.

Freedom came for Ilse when Soviet troops overran the Auschwitz concentration camp in January 1945. She weighed 70 pounds when she was liberated. She was transported to a large refugee camp in the Netherlands and from there made her way to Belgium to search for her husband, father, and brother. There she learned from International Red Cross records that her father had died at Majdanek, a concentration camp in Poland, and that her husband and brother had died at Auschwitz.

She took the necessary steps for immigration to the United States. She did not, however, regard the United States as her country. She told interviewers many years later:

The Statue of Liberty means nothing to me. When we were here on the *St. Louis*, pleading for deliverance from evil, she sent us away. Her tablet says "Give me your huddled masses, yearning to breathe free." We were not a mass. We were just a little over 900 on the *St Louis*. And more than yearning to breathe free, we were yearning just *to breathe, to survive*. To send the *St. Louis* back to Hitler's Europe was a criminal act. It was the greatest cruelty.

Not all Holocaust survivors who had been passengers on the *St. Louis* were bitter toward the United States. Rudi Dingfelder, a German Jew, born in 1924, was a promising student with a knack for machines and math. When the *St. Louis* set sail, he was 15 years old. He and his parents were admitted to the Netherlands when the ship was returned to Europe from Cuba. After the Germans invaded the Netherlands in 1940, Rudi endured unspeakably horrific experiences during the Holocaust, including slave labor at Auschwitz and the murder of his parents. Near death, he was liberated by Soviet troops in 1945.

Rudi's brother, Martin, had immigrated to the United States in 1938 at age 17 and become an American citizen. While serving as a translator for the U.S. Army in Germany after the war, Martin discovered that Rudi had emerged from the Holocaust alive. He located his brother and made arrangements for him to emigrate to the United States.

Rudi Dingfelder changed his name to Robert Felder and became known as Bob Felder. He became a U.S. citizen. Bob Felder married, and the couple raised their two children in West Bloomfield, Michigan. Working as a toolmaker in Detroit, Bob eventually became a design engineer.

Bob Felder said the United States was the only place he ever felt truly free. He was annoyed when people spoke ill of the United States or expressed what he thought were petty complaints about the country. His wife reports that he would say, "You are spoiled. You do not realize how good you have it here, how wonderful this freedom is."

Bob's son, Les, said, "There was never a prouder American." Only once, Les said, did his father mention how the United States had turned its back on the Dingfelder family in 1939. He told his son that the United States might not have done right by Rudi Dingfelder, but that it had done more than right by Bob Felder.

The major sources for this chapter were:

Bolkosky, S. M., Ellias, B. R., & Harris, D. (1987). *Life unworthy of life*. Detroit, MI: Jewish Community Council of Metropolitan Detroit.

Breitman, R., & Lichtman, A. J. (2013). *FDR and the Jews*. Cambridge, MA: The Belknap Press of Harvard University Press.

Ogilvie, S. A., & Miller, S. (2006). *Refuge denied*. Madison, WI: The University of Wisconsin Press.

Thomas, G., & Morgan-Witts, M. (2010). *Voyage of the damned*. New York, NY: Skyhorse Publishing.

LEARNING ACTIVITIES FOR "YEARNING TO BREATHE FREE"

Facts of the Case

1. Why were German Jews traveling to Cuba aboard the *St. Louis* in 1939?
2. What motivated the Nazi government in Germany to send Jews to Cuba aboard the *St. Louis*?
3. Why were passengers aboard the *St. Louis* refused entry to Cuba?
4. How did the U.S. immigration quota system operate in the 1930s?
5. What happened to the *St. Louis* passengers after they were forced to return from Cuba to Europe?

Historical Understanding

1. Briefly summarize the origins of anti-Semitism in Nazi Germany.
2. What was *Kristallnacht*?
3. Briefly describe conditions at the Auschwitz concentration camp in Poland.
4. What was the Holocaust?

Expressing Your Reasoning

Should President Franklin Roosevelt have admitted the Jewish refugees aboard the *St. Louis* into the United States? Why or why not?

Key Concepts from History

What do the following have in common?

1. In 1942 Nazi leaders met at the Wannsee Conference near Berlin where they adopted "The Final Solution to the Jewish Question." The term *Final Solution* was Nazi code for a plan to murder all Jews within reach. This policy of deliberate and systematic annihilation of the Jewish people was carried out in Nazi-occupied Europe during World War II. It culminated in the Holocaust, the killing of 90% of Jewish Poles and two-thirds of the Jewish population of Europe—more than 6 million Jews.
2. During World War I, leaders of the Ottoman government in Turkey set in motion a plan to expel and kill Armenians living in the Ottoman Empire. The killing was carried out in two phases—the wholesale killing of the able-bodied male population through massacre and subjection of army

conscripts to forced labor, followed by the deportation of women, children, the elderly, and the infirm on death marches. Many Armenians sought independence from Ottoman Turkey. The Ottoman government in Turkey regarded the Armenian minority as disloyal and as a security threat during the First World War. Killing and deportation of Armenians in Turkey began in May 1915. *The New York Times* reported almost daily on the mass murder of the Armenian people, describing the process as "systematic," "authorized," and "organized by the government."

3. The Great Famine, sometimes called the *Holdomor* in the Ukrainian language, occurred in the Ukrainian Soviet Socialist Republic of the Soviet Union between 1932 and 1933. Estimates of the number killed from starvation range from 2 to 5 million ethnic Ukrainians. Ukrainian farmers revolted against the Soviet policy of collectivist agriculture. The peasant farmers of the Ukraine preferred their individually owned private farms to the government-controlled collective agriculture ordered from Moscow. The Soviet authorities in Moscow deliberately created the famine. All household food was confiscated by Soviet authorities, outside aid was rejected by the Soviet government, and movement of the Ukrainian population was restricted. Some scholars claim that the famine was a mass murder planned by Soviet leader Joseph Stalin to eliminate a nationalist Ukrainian independence movement. The famine took place against a backdrop of persecution, mass execution, and incarceration aimed at undermining Ukrainians as a national group.

Historical Inquiry

In 2017 there was widespread controversy over admitting refugees to the United States. U.S. immigration and refugee policies have changed since 1939. Would refugees be more likely to be admitted to the United States in 2017 than they were in 1939?

Using online and other sources, test the hypothesis that refugees would be more likely to be admitted to the United States in 2017 than they were in 1939. Compose a short essay in which you accept or reject the hypothesis. Use evidence to support your conclusion. To begin your investigation, the following search terms will be helpful:

- The Immigration and Nationality Act of 1952
- Refugee Act of 1953
- Immigration and Nationality Act of 1965
- The Refugee Act of 1980
- Donald Trump and refugees

CHAPTER 34

Tell Them We Love Them

Japanese Americans During World War II

Family Being Evacuated from Bainbridge Island, Washington, 1942

Courtesy of the Museum of History & Industry, Seattle.

President Franklin Roosevelt proclaimed it "a date which will live in infamy." Without warning, in the early morning of December 7, 1941, a calm and clear Sunday, hundreds of Japanese fighter planes attacked the main naval base of the American Pacific Fleet at Pearl Harbor near Honolulu, Hawaii. Japanese bombers inflicted crushing damage. It was a scene of nearly total destruction.

In two devastating waves, Japanese planes destroyed 19 American naval vessels. Over 300 U.S. airplanes were damaged or destroyed. More than 2,400 soldiers, sailors, and civilians were killed in the attack. America's offensive naval power in the Pacific had been nearly wiped out.

Shiro "Kash" Kashino

Courtesy of Louise Kashino and Vince Matsudaira.

The Empire of Japan was establishing what it called "The Greater East Asia Co-Prosperity Sphere" to dominate Asia and the Pacific. Japan's attack at Pearl Harbor was an attempt to remove the United States as an obstacle to Japanese expansion.

The day following the surprise attack, the United States declared war against Japan. Several days later, on December 11, 1941, Germany and Italy, Japan's allies (the three together were called the Axis Powers) declared war on the United States. The U.S. responded with a declaration of war against Germany and Italy. The nation was now engaged in the Second World War. (The main powers allied with the United States were Great Britain, France, the Soviet Union, and China.) The war was fought in two theaters—against Japan in the Pacific, and against Germany and Italy in Europe and in North Africa.

The attack on Pearl Harbor was a profound shock to all Americans. The whole country was stunned by the surprise attack and gripped by fear that Japan might follow the attack with one on the West Coast. Residents of California, Oregon, and Washington were especially alarmed.

Americans of Japanese ancestry dreaded the domestic aftermath of the attack on Pearl Harbor. They feared that in the panic following the attack, they might

General Jacob L. Devers Presenting American Flag to the Mother of Private First Class Fumitake Nagato at Arlington National Cemetery, 1948

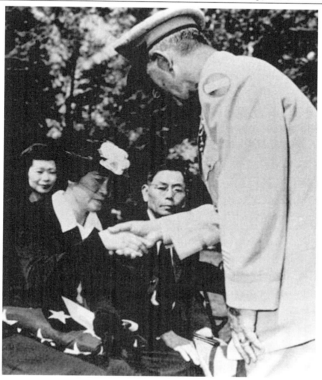

be linked to the Japanese enemy abroad. There was good reason for them to feel anxious. Prejudice against Japanese Americans had been widespread, especially on the West Coast, for a half-century before Pearl Harbor.

Immigration from Japan to the United States was slow through most of the 19th century. In 1891, the number of Japanese entering the United States reached 1,000 for the first time. The new immigrants were largely young, poor, single men. Many came expecting to return to Japan once they earned enough money to buy land there. Unable to save the necessary amount, some became permanent residents in the United States. These young men were prevented by law and custom from marrying White women. Instead, they took "picture brides." On the basis, often, of a photograph, their marriages were arranged by matchmakers in Japan and the young brides-to-be sailed to meet their prospective husbands, sight unseen.

The *Issei*—first-generation, Japanese American immigrants—settled mostly in Hawaii (a U.S. territory at the time, not to become a state until 1959) and in the Pacific coast states of California, Oregon, and Washington. The majority worked in fruit orchards, vineyards, and farms. Others found jobs laboring for the railroads, in canneries, logging, and meatpacking. By the early 1900s, some 150,000 people of Japanese ancestry lived in Hawaii and another 150,000 lived on the U.S. mainland, mainly on the West Coast. They comprised immigrants from Japan and their offspring born in the United States.

At first, local residents welcomed the Issei. There was a high demand for their labor. They were industrious, willing to work for low wages, and did not complain about their working conditions. But as the number of immigrants increased and as the Japanese farm workers began to use their savings to buy land of their own, anti-Japanese sentiment was inflamed among Whites. Unions regarded them as unwelcome competitors for jobs. Local farmers often resented the Issei success at growing citrus fruits, potatoes, and rice.

Some California newspapers began writing about a "yellow peril." This notion suggested that waves of Japanese immigrants would gradually engulf the state. Several writers called for preserving the United States as a "White" country and warned of racial mixing. Japanese immigrants were portrayed as tricky, inscrutable, deceitful, and treacherous.

Official actions were taken against the Japanese. In 1905, the California legislature passed a resolution calling for the legal exclusion of Japanese immigrants. A year later, the San Francisco school board established separate schools for Japanese children. In 1913, California adopted the Alien Land Act. It barred Japanese and other aliens (foreigners who are not citizens of the country where they are living) from owning land. As a result of this law, Issei in California were forced to rely on White friends to hold their property as the "legal" owners, or to register their land in the names of their adult *Nisei* children. (Nisei were those born in the United States of Issei parents. They were citizens. According to the Fourteenth Amendment to the Constitution, anyone born in the United States is a citizen.)

In 1907, pressure exerted (mostly by residents of the West Coast) on President Theodore Roosevelt led to the "Gentlemen's Agreement" with Japan. The Japanese government agreed to reduce immigration to the United States, and in exchange, the United States promised not to adopt laws that discriminated against the Japanese.

That promise was not kept. Asian immigrants (primarily Japanese and Chinese) were discouraged from settling permanently in the U.S. by state laws limiting their ability to own land and property. These laws relied on language from a Supreme Court decision. In 1922, the U.S. Supreme Court had declared Asian immigrants "aliens ineligible to citizenship." Laws that followed that decision, targeting primarily Japanese and Chinese immigrants, prohibited land ownership by "aliens ineligible for citizenship" without naming a particular group. The Supreme Court decision had barred Asians from becoming naturalized citizens, and laws following the decision prevented them from becoming land owners.

The goal of halting Japanese immigration to the United States culminated with the Immigration Act of 1924. That law put quotas on immigration from other parts of the world, but excluded all immigration from Japan (and other Asian countries). The Immigration Act infuriated the Japanese government, which felt the United States had violated the Gentlemen's Agreement.

There were other, extra legal ways to discriminate against Americans of Japanese origin. For example, they were often refused housing in White neighborhoods. A California billboard of the period read: "Japs, don't let the sun shine on you here. Keep moving."

In the days that followed the attack at Pearl Harbor, anti-Japanese sentiment swept the nation. In government halls, newspapers, and on the streets, many Americans expressed hatred toward the Japanese and a desire for revenge. In his testimony before the House Naval Affairs Committee, U.S. Army General John DeWitt, military commander of the newly created Western Defense Command, envisioned immediate dangers on the West Coast. He expected naval attacks and air raids. Adding to the danger, the general believed, was the likelihood that Japanese American residents along the West Coast would commit acts of sabotage (destruction of properties by enemy agents) and espionage (spying to obtain government secrets). He said, "A Jap is a Jap! There is no way to determine their loyalty." (These claims were discredited by both the FBI [Federal Bureau of Investigation] and the FCC [Federal Communications Commission].)

DeWitt's headquarters claimed that there was a "military necessity" to remove everyone of Japanese ancestry from the West Coast, where 90% of mainland Japanese Americans lived. DeWitt and others claimed that it was impossible to distinguish between loyal and disloyal Japanese Americans. The animosity he expressed was not merely national, but racial. In his request to relocate Japanese Americans, made to the War Department (today the Department of Defense), he stated that they were members of "an enemy race," regardless of their citizenship, and that their "undiluted racial strains" made them a risk to national security.

There were similar remarks from many officeholders. For example, John Rankin, U.S. representative and later senator from Mississippi, said, "This is a race war. I say it is of vital importance that we get rid of every Japanese, whether in Hawaii or the mainland. . . . Damn them! Let's get rid of them now."

In January 1942, Earl Warren, then attorney general of California, and later governor of California and chief justice of the United States, declared, "I have come to the conclusion that the Japanese situation as it exists in this state today, may well be the Achilles heel of the entire civilian defense effort. Unless something is done it may bring about a repetition of Pearl Harbor." He then announced his support for evacuation of Japanese Americans from the Pacific Coast.

Growers, merchants, and businessmen along the Pacific Coast who had an interest in removing competition joined in calls for evacuation. For example, in late December 1941, the Los Angeles Chamber of Commerce called for removal of Japanese American citizens and aliens from the city.

Well-publicized remarks by some prominent Americans intensified the panic. For example, both the *Los Angeles Times* and the *San Francisco Examiner* published a column by newspaper writer Henry McLemore that included the following:

> I know that this is the melting pot of the world and all men are created equal
> and there must be no such thing as race or creed hatred, but do these things

go when a country is fighting for its life? . . . I am for immediate removal of every Japanese on the West Coast to a point deep in the interior . . . I don't mean a nice part of the interior either. . . . Personally, I hate the Japanese. And that goes for all of them. . . . Herd 'em up, pack 'em off, and give 'em the inside room in the Badlands. Let 'em be pinched, hurt, hungry, and dead up against it.

There were rumors of Japanese American farmers cutting or burning arrows into their fields to guide Japanese planes to American bases and factories. There were other rumors that Hawaii residents had pointed the way for Japanese pilots at Pearl Harbor, and still others claiming that Pacific Coast residents were signaling enemy ships at sea.

These rumors and other misinformation that Japanese Americans had aided the enemy were all false. Not a single act of sabotage or espionage by a Japanese American in Hawaii or on the mainland was ever proven.

Contributing to anxiety during early months of the war was grim news from the South Pacific. Japanese military forces were making swift progress there. Allied defeats at Manila, Guam, Wake Island, the Philippines, and Hong Kong weighed heavily on the hearts of Americans. Further, government officials learned that Japanese submarines had torpedoed three American freighters near the coast of California.

By February 1942, the military position of the United States in the Pacific was perilous. Secretary of War Henry Stimson believed that an invasion of the West Coast was a real possibility. He decided early in the month that Japanese Americans should be removed from the coast. In his diary he wrote: ". . . we cannot understand or trust even the citizen Japanese."

Some who were close to President Roosevelt advised against evacuation and relocation of Japanese Americans. They included his wife, Eleanor Roosevelt; the U.S. attorney general, Francis Biddle; and other public officials. The dissenters, however, failed to persuade the president. Neither did the American Civil Liberties Union (ACLU) when it protested in a letter to the president that removal of the Nisei would be a violation of the constitutional rights of citizens.

A growing sentiment for evacuation of Japanese Americans soon resulted in government action. In February 1942, President Roosevelt issued Executive Order 9066. It authorized the secretary of war and the military commanders he designated to prescribe military zones "from which any and all persons may be excluded." Although the order did not specify Japanese Americans, its purpose was clearly to give the army the authority to remove them from the West Coast.

There was no outpouring of anti-Japanese hysteria in Hawaii, and no mass evacuation or incarceration. More than 150,000 Japanese Americans resided in Hawaii, 35% of the Hawaiian population. As the largest portion of the plantation workforce on which the economy of the eight Hawaiian islands depended, they were indispensable. They also worked as civilians in the defense industry, unloading ships at Pearl Harbor, and maintaining Hickam Field, the headquarters of the Army Air Force in Hawaii. Although President Roosevelt favored evacuation in Hawaii, it did not happen. The damage would have been too great to the business, government, and military sectors.

FDR's attitude toward Japanese Americans had deep roots in his past. At the outset of his career in public service as undersecretary of the navy, he began to regard Issei immigrants and their Nisei children negatively. He believed that Japanese Americans could not be assimilated (integrated into a wider society or culture) and that they were a source of irritation to their White "American" neighbors. In the 1920s, Roosevelt opposed immigration of Japanese to the United States. Although he did not regard those of Japanese ancestry to be racially inferior, he did regard them as a biologically distinct people, of "oriental blood," incapable of adapting to American society or becoming "true Americans."

The president shared the racism widespread among White Americans of his background and period. In 1942, he assumed that Japanese Americans were potentially disloyal and that preventive measures should be taken. He did not react this way toward Americans of German or Italian ancestry, despite the presence of German agents in the U.S., the sinking of American freighters off the East Coast in January 1942 by torpedoes form German U-boats (submarines), and the existence of expressly pro-Nazi organizations of Americans. An example of such an organization was the German American Bund, with a membership estimated at 25,000.

In March, Congress unanimously passed Public Law 503, which provided for enforcement of the president's executive order. Under the authority of the new law, the army began issuing civilian exclusion orders. The Pacific coastal strip was divided into three exclusion districts: the entire state of California, the western portions of Washington and Oregon, and the southern half of Arizona.

About a week after orders were posted in an area, all Japanese, whether citizens or not, were required to prepare to evacuate. Under authority of Executive Order 9066, during the spring of 1942, the army evacuated more than 110,000 Japanese Americans, two-thirds of them American citizens, from the Pacific Coast states.

One member of each family was required to report for registration. Within 5 days of registration, all Japanese in an area were processed for removal. On the day of departure, they were given identification tags and transported by truck, bus, or train to temporary "assembly centers" along the West Coast. They were to remain there until permanent inland "relocation centers" were ready for them. Although the United States was at war with Germany and Italy, no German Americans or Italian American families were evicted from their homes.

Less than a month following Executive Order 9066 and 3 days after passage of Public Law 503, the first evacuees were ordered to depart, hurriedly leaving their homes, businesses, and farms. The average age of Issei was 58; for Nisei, the average age was 19. With numbered tags hanging from their coats, they were accompanied under armed guard to assembly centers, permitted to bring with them only what they could carry in a suitcase or duffle bag. They were not allowed to bring pets. Some soldiers wept as they guarded the move.

The majority of those evacuated had no choice but to leave their property—their land, their houses, their cars, family heirlooms, and other personal property—behind, entrust it to White associates, or sell it for far less than it was worth. Thousands of families also lost their homes and farms to mortgage foreclosures by banks, because their bank accounts were frozen by government order.

Some evacuees recalled scavengers and bargain hunters driving trucks through their neighborhoods. Bill Hosokawa, one of 271 people (91 aliens and 180 American citizens) exiled from their homes in Bainbridge Island, Washington, remembers drivers shouting from the trucks: "Hey you Japs! You're going to get kicked out of here tomorrow. I'll give you ten bucks for that refrigerator. I'll give you fifteen bucks for your piano. I'll give you two bucks and fifty cents for that washing machine." The value of property losses to Japanese Americans driven from their homes has been estimated to be more than 3 billion dollars in present-day currency value. They were not compensated for these losses.

Some White friends and neighbors kept their promises to take care of the property of those evacuated and returned it intact when the owners came home after the war. Some even operated the farms forcibly abandoned by their owners, paid the taxes, and turned over profits years later when the owners returned home. Much property, however, was lost to theft or vandalism during the absence of its owners. Some of those entrusted with taking care of property were not trustworthy. They sold it or never returned it.

In her book *Desert Exile*, Yoshiko Uchida describes what it was like for her family to be uprooted from their home in 1942. The family lived comfortably in a house on Stuart Street in Berkeley, California. On national holidays, Mr. Uchida hung a huge American flag on the front porch.

The experiences of the Uchidas were typical of Japanese Americans who were evacuated and incarcerated. At 5 P.M. on Pearl Harbor Day, Yoshiko (then aged 20) came home from the library to find an FBI agent in the living room. Her father was gone. As an executive of a Japanese business firm, he was one of many aliens considered especially dangerous by the government. Mr. Uchida was seized immediately after the Japanese attack and sent to an internment camp in Montana.

In April 1942, Yoshiko, her mother, and her sister were ordered to report to Tanforen Assembly Center. They had 10 days to prepare. They desperately tried to dispose of their household possessions. The piano was left with one neighbor; other pieces of furniture with another. Like many others, the Uchidas suffered financial losses in disposing of their property so quickly.

On the day of departure, the three women arrived at their church, the designated assembly point, carrying the few belongings they were permitted to bring. They were taken to a fenced-in camp that had been built at Tanforen racetrack. This was to be their temporary home until the government could construct camps far removed from the West Coast.

It had rained the day before arrival. The grounds had become a mass of slippery mud. The girls helped their mother through the mud past tarpaper barracks until they reached Barrack 16, the one to which they had been assigned. It was a horse stable. Each stall was about 10 feet by 20 feet, empty except for three folded army cots. The stench of horse manure hung in the air. The family stall was cold and dank and afforded almost no privacy.

Meals were served in a mess hall. Their first dinner at Tanforen consisted of two canned sausages, a boiled potato, and a piece of butter-less bread. Meals improved, but most of the time they were skimpy and starchy. Yoshiko and her sister were usually hungry.

Gradually those held at Tanforen, a community of 8,000, worked to improve conditions. A form of limited self-government was set up. Buddhist temples and Christian churches were established. A post office was opened. Education and recreation programs were organized. Yoshiko worked in the elementary school, for which she was paid 16 dollars (240 dollars today) a month. Eventually, her father was allowed to join the family in their stall at the temporary assembly center.

After 5 months, the Uchida family was sent from the Tanforen temporary assembly center to the Utah desert. There they were confined at Topaz, one of 10 relocation centers erected on remote, desolate sites in deserts and swamps where Japanese Americans were incarcerated under armed guard. The 10 relocation camps were operated by a new civilian agency, the War Relocation Authority (WRA). The camps were dispersed among seven states: Arizona, Arkansas, California, Colorado, Idaho, Utah, and Wyoming.

A site survey by the National Park Service offered a bleak description of the interiors of these camps, reporting that they were arranged like prisoner-of-war camps and were not suitable for family living. Tarpaper barracks were grouped into blocks. Each block had a central mess hall, latrine, showers, washbasins, and laundry tubs. Toilets, showers, and bedrooms were not partitioned. There was no water or plumbing in the living quarters. Eight-person families were placed in 20-by-20-foot rooms; six-person families in 12 by 12-foot rooms; and four-person families in 8-by-20-foot rooms. Smaller families and single persons had to share units with strangers. Each detainee received a straw mattress, army blanket, and not much else. There were long lines for eating, washing, and personal needs.

Military police patrolled the barbed wire perimeter of the camp. Inside the perimeter, there were tall towers with armed guards, bayonets on their rifles, and machine guns pointed inward. When someone had to travel from their room to the lavatory at night, often in snow or mud, a searchlight from one of the guard towers beamed on them. Swirling masses of sand in the air constantly coated their bodies and clothing.

The inmates strove for some semblance of normal American life in the camps. Cub Scout packs and Boy Scout troops were organized. There were baseball leagues. Children attended schools. High school yearbooks show photos of teens jitterbugging (a fast dance popular in the 1940s). There were, however, few comforts. Yoshiko, homesick, angry, and despairing, characterized her life at Topaz: "No matter what I did, I was still in an artificial government-sponsored community on the periphery of the real world. I was in a dismal, dreary camp surrounded by barbed wire in the middle of a stark, harsh landscape that offered nothing to refresh the eye or heal the spirit."

Most Japanese Americans spent 3 years in one of the 10 government reloca- tion centers like Topaz. Some, determined by the WRA to be loyal, applied for resettlement and were released sooner to perform certain jobs or attend college under a WRA resettlement program. When the Uchidas were released in 1943, they gradually returned to a comfortable life. The bitterness of their bondage, however, lingered in their memories after the war.

While the majority of Japanese Americans, like the Uchida family, cooperated fully with government authorities during the relocation period, there were excep- tions. At Tule Lake, one of the relocation centers, a militant minority of Japanese Americans was openly pro-Japan during the war. More than 5,000 members of this group renounced their U.S. citizenship. At the end of the war, 4,724 resi- dents (just under 4%) of those who had been held in relocation centers chose to return to Japan.

A small number of Japanese Americans challenged the legality of relocation. Four of their cases reached the U.S. Supreme Court. In early 1942, Gordon Hi- rabayashi, a Nisei and University of Washington student, declined to register for evacuation under Executive Order 9066. He was found guilty of violating the local curfew law. His appeal reached the Supreme Court of the United States. The High Court upheld his conviction for violating the curfew laws that were deemed wartime emergency measures. The Supreme Court decision avoided the issue of whether Executive Order 9066 violated the Constitution.

Mitsuye Endo was a 22-year-old employee of the California Department of Motor Vehicles when she was suspended from her job and confined at Topaz. She argued that the government had no authority to prevent her, as a loyal U.S. citi- zen, from returning to her home in California. By the time that her case reached the High Court in 1944, the WRA had been granting leave from the camps to some who had been cleared as "loyal." The Supreme Court ruled unanimously in the Endo case that whatever power the WRA might have to detain other classes of citizens, it could not confine "concededly loyal" citizens. Endo was permitted to return home, but the narrowly tailored Supreme Court decision in her case, as in the Hirabayashi case, avoided the broader constitutional question of whether the government had the authority to evacuate and relocate citizens in the first place. In an opinion of the Supreme Court, Justice William O. Douglas stated: "We are of the view that Mitsuye Endo should be given her liberty. In reaching that con- clusion we do not come to the underlying constitutional issues which have been argued. . . ."

Those issues were finally addressed by the Supreme Court in the case of *Korematsu v. United States* (1944). Fred Korematsu was born and raised in the

United States. After graduation from high school in Oakland, California, he worked in a shipyard as a welder. At the outbreak of the war his membership in the boilermaker's union was canceled because of his race. He took a job as a gardener. Determined to escape detention, he underwent plastic surgery to his face, changed his name, and posed as a Spanish-Hawaiian. The ruse failed. While leaving a post office near Oakland, he was seized by FBI agents. In federal court, Korematsu was found guilty of breaking the law.

Fred Korematsu appealed his conviction to the U.S. Supreme Court. In 1944, the High Court was asked to decide whether the evacuation and relocation of Japanese Americans violated their constitutional rights. The nine justices of the Court voted six to three to uphold Korematsu's conviction. Speaking for the majority, Justice Hugo Black said:

> Korematsu was not excluded from the Military Area because of hostility to him or his race. He was excluded because we are at war with the Japanese Empire, because the properly constituted military authorities feared an invasion of our West Coast and felt constrained to take proper security measures, because they decided that military urgency of the situation demanded that all citizens of Japanese ancestry be segregated from the West Coast temporarily.

Three justices dissented from the majority opinion. Justice Owen Roberts argued that Korematsu was a loyal citizen of the nation. He added that it was a violation of constitutional rights to imprison a citizen solely because of his ancestry and without evidence of disloyalty. Justice Frank Murphy added strong words in his dissenting opinion. He wrote that the order to exclude all persons of Japanese ancestry from the Pacific Coast "goes over the very brink of constitutional power and falls into the ugly abyss of racism." He continued:

> Being an obvious racial discrimination, the order deprives all those within its scope of the equal protection of laws as guaranteed by the Fifth Amendment. It further deprives these individuals of their constitutional rights to live and work where they will, to establish a home where they choose and to move about freely.

"Racial discrimination in any form and in any degree," added Justice Murphy, "has no justifiable part whatsoever in our democratic way of life."

In the third dissenting opinion, Justice Robert H. Jackson agreed that it was unconstitutional to transplant Americans on the basis of their race. He wrote that by declaring the exclusion order constitutional, the Supreme Court was, for all time, accepting the principle of racial discrimination: "The principle then lies about like a loaded weapon ready for the hand of any authority that can bring forward a plausible claim of an urgent need."

In September 1945, 2 weeks after Japan surrendered, the exclusion orders were rescinded. Many of those who had been incarcerated, however, their homes and jobs lost, could not return to the lives they had been forced to abandon after Pearl Harbor. All camps, except Tule Lake (the camp for "disloyals" not closed until March 1946) were shut down by the end of 1945. The decision in the *Korematsu* case, however, had upheld the constitutionality of excluding Japanese Americans from the Pacific Coast during the Second World War.

After Pearl Harbor, Japanese Americans were barred from serving in the armed forces. At that time, there were more than 1,400 Japanese Americans already serving in the Hawaiian National Guard. They were organized as the 100th Battalion and were shipped to Camp McCoy, Wisconsin, for training. There, they earned a reputation as outstanding soldiers.

In January 1943, policy changed. Secretary of War Simpson issued a press release stating: "It is the inherent right of every citizen, regardless of ancestry, to bear arms in the Nation's battle." Four days later, President Roosevelt went further in an official letter to Simpson:

> The principle on which this country was founded and by which it has always been governed is that Americanism is a matter of the mind and heart; Americanism is not and never was a matter of race or ancestry.

The effect of this reversal was that Nisei in the relocation camps could volunteer to enlist in the army. (They would be permitted to serve only in Europe, and not in the navy, supposedly because they might be confused with the Japanese enemy fighting in the Pacific theater of the war.) Specifically, the president authorized the formation of a segregated regimental combat team made up of volunteers who were "loyal American citizens of Japanese descent." With these words, the all-Nisei 442nd Regimental Combat Team (442nd) was born. There was still, however, the matter of determining who qualified as "loyal American citizens." A loyalty questionnaire was used for that purpose. In it were two key questions, numbers 27 and 28:

27. Are you willing to serve in the armed forces of the United States on combat duty wherever ordered?
28. Will you swear unqualified allegiance to the United States of America and faithfully defend the United States from any and all attack by foreign and domestic forces, and foreswear any form of allegiance or obedience to the Japanese emperor, or any other foreign government power or organization?

Only those who answered yes to both questions could qualify for the 442nd. More than 65,000 Nisei of draft age answered yes to both. Some 13,000 Nisei answered no to one or both questions, nearly 7,000 of them answering no to both questions. The latter were dubbed the "No-No Boys," and they were classified as "disloyals." Nisei communities remained divided between those who answered yes and those who answered no on these two questions.

The army and the WRA expected 3,000 volunteers from the relocation camps. Less than half that number, 1,256 men, volunteered from the 10 camps during the initial call for volunteers. After the shortfall, a draft was instituted, because more soldiers were needed. Some resisted the draft, were convicted of draft evasion, and imprisoned. (The response in Hawaii was different. There, 1,500 volunteers had been expected; an overwhelming 10,000 men crowded recruitment offices on the islands in response to the initial call for volunteers.)

Nisei were also permitted to enlist in the Military Intelligence Service (MIS) to serve in Asia as translators and interrogators. Most Nisei were not well suited for that assignment, because they spoke very poor Japanese or none at all. However, a group called the *Kibei* (Japanese Americans born in the United States and educated in Japan) were fluent in Japanese. They had learned the language during their schooling in Japan. Thousands of them served in the MIS with distinction across the Pacific against Japan, saving many American lives. After the war, the chief of intelligence for General MacArthur (commanding general in the Pacific) said, "Those interpreters and translators saved over a million lives and 2 years."

Those deemed loyal to serve in the 442nd were trained at Fort Shelby in Mississippi. The 100th Battalion, made up of former Reserve troops from Hawaii, was shipped from its training base in Wisconsin to Fort Shelby, where the Hawaiian unit was designated a separate battalion within the 442nd Regimental Combat Team. While training together, the Hawaiian soldiers clashed with those from the mainland. Having grown up in different social environments, there were cultural differences between them, including the Hawaiians' speaking a pidgin English, while those from the continental states spoke more standard English. The two groups created unflattering nicknames for each other. Those from the mainland referred to the Hawaiians as "Buddaheads" (a term derived from the pidgin term *buta-head*, meaning "pig-headed"). The Hawaiians called their mainland counterparts "Kotonks" (derived from the hollow sound of a coconut hitting the ground, applied derisively to the "thump of a blow to the hollow head of a mainland Japanese American"). Tensions between the two erupted into fistfights and brawls. The army considered disbanding the 442nd.

An officer got an idea for a way to ease the tensions. A group of the Hawaiians would be sent on an excursion of 250 miles from Camp Shelby to Jerome, Arkansas, the site of Rohwer, the nearest relocation camp for Japanese Americans. The mainlanders had never revealed to their Hawaiian counterparts the conditions under which their families and other mainland Japanese Americans were forced to live. The Hawaiian members of the 442nd assumed that they had been invited to visit Arkansas because there was a town there with an unusually large Japanese American community. They were looking forward to a weekend of good food, dances, and pretty girls.

When the soldiers arrived at the Rohwer Relocation Center, their fantasy was abruptly shattered. Daniel Inouye, a Hawaiian member of the 442nd (and later U.S. Senator from Hawaii), recalled what he witnessed upon arriving at Rohwer:

> In the distance we could see rows of barracks surrounded by high barbed-wire fences with machine-gun towers. . . . When we finally came to the gate, we were ordered to get off the trucks. We were in uniform and confronted by men with similar uniforms but they had rifles with bayonets.

The residents of Rohwer had rationed their food in order to have something to share with their visitors. They invited the visiting soldiers to sleep in their cramped barracks while they slept on the mess hall floor, but the soldiers declined and slept in their trucks. That evening the residents threw a party for the Hawaiians. It was a somber event. Recalling the evening decades later, Inouye said, "How can you dance under those circumstances?"

When the soldiers departed the next morning, the laughter and singing that had filled their trucks on the way to Arkansas was replaced by silent reflection. Inouye believed that they were all wondering whether, if they and their families had been torn from their homes, and locked up in one of those dreary camps, they would still have volunteered to fight. He would later say that he was haunted by the thought: "Would I have volunteered if I were from that camp? I don't know. I might well have said, 'Nuts to you.'"

After the trip to Rowher, the "Buddaheads" never again viewed the "Kotonks" in the same light. Inouye reports, "Suddenly our respect, admiration, and love for our brothers . . . rose to phenomenal heights. From that day forward, the soldiers of the 442nd had become united with a new cohesion."

The all-Nisei 442nd Regimental Combat team fought against the Germans in Italy and in France with extraordinary bravery and effectiveness. General George C. Marshall, army chief of staff, declared, "The Japanese regiment was spectacular." It was the most highly decorated unit, for its size and length of service, of any unit in American military history. The unit earned more than 18,000 decorations including 21 Congressional Medals of Honor, the highest decoration that can be awarded to an individual. Seven hundred Nisei were killed in Europe, 67 were missing in action, and more than 9,000 were wounded.

In March 1945, President Roosevelt awarded a Presidential Distinguished Unit Citation, the nation's top award for combat units, to the 442nd. Mark Clark, commanding general of the Fifth Army, of which the 442nd was a part, wrote, "The heroic exploits of the Japanese American soldier should be an inspiration to all of what courage, loyalty, honesty, and devotion to America and its democratic ideals can achieve." After the War, in 1946, President Truman invited the 442nd to the White House and told the Nisei soldiers: "You fought not only the enemy, but you fought prejudice—and you have won."

In autumn 1944, the Germans were defending one of the most formidable natural barriers in the region, the Vosges Mountains in eastern France. German dictator Adolf Hitler had personally ordered German troops to defend the Vosges at all costs. The 442nd led the Vosges assault against the Germans up steep, heavily forested slopes, in cold, slippery-wet weather, and under an overcast sky with no air cover. They were bombarded with a hail of hot steel fragments and wood spikes as German artillery shells exploded in the dense canopy of the dark forest overhead. The 442nd fought valiantly, liberating the Vosges town of Bruyères in October 1944 and driving the Germans farther east. The casualty list for the 442nd named approximately 150 killed and 1,800 wounded in the Vosges campaign—in just 4 weeks of fighting.

The men of the 442nd found little comfort in thoughts of home. First Sargent Jack Wakamatsu reported that one night in a foxhole he heard an infantryman quietly sobbing after reading a letter from his parents in a relocation camp. The letter reported that the house they had left behind in rural California "had been burned down by the people of the community." Wakamatsu later wrote, "We often wondered who our real enemies were, and why we were fighting here in France . . . risking everything trying to free this place from the enemies of freedom, while our own people in America imprisoned our families and now were destroying our homes there."

George Saito, while fighting in Italy with the 442nd, wrote a letter home to his father about the death of his brother Calvin who had just been killed in combat:

> Dad, this is not the time to be preaching to you but I have something on my chest that I want you to hear—In spite of Cal's supreme sacrifice. Don't let anyone tell you that he was foolish or made a mistake to volunteer. Of what I've seen in my travels on our mission I am more than convinced that we've done the right thing in spite of what has happened in the past—America is a damned good country and don't let anyone tell you otherwise.

Three months later, George Saito was killed in action.

Nothing contributed more to the fame of the 442nd than its rescue of the "Lost Battalion" (sometimes called the "Alamo Regiment," because it was originally a Texas National Guard unit and comprised primarily soldiers from Texas). The 442nd was assigned to break through the reinforced German line of resistance in the Vosges Mountains and rescue the Alamo Regiment stranded behind enemy lines. Two hundred seventy-five Texans—cold, wet, hungry, out of supplies, and running low on ammunition—were surrounded by at least 700 Germans occupying the high ground with tanks and heavy armor. Several rescue missions had already failed to reach them. Under brutal battle conditions—mortar shells whistling through the air, artillery explosions raining down, unrelenting fire from automatic rifles and camouflaged machine gun nests, detonating landmines—the 442nd pushed forward up steep, rugged terrain, often face down in the mud and underbrush.

On October 30, 1944, the soldiers of the 442nd reached the Lost Battalion. The beleaguered Texans peered from their foxholes as the Germans withdrew. "The chills went up our spines when we saw the Nisei soldiers," said the lieutenant commanding the Texans. After 2 weeks of bloody fighting, 211 men of the Lost Battalion were rescued. Rescuing them, the 442nd suffered 51 killed in action and an estimated 293 wounded. At 4:00 P.M., the final radio transmission was sent by the rescued Lost Battalion to the commanding general at headquarters: "Patrol 442 here. Tell them we love them."

Following the Vosges campaign in France, the 442nd was dispatched to Italy to lead the final attacks on the heavily fortified Gothic Line, a line between Italy and Austria that Hitler called the last barrier between Allied forces and the German homeland. There the 442nd played a key role in the fighting that broke the Gothic Line and sent the German army into retreat, leading to the surrender of Germany and the end of the war in Europe.

The well-documented experiences of Shiro "Kash" Kashino, a member of the 442nd, can be used to exemplify the service of the storied regiment. Kash was born to Issei parents in Seattle in 1922. He was a star football player at Seattle's Garfield High School. After high school, he worked in a hardware and tackle store. His parents died in the early 1930s, and Kashino said that his older brothers and sisters raised him. Soon after Pearl Harbor, he and his sisters and brothers were ordered to leave Seattle for the Puyallup Assembly Center in Puyallup, Washington, where they and other evacuees were housed in animal stalls and barracks. From there, they were soon moved to Minidoka in the Idaho desert, a relocation camp with about 10,000 Japanese American inmates. Kashino met his wife, Louise, at the assembly center in Puyallup from where she was also moved to Minidoka. They were married at the war's end in 1945, and they celebrated their golden wedding anniversary 2 years before Kashino's death in 2007.

In March 1943, while at Minidoka, Kashino volunteered for the 442nd. He said, "We had to do something to prove our loyalty to America." His orders to report for duty arrived in September. He trained at Camp Shelby in Mississippi and was shipped to Europe, where he fought in the Vosges Mountains, participated in the rescue of the Lost Battalion, and helped break through the Gothic Line. He earned a reputation for bravery and for never leaving a wounded comrade behind. His fellow soldiers, some of whom claim he saved their lives, remember Kash as big and strong, a brave and tough soldier who was also a gentle and caring person. Awarded six Purple Hearts (a U.S. military decoration for soldiers wounded or killed in battle), a Silver Star. and two Bronze Stars for gallantry, Kashino was one of the most accomplished soldiers of the Second World War.

In the fight to rescue the Lost Battalion, provisions were a problem for the 442nd. Kashino agreed to lead a ration detail to a convoy of supply trucks that could not reach them and to bring back what they could carry. The battalion commander, Lieutenant Colonel Alfred Pursall, ordered the men to move down the hill to meet the convoy. Kashino thought the Germans would hear the moving trucks and figure out the exact route the detail would take to get to them. He urged Pursall to wait at least an hour, when it would be less dangerous, before having the detail move out. The colonel insisted that they depart immediately. Under protest, Kashino led his men down to the road where the trucks were pulling up. The Germans unleashed a thunderous artillery barrage illuminating the detail and engulfing the 12 men of the ration detail in flames. Quickly there were casualties. Eight of the 12 men of the ration detail were killed.

When Kashino returned to the battalion command, he complained bitterly to Pursall about his order sending the men into danger. He said, "any one of us would rather starve than suffer the casualties that occurred due to your orders." It was not an acceptable way for a staff sergeant to speak to a lieutenant colonel. Pursall considered it insubordinate, and it would come to haunt Kashino in the future.

After being wounded three times in southern France, Kashino was reduced in rank from staff sergeant to private for taking part in a bar brawl while off duty. He claimed that he had been acting as a peacemaker in the bar, but the next morning he was placed in the stockade. He suspected that he was being punished by Lieutenant Colonel Pursall for telling him off after the shelling of the ration detail he had led. Kashino was released from the stockade to return to active duty.

The 442nd continued to fight immediately following the German retreat from the Gothic Line. During that fighting, Kashino encountered a badly wounded fellow soldier. He tied a tourniquet on the soldier's leg and then proceeded to attack a nearby German machine-gun nest. He then returned to the wounded soldier and carried him to safety. For his gallantry in action, Kashino was awarded a Silver Star, the U.S. military's third highest decoration for valor in combat.

When the fighting in Europe ended, Kashino was assigned to guard German prisoners. He commented that the prisoner of war camp, with its guard towers and barbed wire, reminded him of the Minidoka incarceration camp: "This is exactly what they had built for us in the desert of Idaho."

When the war ended, Kashino expected that the old charges stemming from the bar scuffle would all be dropped. They were not. In May of 1945, he and another soldier were brought before a court-martial (a judicial court for trying members of the armed services), found guilty, sentenced to 6 months, and reduced to the rank of private. Kashino's sentence was suspended for time he served previously in the stockade and in combat. Soon after the court-martial he was discharged from the army.

After his discharge, he and Louise went to Chicago, where Kashino attended technical school to learn to be a refrigeration and air conditioning technician. The union, however, discriminated against Japanese Americans and denied him membership. Consequently, he could not find a job. Kash and Louise then moved to Seattle, where they had been born and raised, but Kashino could not find a job there, again because of racial discrimination by the union.

Eventually, Kashino became one of the managers of the Ford dealership in Lake City, Washington, where the owner respected him and appreciated his military service. Over the years, some of Kashino's friends urged him to petition for a review of his court-martial and restoration of his rank as a staff sergeant. At first Kashino declined, but then, for the sake of the legacy to be left for his two daughters, he consented.

Upon review of the records for his case, in 1997, the army overturned his conviction and restored his rank. Kashino never knew that he had been exonerated. He died the day the affidavit clearing him arrived from the army. Ultimately, the judge advocate general (chief legal officer) of the U.S. Army expunged the record of Kashino's court-martial and vindicated him. In a personal handwritten note at the bottom of the official letter to Louise Kashino clearing her husband, the judge advocate general wrote, "Your husband was an American Hero and that is how he should be remembered."

Some of the Japanese American soldiers returning from the War were recognized as heroes by their fellow citizens, but others were met with hostility. There were hundreds of violent incidents as the Japanese Americans came home from the camps and from the war. For example, three men fired shots at the Lamar, Colorado, farmhouse of a returning Issei and burned down his packing shed, leaving sticks of dynamite at the scene. When the farmer's son, a veteran of the 442nd, came home, his mother showed him the holes from the shotgun pellets. He said:

> I was getting shot at from the enemy, and then at home in my own country, people were shooting at my dad. I was risking my life for this country, and my government was not protecting my folks. And they came home from camp with nothing.

The attackers were acquitted after their defense attorney told the jury: "This is a White man's country."

In early 1945, Hood River, Oregon, a town of 3,000, became a national symbol of bigotry. Before the war, Hood River, located in a valley above the Columbia River Gorge and under Mount Hood, was home to a Japanese American community. Many of them were farmers who had made Hood River cherries and apples famous around the country. In 1945, the honor roll of local men in service inscribed on the outside wall of the Hood River courthouse was defaced with black paint to cover up 16 names, all Japanese Americans. The defacement was done by members of the local post of the American Legion (a national veterans' organization). The mayor of Hood River said, "90% of us are against the Japs. . . . We must let the Japanese know they're not welcome here."

News of the defacement of the Hood River courthouse spread and was widely condemned in newspapers across the country, some comparing the Legionnaires with Nazis. Some White soldiers from Europe wrote letters to newspapers saying they would be dead if not for the bravery of their Nisei comrades. Three White soldiers from Hood River wrote from Europe that they wanted their names removed from the courthouse wall unless the Japanese American names were restored.

The American Legion post did not back down. They issued a public statement to returning "Japanese" that featured these words in capital letters: "FOR YOUR OWN BEST INTERESTS, WE URGE YOU NOT TO RETURN." While many American Legion posts condemned what had been done at Hood River, more than a dozen in other states took Japanese names off their own honor rolls. Under pressure, including boycotts by grocery chains of Hood River's famous apples, and refusal by bankers in Portland to lend money to some Hood River farmers, the Hood River American Legion post finally restored the names of the 16 Nisei.

Responses to returning veterans varied. One returning veteran told of his experience boarding a bus in Los Angeles. He was wearing his new paratrooper uniform with campaign medals and awards, proudly displayed on his chest. As he boarded, a woman in the front row said, "Damn Jap." The bus driver stopped the bus and said, "Lady, apologize to this American soldier or get off my bus." She got off the bus.

When he returned from the war, a Nisei soldier awarded the Congressional Medal of Honor went to get a haircut outside San Francisco. He had received a battlefield promotion in Europe from sergeant to lieutenant and was wearing his medals on his uniform. He was also wearing a metal hook in place of the hand he had lost to a German grenade. As he entered a barbershop, he was turned away with the words: "You're a Jap and we don't cut Jap hair." The soldier walked away. He was Daniel Inouye, who became the first U.S. representative from Hawaii when it became a state in 1959 and then one of its U.S. senators, serving 49 years in the Senate, the longest serving U.S. senator in history.

Wilson Makabe of Loomis, California, returned stateside after serving with the 442nd. He had spent 2.5 years in hospitals from wounds suffered in Italy. He lost one leg, and the other one was in a long brace. He could walk only with great difficulty. When he got home, his brother told him that the family house had been set on fire within hours after the closing of the relocation camps had been announced on the radio. Makabe later said, "All the time in the hospital I don't remember shedding a tear, but I cried that night. You wonder if it was worth going through all that."

When he got back to Loomis, Makabe drove to a local gas station. He recalled what the owner said to him:

> When he saw me at the service station getting out, struggling to get out of the car, to fill it with gas, he came out. After I was all through he said, "I'd like

to talk to you." I said, "Hop in." He traveled with me down the road from the station. He said, "Y'know, I was one bastard. I had signs on my service station saying 'No Jap trade wanted.'" He said, "Now when I see you come back like that, I feel so small." And he was crying.

Minoru Kiyota had been jailed at the Tule Lake camp as a "disloyal," and, like many others, was so angry that he renounced his American citizenship. A bitter man, he was released in March 1946. Soon afterward, waiting for a train in Oakland, California, he entered the station's coffee shop, which was filled with American servicemen on their way home from the Pacific. As he started to take a seat, the man behind the counter pointed to a sign: NO JAPS ALLOWED.

Kiyota got up to leave but was stopped by a hand on his shoulder. It was a young U.S. marine sergeant. "Be my guest," said the marine, motioning Kiyota to a table with four other marines. "Mister," said the sergeant in a sharp voice. "Give this man some ham and eggs and a cup of hot coffee and be quick about it."

The marines conversed with Kiyota. He told them that he had just been released from a detention camp. "A what?" said one of the marines. "But you're an American citizen." After breakfast, as Kiyota thanked the marines and walked out, he noticed that one of them stood up and ripped the NO JAPS ALLOWED sign from the wall.

In 1948, the remains of two soldiers, Fumitake Nagato and Saburo Tanamachi, were transferred from an American cemetery in France, to Arlington National Cemetery. Both had been killed in the Vosges Mountains during the rescue of the Lost Battalion. They were the first persons of Japanese ancestry to be buried at Arlington, the shrine of national heroes. At the gravesite, Private Nagato's mother was presented with the American flag that had draped his coffin.

Former chief justice of the U.S. Supreme Court Earl Warren is remembered most for the several landmark decisions made by the Warren Court (1952–1969) upholding the rights of citizens. One of the most famous and far-reaching of those decisions was *Brown v. Board of Education* (1954), which declared racial segregation in public schools a violation of the U.S. Constitution. In 1971, Warren was being interviewed as part of an oral history for the University of California. The interviewer asked him about his involvement, as attorney general and later governor of California, in the evacuation of Japanese Americans. He broke into tears. The interview stopped.

In his memoirs 7 years later, the former chief justice wrote that he:

> . . . deeply regretted the removal order and my own testimony advocating it, because it was not in keeping with our American concept of freedom and the rights of citizens. . . . Whenever I thought of the innocent little children who were torn from home, school friends, and congenial surroundings, I was conscience-stricken. . . .

Some have drawn a connection between Warren's remorse over the incarceration of Japanese Americans and his avid support for the racial integration ordered by the Court's unanimous *Brown* decision. Another justice, William O. Douglas, who had voted with the majority in the *Korematsu* case, said in retrospect that the decision in the case "was ever on my conscience."

In 1988, Congress passed, and President Ronald Reagan signed, the Civil Liberties Act. It provided $1.2 billion to enable payments of $20,000 to each of an estimated 80,000 Japanese American relocation camp survivors. Also in the law was a formal apology to those who were displaced. According to the act, "Congress recognizes that . . . a grave injustice was done to both citizens and permanent resident aliens of Japanese ancestry by the evacuation, relocation, and internment of civilians during World War II."

Eric Shinseki was a former army chief of staff and U.S. secretary of veteran affairs. As a four-star general he is the highest-ranking officer of Japanese ancestry in the history of the U.S. Army. While growing up in Hawaii, he overheard 442nd veterans in his family reminiscing when they gathered occasionally at his family home. Like most Japanese American veterans, they were humble and rarely spoke to others of their wartime experiences. In 2017, General Shinseki spoke of the 442nd at a program for the National Museum of the U.S. Army. He said:

American soldiers of Japanese Ancestry delivered a powerful lesson in citizenship during World War II. Their values—loyalty, courage, patriotism—are timeless statements about being American. Rising above fear and prejudice, they wrote an unrivaled battle history that remains legendary, even today. It's an American story for the ages.

The major sources for this chapter were:

Asahina, R. (2006). *Just Americans: How Japanese Americans won a war at home and abroad*. New York, NY: Gotham Books.

Commission on Wartime Relocation. (1982). *Personal justice denied: Report of the commission on wartime relocation and internment of civilians*. Washington, D.C.: U.S. Government Printing Office.

Matsudaira, V. E. (Director). *Kash: The legend and legacy of Shiro Kashino*. United States: eShadow Productions.

Korematsu v. United States, 323 U.S. 214 (1944).

Reeves, R. (2015). *Infamy: The shocking story of the Japanese American internment in World War II*. New York, NY: Henry Holt and Company.

Robinson, G (2001). *By order of the President*. Cambridge, MA: Harvard University Press.

Uchida, Y. (1982). *Desert exile: The uprooting of a Japanese American family*. Seattle, WA: University of Washington Press.

LEARNING ACTIVITIES FOR "TELL THEM WE LOVE THEM"

Facts of the Case

1. What was Executive Order 9066?
2. What reasons were given for removing Japanese Americans from the West Coast?
3. What was Topaz and what were the conditions there?
4. What was the 442nd Regimental Combat Team?
5. How did Shiro "Kash" Kashino distinguish himself as a soldier?

Historical Understanding

1. What was the decision in the case of *Korematsu v. United States* (1944)?
2. What do the opinions of the three dissenting Supreme Court justices in the *Korematsu* case have in common?
3. Briefly describe mistreatment of Japanese Americans on the West Coast before the attack on Pearl Harbor.
4. How were Japanese American veterans treated when they returned from the War?

Expressing Your Reasoning

Should Shiro "Kash" Kashino have volunteered to serve in the 442nd Regimental Combat Team? Why or why not?

Key Concepts from History

What do the following have in common?

1. Opened in 1940 and located approximately 37 miles west of Krakow, Poland, Auschwitz was the largest compound of its kind established by the German Nazi regime. Prisoners kept there were used for forced labor if not selected for immediate killing. Conditions for the prisoners were savagely brutal. They were tattooed with identification numbers; starved; beaten; allowed only tattered prison uniforms for clothing, no matter how cold the weather; given virtually no medical care; crowded into unsanitary barracks for sleeping, several to a bunk; allowed no freedom of movement; abused by guards, and murdered in gas chambers, with their corpses burned in ovens. Nazi doctors used some prisoners as the subjects for inhumane medical experiments. It is estimated that the Nazis deported at least 1.3 million people to the Auschwitz complex between 1940 and 1945. Of these, authorities murdered

approximately 1.1 million. The majority (960,000) of those who died at Auschwitz were imprisoned there because they were Jews from various European countries occupied by Nazi Germany. Jews were considered enemies of the Nazi state. Poles, Roma, other nationalities, and Soviet prisoners of war were also sent to Auschwitz, and many of them (135,000) died there.

2. Manzanar was the first of 10 American relocation centers where Japanese Americans were incarcerated during World War II. It was located in a valley of the Sierra Nevada, approximately 230 miles north of Los Angeles. The compound was built to confine persons of Japanese descent living on the West Coast of the United States who had been forcibly removed from their homes by U.S. government authorities. At its peak, Manzanar had more than 10,000 inmates. These Japanese Americans were held at Manzanar behind barbed wire and under armed guard. They were housed in crowded tarpaper barracks with a lack of privacy. With no kitchens or bathrooms in their barracks, they ate in communal mess halls and used communal latrines. After being uprooted from their homes and communities, the incarcerees endured primitive, sub-standard conditions. They had to wait in one line after another for meals, at latrines, and at the laundry room. Most inmates were employed at various jobs within Manzanar to keep the camp running. Some worked in schools and medical facilities. They were paid modest wages and each person received $3.60 per month ($53 per month as of 2017) as a clothing allowance. The inmates made Manzanar more livable through recreation. They participated in sports, including baseball, football, and martial arts. They also personalized and beautified their barren surroundings by building elaborate gardens, which often included pools, waterfalls, and rock ornaments.

3. Omarska was a detention center run by Bosnian Serb forces in the mining town of Omarska. It was set up for Bosniak and Croat men and women captured during the first months of the Bosnian War in 1992 in the ethnic cleansing (mass expulsion or killing of members of an unwanted ethnic or religious group) of Prijedor, a town near northern Serbia. Around 6,000 Bosniaks and Croats were held in appalling conditions at the camp for about 5 months in the spring and summer of 1992. Guard posts and anti-personnel landmines were set up around the compound. The conditions in the camp were horrible. The heat was unbearable. The detainees at Omarska had one meal a day. Meals were often accompanied by beatings. The toilets were blocked and there was human waste everywhere. Precise figures are not available, but it has been estimated by official sources that hundreds and possibly thousands perished at Omerska, mostly Bosniaks and Croats. In a 2007 decision, the International Court of Justice proclaimed that Bosniaks and Croats held forcibly by Serbs at detention camps, including Omerska, were systematically victims of massive mistreatment, beatings, rape, and torture causing serious bodily and mental harm.

Historical Inquiry

In his dissenting opinion in the case of *Korematsu v. United States* (1944), Justice Robert Jackson wrote that by declaring the exclusion order (Executive Order 9066) constitutional, the Supreme Court was, for all time, accepting the principle of racial discrimination: "The principle then lies about like a loaded weapon ready for the hand of any authority that can bring forward a plausible claim of an urgent need."

Is the weapon still loaded? Has the precedent set by the *Korematsu* decision been overturned, or does it still stand?

Using online and other sources, test the hypothesis that the precedent still stands, i.e., that the relocation and detention of Americans of a particular ethnic or racial group is still permitted under the U.S. Constitution. Compose a short essay in which you accept or reject the hypothesis. Use evidence to support your conclusion. To begin your investigation, the following search terms will be helpful:

- *Korematsu v. United States*
- *Korematsu v. United States* PBS
- Korematsu Supreme Court ruling *Los Angeles Times*
- *Korematsu v. United States* Densho Encyclopedia
- A discredited Supreme Court decision *The New York Times*

CHAPTER 35

Naming of Names

The Testimony of Elia Kazan

Elia Kazan Holding His Oscar

There was turmoil outside the Dorothy Chandler Pavilion on Wilshire Boulevard in Los Angeles on Sunday, March 21, 1999. It was the night of the 71st annual Academy Awards ceremony. Legendary film director Elia Kazan was to be presented an honorary lifetime award from the Academy of Motion Picture Arts and Sciences.

Why were there more than 300 demonstrators across the street from the fabled red carpet where celebrities paraded before cameras as they entered the pavilion? Two-thirds of the crowd noisily protested the award for Kazan; others expressed their support for it. An elderly woman haltingly walked along the boulevard with her three-legged cane in one hand and a huge placard in the other. The placard read, "Kazan is a Rat." One protest banner read "Kazan: Snitch" and another: "Elia Kazan: Benedict Arnold." Several fights broke out between anti- and pro-Kazan factions, prompting police to separate protesters and disperse the crowd.

The 39-member Academy board had voted unanimously in January to give Kazan the honorary award. Many Academy members, and others, opposed that decision. Much publicity about the honorary Oscar had preceded the Academy Awards event and opinion outside the film industry was also divided.

Kazan, who would turn 90 in September, was regarded as one of the greatest film directors of all time and had received many awards, including two Oscars for best director. Those who considered him unworthy of this lifetime award, however, could not forgive a decision he had made 47 years earlier.

Elia Kazan was born in 1909 as Elias Kazancoglu, child of Greek parents in Turkey. To escape tyranny in their native land, his parents immigrated to the United States when Elia was 4 years old.

His father expected Elia, like his brother, to join him in the family business, the Kazan Carpet Company in New York. Elia's mother had other ideas for the younger son. Secretly, she worked with one of Elia's Long Island high school teachers to gain admission for her son to a good college.

Elia, dreading the carpet business, joined the conspiracy by working after school and on summer vacation to earn money for his tuition. He was admitted to Williams College, an elite private college in Williamstown, Massachusetts. When his disapproving father learned of his college acceptance, he struck his wife so violently that she was knocked to the floor. In the fall of 1926, both parents nevertheless accompanied Elia to enroll at the idyllic Williams campus.

At Williams, Kazan helped pay his expenses by waiting tables at fraternity houses. He saw himself as an immigrant outsider who was self-consciously shy, intense, short (5 foot, 6 inches), and dark with a large nose. He contrasted this self-image to the handsome, confident, carefree, and affluent fraternity boys whose meals he served. He was also jealous of them for the pretty blond young women they dated. He became resentful. As he wrote in his autobiography:

> It made me rebellious. It also made me join the Communist Party at a certain time because I got resentful of being excluded. I was an outsider . . . but I was also sympathetic with people that were struggling to get up, because I was struggling to get up.

When he graduated from Williams in 1930, Kazan had no clear purpose in mind. He drifted to Yale Drama School, mostly because a friend enrolled there. He did not much care for Yale. He studied there for 2 years and departed a year before he was due to receive his graduate degree. He thought the acting classes focused on imitations of real life rather than on expression of genuine emotion.

While at Yale, Elia was attracted to Molly Day Thatcher, 3 years older than he. Though opposites in many ways, they were drawn to each other. Kazan saw himself as an outsider. Molly was not, and that was part of his attraction to her. He described her as blond, slender but "voluptuous," and "impeccably WASP" (White Anglo-Saxon Protestant in heritage). Her grandfather had been president of Yale.

Elia and Molly married in 1932. The first of Kazan's three wives, Molly was to have a profound influence on his career. (Kazan considered himself truthful and "rigorously moral," but he said: "There is one thing I have lied about consistently and that is my relationships to women out of wedlock. I have again and again lied to my wives about this.")

Soon after Kazan left Yale in 1932, he joined the new experimental Group Theater (the Group) in New York. As an actor and director with that company, he practiced what later became the highly influential "Method" technique of acting, which encourages actors to draw on their personal experiences and to express themselves with raw emotion on stage. Method actors summoned emotions from their own lives to illuminate their stage roles. As Kazan expressed it: "It is turning psychological events into behavior, inner events into visible, external patterns of life on stage."

Kazan joined the Communist Party in 1933, and he was recruited to join the theater company's Communist unit, or cell. Eight members of the Group joined its Communist Party cell. In his autobiography, he wrote:

> I knew the kind of films and plays I wanted to make; I'd seen them made by Russians, films about the one enduring drama of our time, the class struggle, the final conflict. . . . The only people you could trust are members of the working class.

In his diary, he wrote: "The revolution I want is a society where everybody works to produce enough for everybody but not for profit."

Early in his career, Kazan was drawn to the Left-wing theater movement emerging in New York City. In the depths of the Great Depression, while a member of the Group, he also taught directing classes for the League of Workers Theatre. Organized in 1935, it was a Left-wing federation of little theaters and amateur theatrical groups that produced plays. Its slogan was: "Theatre is a weapon." The League was a communist-front organization (responsive to instructions from the communist government of the Soviet Union).

In 1934, Kazan directed and acted in a play called *Waiting for Lefty*. It received good reviews and ignited his first spark of fame. Referring to Kazan's leading role in that play, one reviewer referred to him as the "Proletariat Thunderbolt." (*Proletariat* means "working class" and is a term central to Marxist ideology.)

The same year, Kazan became one of the Group's leaders and also the leader of the Group's Communist Party cell. Kazan was told by a local Communist Party leader that the Group's three-member leadership team should be replaced by an actors' cooperative so that it would be a theater run by its actors. Kazan was also told that the Group should produce more overtly pro-communist propaganda plays. Kazan did not approve of the dictates, and his wife Molly expressed her outrage to him over the meddling of the Communist Party in theater matters. At the Group's next regular cell meeting, Kazan put forward the party's demands without enthusiasm. His presentation did not satisfy some members who reported his "failure of leadership" to party headquarters.

Another meeting of the cell was scheduled. A leading communist organizer was dispatched from Detroit to take charge of the meeting. His task was to get unanimous approval of the party line. He criticized Kazan's leadership and gave him a stark choice between his loyalty to the Group at large or to its communist faction. Kazan was told that forgiveness was possible if he confessed the error of his ways. None of the Group members spoke up for him. The next day, Kazan sent his letter of resignation from the Communist Party. Later, referring to the man from Detroit, Kazan wrote, "I understood the police state from him."

He continued to believe in the general principles endorsed by official communism, but he rejected party discipline. He would later write:

> the Party had at heart the cause of the poor and unemployed people whom I saw on the streets about me and . . . by fighting for them I would be acting for the good of the American people . . . . [Looking back late in life, he told an interviewer: "For years after I resigned, I was still faithful to their way of thinking. I still believed in it."]

During World War II, Kazan served in the South Pacific. Though close to the horrendous fighting and deeply affected by it, his task was not dangerous. He was assigned to evaluate government entertainment for the troops overseas. Kazan went on to a storied career as a director, on stage and screen. His first major success on Broadway had come in 1941. That year, he directed Pulitzer Prize–winning playwright Thornton Wilder's *The Skin of Our Teeth*. It made him a directorial star.

Following his first big hit, Elia Kazan enjoyed roughly 15 years of success. Between 1943 and 1954, he directed 14 plays and 10 movies: Of the plays, nine were long-running hits on Broadway. He collaborated with the great playwrights of the era, including Arthur Miller and Tennessee Williams. He discovered major stars including Marlon Brando, James Dean, Lee Remick, and Warren Beatty. He also helped actors who had labored relatively unknown to achieve stardom. He directed *Death of a Salesman* (Miller) and *A Streetcar Named Desire* (Williams). And there were the movies, including *A Tree Grows in Brooklyn* and a film boldly exposing anti-Semitism, for which he won his first Academy Award, *Gentlemen's Agreement*. But Kazan's involvement with the Communist Party was to deform the shape of his career.

During World War II, the Soviet Union had (eventually) been on the side of the Allies, and its grueling fighting on the Eastern Front of the war in Europe was essential to their victory. But the USSR extended control over much of Eastern Europe, including part of Germany itself: At the end of World War II in 1945, troops of the Soviet Union invading from the east met American troops invading from the west at the Elbe River in Germany, and soon after, Germany was divided into two countries: the pro-Soviet, communist German Democratic Republic in the east and the pro-Western, democratic Federal Republic of Germany in the west. In 1946, former prime minister of Great Britain Winston Churchill coined an enduring term for the division when he said: "an *iron curtain* has descended across the continent." The Soviet Union and the United States came out of the war as the two world superpowers, and their competition for power and influence across the globe was given the name of the Cold War, a state of political hostility, short of open warfare, between the Eastern Bloc (the Soviet Union and its satellite countries and the Western Bloc the United States and its allies.)

The spread of communism in the countries of Eastern Europe occupied by the Soviet Army at the end of World War II threatened and frightened Americans. In 1949, the Soviet Union exploded an atomic bomb, ending the American monopoly on nuclear weapons. That same year, communist forces, led by Mao Zedong, declared victory over opposing forces in the Chinese Civil War and established the People's Republic of China. The U.S. had supported the defeated opposition. The Korean War began in June 1950 when communist North Korea invaded South Korea. The United Nations, with the United States as the principal force, came to the aid of South Korea. China aided North Korea, and the Soviet Union provided assistance to the communist forces.

American fear of communism was heightened by news of widespread pro-Soviet spying during the Cold War. Perhaps the most notorious spy case was that of American communists husband and wife, Julius and Ethel Rosenberg. Convicted of divulging atomic secrets to the Soviet Union, the Rosenbergs were sentenced to death and electrocuted in 1953. Growing apprehension about the domestic influence of communism spurred national security measures at home by the federal government.

Amid a political climate of fear and dread, Joseph McCarthy, the junior senator from Wisconsin, further inflamed public fear of communism. In 1947, he initiated what has come to be called the Second Red Scare (the promotion by a state or society of widespread fear of a potential rise of communism, anarchism, or radical leftism). (The First Red Scare had occurred immediately after World War I. It was spurred by perceived threats from the 1917 Bolshevik Revolution in the Soviet Union, the American labor movement, anarchist revolution, and political radicalism.)

Senator McCarthy spent almost 5 years exploiting the fear of communism. He pressed on with accusations that communists had infiltrated the federal government, universities, the film industry, and elsewhere. Insinuations of disloyalty were enough to convince many Americans that their government and other institutions were packed with traitors and spies. In February 1950, in Wheeling, West Virginia, McCarthy gave a speech that propelled him into the national spotlight. Waving a piece of paper in the air, he declared that he had a list of 205 known members of the Communist Party who were "working and shaping policy" in the State Department. The next month, a Senate subcommittee launched an investigation.

At the beginning of his second term as senator in 1953, McCarthy was put in charge of the U.S. Senate Committee on Government Operations. That chairmanship allowed him to launch expansive investigations of the alleged communist infiltration of the federal government. In hearing after hearing of the committee, he aggressively interrogated witnesses. More than 2,000 government employees lost their jobs as a result of McCarthy's investigations. At the time, people, including fellow senators, were afraid to stand up to McCarthy for fear of being labeled communist sympathizers.

Even before McCarthy began his work, the Committee on Un-American Activities (HUAC) was created by the House of Representatives in 1946 to investigate alleged disloyalty and subversive activities on the part of private citizens, public employees, and those organizations suspected of having communist ties. Committee members quickly settled their gaze on the Hollywood film industry, which was seen by committee members as a hotbed of communist activity. This reputation originated in the 1930s, when the economic difficulties of the Great Depression had increased the appeal of Leftist organizations for many struggling actors and studio workers (including Elia Kazan). In October 1947, more than 40 people with connections to the movie industry received subpoenas to appear before HUAC on suspicion of holding communist loyalties or being involved in subversive activities.

Aware that their answers to committee members' questions could ruin their reputations and careers, most individuals either sought leniency by cooperating with investigators or, citing their Fifth Amendment constitutional right against self-incrimination, remained silent.

One group of 10 Hollywood screenwriters and directors, however, took a different approach. They openly challenged the legitimacy of the committee investigations. These men, who became known as the Hollywood Ten, not only refused to cooperate with the investigation but also denounced the HUAC anticommunist hearings as an outrageous violation of their civil rights. They insisted that the First Amendment to the U.S. Constitution gave them the right to belong to any political organization they chose. Some compared the committee's coercive methods and intimidating tactics to the oppressive measures enacted in Nazi Germany. "I am not on trial here," asserted one screenwriter during a HUAC hearing. "This committee is on trial."

The Hollywood Ten paid dearly for their defiance at the HUAC hearings. In November 1947, they were cited for contempt of Congress. Following a trial on that charge in April 1948, each of the men was found guilty, fined, and sentenced to prison.

A more lasting punishment came in the form of a movie industry blacklist. Executives did not want their studios associated with radical politics in the minds of the movie going public. They agreed not to employ the Hollywood Ten or anyone else suspected of being affiliated with the Communist Party whose name appeared on a blacklist. The motion picture industry blacklist grew steadily larger as Congress continued its investigations into the 1950s. More than 300 writers, actors, and directors were denied work in the United States because they were listed on the (unofficial) Hollywood Blacklist.

At the height of the Red Scare, Elia Kazan's brief flirtation with communism 16 years earlier came to light. He received a subpoena and appeared before HUAC on January 14, 1952. In his testimony, he spoke freely of his own membership (1934 to 1936) in, and subsequent disillusionment with, the Communist Party. He refused, however, to name the other communists in his cell. He was defiant and resolved never to bow to HUAC. As he wrote in his autobiography:

> I'd made up my mind that when the time came, I'd simply say yes, I had carried a card (Communist Party membership) for a year and a half. I wouldn't hide anything that concerned me. I wouldn't "take the Fifth" (invoke the Constitution's Fifth Amendment right to remain silent), but I would not, under any pressure, name others. That would be shameful; it wasn't an alternative worth considering.

The night preceding his appearance before HUAC, Kazan's wife, Molly, had expressed her contrary opinion: "I can't say much for their procedures, but it's the duty of this Congress to find out all there is to find out about the Party and what they're up to and to ask people like you what you know. I hope you tell them the truth."

The committee recalled Kazan to testify again under oath. Kazan conferred with his friend, 20th Century Fox Hollywood producer Darryl Zanuck, a leading figure in the Hollywood film studio system who produced several of Kazan's films. Zanuck advised Kazan: "Name the names for chrissake." Kazan later quoted him as saying: "Who the hell are you going to jail for? You'll be sitting there and someone else will sure as hell name these people. Who are you saving?" Kazan protested that these people were once his good friends.

In March 1952, between his first and second appearances before HUAC, Kazan attended the Academy Awards ceremony in Hollywood. The film version of Tennessee Williams's *A Streetcar Named Desire*, which Kazan had directed, had been nominated for 12 Oscars. Kazan and the Hollywood press expected a sweep. His testimony before HUAC was supposed to have been secret; it became public when it was leaked to a Hollywood trade publication, *Hollywood Reporter*. *A Streetcar Named Desire* received only four Oscars, none of them awarded to Kazan. He viewed the rejection as a warning from powerful figures in Hollywood who expected him to cooperate with HUAC.

Kazan was in the clutch of a dilemma. He lamented that he had no good choice. To name his former colleagues would be a betrayal that would bring severe criticism from friends and colleagues in the film industry. Refusing to name them would threaten his career and possibly land him on a Hollywood blacklist. He hated the Communist Party, but he resented HUAC.

Elia came to agree with Molly that it was the duty of the government to investigate the communist movement in the United States. In retrospect, he wrote that there was no way he could go along with claims that the Communist Party was nothing but another political party, like the Republicans and Democrats: "I knew very well what it was, a thoroughly organized, worldwide conspiracy. This conviction separated me from my old friends."

Kazan especially bristled at efforts of the communists to suppress free expression in the name of "party discipline." His view of the Soviet Union had also evolved: "After 17 years of watching the Soviet Union turn into an imperialist power, was that truly what I wanted here? Hadn't I been clinging to once-held loyalties that were no longer valid?"

During his second appearance before HUAC on April 10, 1952, in the House Office Building in Washington, Kazan named eight former Group Theater members whom he said had been communists. "Why," he later wrote, "had I tried so hard and for so long to stay in good with my old comrades when I no longer believed in anything they stood for?" He also named nine Communist Party officials. All 17 of these individuals had been named previously by other HUAC witnesses.

Early in the spring of 1952, before his HUAC testimony, Kazan had anticipated the consequences of refusing to identify communists. In a conversation with his friend, playwright Arthur Miller, he expressed his misgivings. Here is Kazan's diary entry about that conversation:

> (I) told Art I'd prepared myself for a period of no movie work or money, that I was prepared to face this if it was worthwhile. But I didn't feel altogether good about such a decision. That I'd say (to myself) what the hell am I giving all this up for? To defend a secrecy I didn't think right and to defend people who'd already been named or soon would be by someone else? I'd said I'd hated the Communists for many years and didn't feel right about giving up my career to defend them. That I would give up my film career if it was in the interests of defending something I believed in but not this.

Kazan's decision to name fellow communists from his Group Theater days came at a high price. News of his HUAC testimony appeared on the front page of *The New York Times*. It was followed by a storm of anger. Many of his colleagues from film and theater considered his testimony shameful. Some colleagues became lifelong enemies. Close friends were heartsick, and some snubbed and scorned him.

Initially ambivalent about his testimony, Kazan was miserably depressed in its immediate aftermath, and reported that he felt guilty and was not sleeping well. He was also anguished to think that he would be leaving a legacy of shame for his then four children.

Kazan and his wife, Molly, composed a statement to justify his naming of communists. The statement was placed as a paid advertisement in *The New York Times*. It argued that most Americans casually and openly state their political affiliations. Why, the statement asked, would communists want to maintain secrecy? The statement also alleged that the American Communist Party had become a tool of the Soviet Union, the business of which was to pilfer state secrets and undermine the United States. Kazan's statement also addressed what he, as an artist, considered to be especially dangerous—attempts by the Communist Party to control thought and suppress personal opinion.

Kazan's supporters characterized his decision to divulge names as a forced choice: betrayal of former colleagues who, at one time, had betrayed him, or abandonment of his career to defend people he no longer respected and whose views he had come to despise. One prominent historian, Arthur Schlesinger, Jr., argued that communism was an international movement led by Moscow and that it was the enemy of American democracy. According to this view, Kazan's testimony had exposed spies and enemies threatening the United States.

Kazan's critics thought him guilty of fanning Cold War hysteria. He had added, his critics claimed, to the climate of fear and suspicion that was sweeping the country. He had exposed his friends, and others, to the self-appointed "watchdogs" who were hounding them, blackballing them from Hollywood and university campuses, and threatening them with contempt charges that would land them in prison.

A director named by Kazan who fled the country said: "Elia Kazan too was a traitor. Some of those betrayed were his close friends. Their lives and futures were destroyed. He became ally and accomplice to an infamous committee which shamed his country."

Arthur Miller regarded the testimony as a betrayal of friends, country—and of Kazan himself. Miller cut off contact with Kazan. Though they worked together 10 years later, the two never reconciled. Shortly after Kazan testified, Miller wrote a play, *The Crucible*, dramatizing the Salem witch trials of 1692–1693 in Massachusetts Bay Colony. In the play, Miller portrays the horrific consequences of falsely accusing innocent people of being witches. *The Crucible* was inspired by what Miller considered the parallel of the anti-communist witchhunt of the Cold War, including his friend's, and others', naming of communists. In 1956, Miller, though never a member of the Communist Party, was questioned by HUAC and convicted of contempt of Congress for refusing to name others at meetings he had attended. Kazan rejected the playwright's metaphor, asserting that witches do not exist, but comrades (Communist Party members) did.

Kazan's testimony also inspired creative work on his own part. One work in particular affirmed his HUAC testimony. He had come to believe that he was right to have given it. His most acclaimed film, *On the Waterfront*, opened in July 1954. It focuses on union violence and corruption among longshoremen (dock workers) on the waterfronts of Hoboken, New Jersey. The main character, a longshoreman, informs on corrupt union officials in his official testimony against union corruption and violence. He is depicted heroically in the film.

In his autobiography, Kazan acknowledged that he identified with that character. He wrote, "*On the Waterfront* was my own story; every day I worked on that film, I was telling the world where I stood. . . . " *On the Waterfront* was a spectacular critical and commercial success. It received 12 Academy Award nominations, winning eight Oscars, including Best Picture, and Best Director for Kazan. Kazan felt vindicated.

Yet Kazan's ambivalence over his HUAC testimony lingered. His wife, Molly, died in 1963 at age 56. Soon afterward, Kazan received a compassionate letter of condolence from one of the people he had named in his testimony, actor and director, Tony Kraber. He had not heard from Kraber since that time. The letter moved Kazan deeply and prompted a reflection on his testimony. He wrote,

> I felt ashamed. . . . He was human and I'd hurt him . . . I felt that no political cause was worth hurting any other human for. What good deeds were stimulated by what I'd done? What villains exposed? How is the world better for what I did? It had just been a game of power and influence, and I'd been taken in and twisted from my true self. I'd fallen for something I shouldn't have, no matter how hard the pressure. . . .

Kazan's remarkable work continued following the HUAC uproar. He went on to direct highly successful plays as well as films. He also authored best-selling novels. Several of his productions won Tony Awards, Golden Globe Awards, Academy Award nominations, and other honors. To many critics, Kazan was one of the great American artists of the 20th century. His HUAC testimony, however, continued to shadow him, and nearly a half-century later, that cloud hung over the bitter controversy, both inside and outside the Dorothy Chandler Pavilion, on March 21, 1999. That was the night that Kazan, then age 89, was to receive his honorary lifetime award from the American Academy of Motion Picture Arts and Sciences for his extraordinary achievement in film.

To avoid the protesters, Kazan entered the pavilion discreetly through a back door. When he appeared on stage to accept the gold statuette, about half of those in the auditorium rose to greet him with applause. An almost equal number remained seated and did not applaud, some grim-faced in stony silence with crossed arms. In his brief acceptance remarks, Kazan did not address the controversy.

Haskell (Pete) Wexler, one of the Academy's governors, had voted to bestow the honorary award on Kazan. Wexler wrote to Kazan suggesting that he make some kind of reconciliatory gesture to his enemies, something short of a full-scale apology. Kazan wrote a three-word reply: "Fuck you, Pete."

In some circles, Kazan's refusal to apologize for his testimony or for the hardships it caused made him an outcast, a pariah. Many writers, actors, directors, and others whose careers were destroyed when they were blacklisted have never forgotten nor forgiven him. One writer who had been blacklisted said at the time, "Like Judas. Informers are never forgiven."

The major sources for this chapter were:

Epstein, M. (Director). (2003). Arthur Miller, Elia Kazan, and the Blacklist: None without sin. [Television series episode]. New York, NY: Public Broadcasting System.

Kazan, E. (1988). *Elia Kazan: A life*. New York, NY: Alfred A. Knopf, Inc.

Schickel, R. (2005). *Elia Kazan: A biography*. New York, NY: HarperCollins.

LEARNING ACTIVITIES FOR "NAMING OF NAMES"

Facts of the Case

1. What were Elia Kazan's professional achievements?
2. What testimony did Kazan give to the House Un-American Activities Committee (HUAC) in 1952 about communists and communism?
3. What justification did Kazan offer for his HUAC testimony in April 1952?
4. Why did Kazan's friend, playwright Arthur Miller, disapprove of Kazan's HUAC testimony?
5. What was the response to Kazan's honorary lifetime achievement Oscar awarded by the American Academy of Motion Picture Arts and Sciences?

Historical Understanding

1. What was the Cold War?
2. What gave rise to the "Second Red Scare"?
3. What was the Hollywood Blacklist?
4. How did the House Un-American Activities Committee (HUAC) respond to communism?
5. Who were the Hollywood Ten?
6. How did Senator Joseph McCarthy contribute to the "Second Red Scare?"

Expressing Your Reasoning

Should Elia Kazan have named communists in his testimony before the House Un-American Activities Committee? Why or why not?

Key Concepts from History

What do the following have in common?

1. John Garfield, once a member of the Group Theater, was a Hollywood movie star famous for playing tough guys. He set up his own production company in 1947 and produced *Body and Soul*, one of the most highly regarded boxing films ever made. It was a huge critical and commercial success nominated for three Oscars. In 1951, Garfield was subpoenaed by the House Un-American Activities Committee (HUAC). He was not and had never been a communist, but he declined to name people who might have been. The experience ruined his career. He was blacklisted, and Hollywood studios barred him from appearing in their films. Garfield died of a heart attack in 1952 at the age of 39.

2. The Lavender Scare is a term for the mass firings of gay people from the United States government during the Second Red Scare of the 1950s. Gay men and lesbians were said to be security risks and communist sympathizers, which led to the call to remove them from government employment. At the time, the Republican national chairman said that "sexual perverts who have infiltrated our Government in recent years" were "perhaps as dangerous as the actual Communists." They were considered to be more susceptible to blackmail and thus were labeled as security risks. Senator Joseph McCarthy, with the enthusiastic support of FBI Director J. Edgar Hoover, was responsible for the firing of scores of gay men and women from government employment.

3. Paul Robeson was an African American who had an international career as a famous singer as well as a theater and movie actor. He received an academic scholarship to Rutgers University, where he was an All-American football star and graduated as class valedictorian (academically first in his class). He received his law degree from Columbia University while playing in the National Football League. He was politically involved and fought fervently against social injustice at home and abroad. He supported America's war efforts during World War II. He spoke out against racism and advocated extensively for the civil rights of African Americans. He actively opposed colonialism in Africa. He criticized policies of the United States government, especially those that he believed failed to provide for racial equality or that threatened world peace. His public praise for some policies of the Soviet Union and for the communist ideal of racial equality were widely reported. He visited the Soviet Union, and was honored by its government. His communist sympathies and pro-Soviet conduct brought FBI scrutiny. In 1956, Robeson was called before HUAC after he refused to sign an affidavit affirming that he was not a communist. In his testimony, he invoked the Fifth Amendment and refused to reveal his political affiliations. At that hearing, Robeson said, "Whether I am or not a Communist is irrelevant. The question is whether American

citizens, regardless of their political beliefs or sympathies, may enjoy their constitutional rights." Robeson was blacklisted and his passport was revoked for 8 years. After his HUAC hearing, his recordings and films were largely removed from public distribution, and he was widely condemned in the U.S press. During the height of the Cold War, it became increasingly difficult in the United States to hear Robeson sing on commercial radio, buy his music, or see his films.

Historical Inquiry

In 1953, husband and wife Julius and Ethel Rosenberg were executed as spies for passing atomic secrets to the Soviet Union. Following their sensational trial, some protested that they were innocent, and these claims continue to be argued. When the couple was electrocuted, their sons Michael and Robert were, respectively, 10 and 6 years old. Both brothers fought for years to clear their parents' names.

Using online and other sources, test the hypothesis that Julius and Ethel Rosenberg were guilty of espionage as charged. Compose a short essay in which you accept or reject the truth of the claim. Use evidence to support your decision.

To begin your investigation, the following search terms will be helpful:

- Julius and Ethel Rosenberg
- Robert Meeropol
- Michael Meeropol
- David Greenglass
- Ruth Greenglass
- Guilt of the Rosenbergs

CHAPTER 36

Crime After Crime

Burglary of the FBI

FBI Sketch of Bonnie Raines

In late 1970, when protests against the Vietnam War were raging across the country, William Davidon, a professor of physics at Haverford College in Pennsylvania, posed this startling question to a small group of people: "What do you think of burglarizing an FBI office?"

Those asked were stunned. What, they wondered, could be gained by breaking into an FBI office? The Federal Bureau of Investigation (FBI), headed for nearly half a century by legendary director J. Edgar Hoover, was revered as the agency that protected Americans from crime. Further, they thought, security of

FBI offices would be so tight that anyone who dared to attempt to break in to one of them would surely be caught and sent to prison.

Professor Davidon had come reluctantly to the idea of such a burglary. He believed that the FBI was spying on Americans and violating their constitutional right to dissent. The agency that was supposed to fight crime, Davidon suspected, was committing crimes. Breaking into an FBI office would be a crime to expose what he considered a crime against democracy.

Davidon approached nine people with his burglary suggestion. Only one of them turned him down. The other eight trusted him, and although shocked, listened to his explanation. They respected him and believed that he would engage in high-risk protest only if it promised to be effective.

The group met for the first time shortly before Christmas of 1970. Repugnant as a burglary was to them, they thought it might be the only way to expose evidence that the FBI was violating the right of Americans to dissent. As passionate opponents of the Vietnam War, all of them suspected that the FBI was suppressing protest against the war.

The preceding year had been one of deep division, unrest, and violence across the country. In November 1969, the nation was horrified to learn that American soldiers had massacred 504 Vietnamese, including children, women, and elderly people, in the small hamlet of My Lai. The commander of the soldiers accused of the massacre, Lieutenant William Calley, was convicted of murder and sentenced to life imprisonment at hard labor. President Nixon reduced the sentence to 3 months and ordered that Calley serve his sentence under house arrest rather than in prison.

In March, three members of a violent protest group known as the Weather Underground were killed in an explosion they accidentally set off while making a bomb in a New York town house.

In a speech in April, President Nixon announced that the United States was invading Cambodia after months of bombing it secretly. The announcement set off more antiwar protests than ever before.

Two days following the president's speech, James Rhodes, the governor of Ohio, declared martial law at Kent State University and ordered the Ohio National Guard to patrol the campus. The governor called protesting students "the worst kind of people we harbor in America." The next day, four students were killed and nine injured by National Guard gunfire on the Kent State campus. It was the first time that Americans were killed while protesting the war. Several days after the Kent State shootings, two students were killed by police on the campus of Jackson State University, an historically Black college in Mississippi.

The following Friday, hundreds of construction workers in the financial district of New York City attacked scores of students gathered for a vigil to mourn the students killed at Kent State. The attackers used crowbars and other heavy tools wrapped in American flags to beat the students. From their office windows high above, financial district workers tossed ticker tape to celebrate the violence in the streets below them. Vice President Spiro Agnew wrote a letter to the union official who organized the attacks on the students congratulating him for "his impressive display of patriotism." Many public officials lashed out at war protesters. One of the more extreme attacks on antiwar activists came in 1970 from Governor Ronald Reagan of California. He said, "If it takes a bloodbath to silence the demonstrators, let's get it over with."

In the middle of the night of August 24, 1970, a bomb exploded in front of Sterling Hall on the campus of the University of Wisconsin at Madison. Sterling Hall housed the Army Mathematics Research Center. A 33-year-old physics researcher, the father of three young children, was killed by the blast, and four people were injured.

Davidon was distressed by the increase of violence in the country and believed that the Vietnam War was a major cause of it. He wanted to step up protest against the war. At the same time, his suspicion was growing that the government was unlawfully suppressing protest.

At first, he was skeptical of rumors he heard from members of various peace groups that there were FBI spies in their midst. As the rumors persisted, Davidon came to believe that they were probably true, that peace organizations were being infiltrated by informers. He feared that FBI Director Hoover was using his power to spy on those who opposed the war. With freedom to dissent obstructed by the government, Davidon thought, free expression became meaningless. How, he wondered, could a government that claimed to be fighting a war for people's freedom in another country at the same time suppress dissent by its own people?

He was, however, not sure that the FBI was suppressing dissent against the war. So far there were only rumors and suspicions. He now focused his mind on how to prove or disprove the rumors. As he framed the problem, he came to the conclusion that he needed hard evidence. Assumptions would not do. To convince himself, he would have to find evidence of official suppression of dissent. Government spies, informants, tapping of telephones, threats to antiwar activists, or other actual surveillance measures by government agents to intimidate protesters would have to be uncovered for Davidon to confirm his suspicions. If he could find evidence of such tactics and present it to the public, he was confident that people would demand that the suppression be stopped.

This perplexing problem led Davidon to consider burglary. He disliked it as a tool of resistance—as he had when he had used it before. Early in 1970, he had joined Catholic antiwar activists in raiding draft board offices to destroy records of young men eligible to be drafted into compulsory military service. It seemed to him, however, that there was no other way now to get documentary evidence of FBI operations except by breaking into an FBI office and stealing files.

John and Bonnie Raines were two of the nine people approached by Bill Davidon. John had experience with resistance during the civil rights movement. Beginning in 1961, he went south nearly every summer to protest racial discrimination. As a Freedom Rider he had tested integration of interstate buses traveling between cities of the South. One night in a small southwestern Georgia town he had been arrested and jailed. He was rescued by a local Black farmer who, fearing for Raines's safety alone in a jail cell, put up his small farm as bail so that John could be released and leave town.

Tall, blond, and handsome, with striking blue eyes, John Raines, the son of a prominent Methodist pastor, had been raised in an affluent, liberal area of Minneapolis. He referred to his upbringing as "firmly inside a world of privilege and power." Minneapolis mayor, future U.S. senator, vice president, and Democratic nominee for president Hubert Humphrey had been a neighbor who occasionally dropped by his family's home.

Bonnie Raines, warm and engaging with long black hair and a radiant smile, grew up in Grand Rapids, Michigan. She attended Michigan State University where she was a good student and a cheerleader. To earn money for college, she worked summers as a waitress at a stately resort in Glen Arbor, Michigan, where John's family had a vacation cottage overlooking beautiful Glen Lake.

One summer night in 1961, John went to the resort for dinner and sat at one of the tables Bonnie was serving. They were attracted to each other, fell in love, and married a year later in Grand Rapids. After their wedding, they moved to New York. By 1970 they had three children.

John became a professor of religion at Temple University in Philadelphia. Bonnie was the director of a day care center and studying toward a graduate degree in child development at Temple. The evening they met with Davidon at his home, they were stunned by his question. As Davidon explained his thinking about a burglary that evening, John and Bonnie found themselves agreeing with him. They felt deeply about the constitutional right to protest and, if government officials were trying to silence protesters, they wanted them exposed.

Every evening for a week the Raineses discussed Davidon's question with each other after dinner as their three children, ages 7, 6, and 1, slept upstairs. With deep anguish they grappled with the conflict between their ideals and the well-being of their children. Were they willing to threaten the future of their family? Finally, though skeptical that an FBI office could be burglarized, they called Davidon to tell him that they would take the risk and join in his search to determine whether the rumors of infiltration by government spies were true. Before committing, they asked John's brother and sister-in-law whether they would raise the three Raines children if Bonnie and John went to prison. The children's aunt and uncle promised that they would.

With John and Bonnie on board, before the December holidays, Davidon recruited six more people for the burglary. All members of the group were passionate opponents of the Vietnam War. They confronted a disturbing spiral of casualty numbers: In some months, more than 500 American soldiers were killed. (In the end, more than 58,000 Americans, 1.1 million Vietnamese military, and widely ranging estimates of up to 2 million Vietnamese civilians from both sides combined were killed in the war.) Group members were also mindful of growing opposition to the war, including hundreds of thousands of young men who refused the draft and a half-million troops who deserted by 1971. They were inspired by the example of Martin Luther King, Jr.'s 1963 "Letter from a Birmingham Jail," in which he called for nonviolent civil disobedience in protest of unjust laws.

The prospective burglars were fully aware of the danger in what they were plotting to do. They could lose their freedom and possibly their lives. In December 1970, pledging strict secrecy to one another, they began meeting in the third floor attic of the Raineses' home in Germantown, a suburb of Philadelphia, to make their plans. They named their group the Citizens' Commission to Investigate the FBI. Their goal was to break into the FBI office in Media, Pennsylvania, a sleepy town 15 miles southwest of Philadelphia; take as many files as they could carry away; review the files; and, if they contained information the group believed the public ought to know, distribute them to the public.

Their first task was to choose a night for the burglary. They chose March 8, 1971, because that was the night of the highly anticipated world heavyweight championship boxing match between Muhammed Ali and Joe Frazier. The burglars hoped that the nation would be riveted to the fight at Madison Square Garden the night they were breaking into the FBI office.

The nights of their planning meetings, the group would have dinner at the Raineses' house. After dinner a babysitter arrived. John, Bonnie, and the other plotters adjourned to the attic. Following their meeting, two to a car, the burglars would drive to Media to case the area near the FBI office. They would often sit for hours in their cars during bitter cold nights of January and February. Afterward, they would return to the attic to discuss what they had discovered.

While casing in Media, they carefully monitored many conditions, including parking of vehicles near the FBI office; movements of residents in and out of the building, as well as people who worked in offices located on the first and second floors of the residential apartment building in which the FBI office was located; schedules and routes of local police who patrolled the neighborhood; lighting patterns in the FBI office and nearby offices; closing times of nearby restaurants and bars; and the schedule and movement of the county courthouse guards across the street from the FBI office.

During one of the planning sessions in the attic, it was suggested that a crowbar be used to break into the FBI office. One member of the group thought that would be too noisy. Instead, he said that he would learn to pick the lock. He then joined a locksmith association and researched locksmithing in the library of the association. He had walked by the FBI one day after Davidon invited him to join the group, and he observed that the lock on the door was a simple five-tumbler lock, easy to pick.

Thorough as the burglars were casing the area outside the FBI office, they needed also to inspect it carefully from inside. For that they turned to Bonnie Raines. The scheme was for her to masquerade as a college student.

Not many people visited FBI offices. Bonnie needed a way for her to visit without arousing the suspicion of agents. There were key questions that had to be answered: Were the cabinets and desks locked? Were the floors carpeted? Was there an alarm system or surveillance cameras in the office?

Bonnie was a very youthful-looking 29 years old. Posing as a college student, she called the FBI office to ask for an appointment and requested of the agent in charge a half-hour interview. As a student in a local college, she said, she was doing research for a class assignment about hiring practices. The agent agreed to meet with her at 2:00 a few days later.

The burglars spent time preparing for Bonnie's bogus interview. They prepared questions for her to ask. They considered what her personal appearance would be—for example, how she should wear her long black hair. She often wore it in long pigtails. For her visit to the FBI office, it was decided that she would wear her hair pulled back in a barrette and tucked under a wool hat. She wanted to reduce the chances that she might later be recognized from photographs that the group assumed law enforcement officers might have taken at antiwar demonstrations Bonnie had attended. She decided to add a pair of horn-rimmed glasses to her disguise. To avoid leaving fingerprints, she would wear gloves. Following the advice of the group, Bonnie dressed for the interview as a nerdy coed, dressed in a skirt, sweater, and long winter coat.

The afternoon of her appointment, Bonnie arrived, as planned, 15 minutes early. She excused herself for arriving early by saying that the bus she took arrived earlier than expected. (Actually, John had driven her and dropped her off out of sight of the FBI office.) The early arrival was a ruse for her to sit and survey the office carefully while waiting for the agent to start the interview. While waiting, she asked one of the agents if she could see an employment application form. The purpose of her request was to observe whether the agent would have to unlock a file cabinet to get the form. She was relieved to see that the file cabinet was not locked.

From where she sat while waiting, she saw two other rooms in the office. She noticed open blinds covering the windows. If the burglars were to use flashlights, she noted, they would have to do so carefully to avoid streaming light between the slats.

During the interview with the agent in charge, Bonnie thought he was a nice guy, the kind of person one might like to have as a neighbor. He didn't seem to suspect anything unusual. Her gloved hands seem to arouse no suspicion while she took notes during the conversation.

The offices had wall-to-wall carpeting that would help muffle any noise made by burglars. The interview lasted an hour. While taking leave, Bonnie asked where the restroom was located. An agent told her the restrooms were outside the office, gave her a key, and pointed down the hall. The burglars wanted to know whether there would be an open restroom where they could hide if necessary. Knowing now that a key was needed, Bonnie realized that there would be no place to hide on the night of the burglary.

She tracked the paths of all electrical cords in the office and discovered that none led to an alarm system. She saw no surveillance cameras. She checked the lock on the office door and confirmed that it was a simple lock that could easily be picked. She also noticed that the second door that opened into the external hallway was blocked on the inside by a large file cabinet. The burglars would have to enter, as she had, through the main entrance.

After exiting the building, Bonnie walked to the spot where John was waiting with the car. She told John that she was now sure the burglary could be done. John was buoyed by her optimism, but he also felt deep foreboding. He especially feared what might happen to his children if the burglars were caught.

Two challenges were daunting. First, residents of the apartment building might come or go through the building entrance and open stairwell at any time. Second, across the street from the FBI office, a guard was stationed around the clock inside the glass door at the Delaware County courthouse. The burglars would be visible to the guard when they entered the FBI office building.

A few days before the burglary was to take place, one of the members of the group announced that he was quitting and left the meeting. He knew all the details of the plan, and the remaining burglars were haunted by the possibility that he would reveal their plot.

At 6:30 P.M. on March 8, the Raineses greeted the babysitter and hugged their young children. It was time to go to meet their co-conspirators at the motel room they had rented as a staging site for the night of the burglary. They drove to the motel in their family station wagon and met their six accomplices at the motel at 7:00.

The locksmith and the four members of the inside team—those who would enter the office and steal the files—wore "uptown" clothes so they would blend with residents of the neighborhood. The locksmith, Keith Forsyth, who would enter the office first, wore a long topcoat to conceal his burglary tools.

Forsyth and John Raines left the motel room in separate cars between 7:30 and 8:00 P.M. Forsyth drove to Media to break into the FBI office. John Raines drove to a parking lot at Swarthmore College, where he would wait for the burglars to arrive with stolen files to be transferred to his family station wagon, now being used as a getaway car.

Forsyth parked a short distance from the FBI office. He entered the apartment building, headed upstairs to the second floor, and walked directly to the FBI office door. He expected to pick the lock in 30 seconds, but he was suddenly shocked to discover that he would be unable to pick it at all. There was now a second lock on the door, a high-security lock on which his tools would be useless. Stymied, he walked to a phone booth and called the motel. Davidon told him to return to the motel.

The group was alarmed. Why, they wondered, was there a second lock on the door? Had it been overlooked before? Had Bonnie Raines's interview visit prompted the FBI to add a second, more secure lock? Had the conspirator who dropped out betrayed them? Were there armed agents waiting inside the office for the burglars?

Bonnie was closely questioned about what she remembered about the second external FBI office door. It was barricaded on the inside by a tall metal cabinet. She thought it would be very difficult to enter through that door. Nonetheless, she saw it as their only chance to succeed, and the others agreed to go ahead.

Forsyth drove back to the FBI office and arrived at 10:40, just as the bell rang to start the Ali-Frazier fight, later than the burglars had expected. This time the locksmith carried a crowbar with him. He easily picked the simple lock on the second door. Next, using the crowbar, he popped out the deadbolt lock at the top of the door. He pushed on the heavy wooden door, but it would not move. He couldn't apply enough force. He needed a heavier tool. He went to the trunk of his parked car and brought back the bar used with a jack stand. Back at the office door he was terrified. Residents could walk by at any moment as he lay on the floor trying to nudge the door open with the bar. If he knocked over the cabinet on the inside, it would make a loud noise, surely to be noticed by the building caretaker who lived in the apartment directly below the office.

Amid his terror, Forsyth remembers taking a small measure of comfort while lying on the floor and prying the door open. He could hear sounds of the Ali-Frazier fight crackling in the hallway from apartment residents listening on their radios. As the burglars had hoped it would, the fight was providing some cover for their break-in.

For several minutes, Forsyth slowly and cautiously pushed the door until it was open barely enough for him to squeeze inside. He then drove back to the motel, where everybody was relieved to see him and delighted to learn that the door was unlocked. The FBI office was ready to be entered.

The inside crew of four burglars was driven to the Media office. Each of the four carried two large suitcases through the front door and into the building. They entered the office through the door that Forsyth had dislodged. In the dark, except for a cautiously used flashlight, they opened every cabinet and broke locks as necessary to open locked drawers.

When every drawer, shelf, and cabinet had been emptied, one of the burglars called the motel to give a cryptic signal that the inside crew was ready to be picked up. Their suitcases were bulging with all the files in the Media FBI office. They were picked up in two getaway cars and, switching cars as a precaution en route, set off to the remote farmhouse where the burglars had planned to sift and winnow the stolen files.

Over the next several days and nights, the burglars discovered files that described surveillance and intimidation by the FBI, including eavesdropping, entrapment, and the use of informers. What they found confirmed suspicions that the nation's leading law enforcement agency was engaged in illegal political spying.

FBI Director Hoover was infuriated when he learned of the Media burglary the morning after it occurred. He set in motion one of the most extensive investigations in the history of the FBI. During the course of the FBI investigation, nearly 200 agents were transferred to Philadelphia to work on the case.

Having completed what they set out to do, the burglars agreed never to meet with one another again. John Raines drove to Princeton and dropped five packets of FBI documents in a mailbox, addressed to U.S Senator George McGovern of South Dakota, U.S. Representative Parren Mitchell of Maryland, columnist Tom Wicker of *The New York Times*, investigative reporter Jack Nelson of the *Los Angeles Times*, and reporter Betty Medsger of the *Washington Post.*

Senator McGovern condemned the burglary, refusing to be associated with what he called an "illegal action by a private group." Congressman Mitchell turned the documents over to the Department of Justice, while declaring both the burglary, and the FBI surveillance of student and peace groups it exposed, crimes to be dealt with.

The mailed documents revealed that the FBI had been monitoring student groups, especially those of Black students. The bureau had paid informers who reported on the activities of students and professors. The stolen files also revealed that personal records of people not linked to any criminal activity—for example, phone records and checking account records had been procured by agents without subpoenas. There was also evidence that banks, credit card agencies, employers, landlords, law enforcement officers, and military recruiters provided confidential files to the FBI, without regard to privacy rights.

It was the *Washington Post* that first published the stolen files. The attorney general of the United States, John Mitchell, tried to deter the paper's publisher. He warned that public release of the files taken from the Media FBI office could endanger the lives of federal agents and the security of the United States.

This was the first time that a journalist had been given secret government documents by sources outside government who had stolen them. Possessing stolen documents was a federal crime. The attorney general threatened to deny broadcast licenses for stations owned by the *Washington Post* if the paper went ahead with publication of the Media burglary documents. Contrary to the advice of its attorneys, the publisher and editors of the *Washington Post*, acting boldly and asserting the constitutional right to a free press, decided to publish the documents.

Other newspapers across the country followed the lead of the *Post*. A storm of criticism of the FBI and Director Hoover followed. For example, the *Philadelphia Inquirer*, long an admirer of Hoover as an anti-communist watchdog and crime fighter, declared that the questions raised by the stolen documents "are questions too fundamental in a free society, with implications too suggestive of police state tactics, to be brushed lightly aside."

One of the stolen documents, a simple routing slip, contained the mysterious word COINTELPRO. Journalist Carl Stern of NBC, using the Freedom of Information Act (a law giving citizens a right to access information from the federal government), persisted against determined resistance by the FBI to uncover the meaning of the term.

He discovered that COINTELPRO was an acronym (Counter Intelligence Program) for a series of highly secret and sometimes illegal projects conducted by the FBI beginning in 1956. Americans who criticized the Vietnam War or were considered "subversive" were targeted for spying. They included U.S. senators, civil rights leaders, journalists, and athletes. Among them were Dr. Martin Luther King, Jr.; Albert Einstein; and Eleanor Roosevelt. Groups deemed subversive were infiltrated by FBI informers.

COINTELPRO tactics included not only infiltration of groups but also planting false media stories, forging of correspondence, disrupting meetings, accusing activists of crimes they did not commit, opening mail, conducting wiretaps, giving perjured testimony and false evidence, and illegal break-ins.

The revelations, exposed by the stolen files, created a national uproar. For the first time, there were widespread calls from members of Congress and newspaper editorials for investigation and oversight of the FBI and its powerful director. In response, Congress authorized the Select Committee to Study Governmental Operations with Respect to Intelligence Activities, known as the Church Committee for its chairman, Senator Frank Church, Democrat of Idaho. Following extensive investigations, the Church Committee concluded that the FBI had "violated specific laws and infringed constitutional rights of American citizens." It recommended legislation that was adopted to create permanent intelligence oversight committees in both houses of Congress. Also established under the Foreign Intelligence Surveillance Act (FISA) was a special court to control electronic surveillance by intelligence agencies.

Although there were close calls, none of the Media burglars was caught. FBI agents missed encountering Bonnie Raines only by minutes. Two agents had come to the Raineses' house to question them about the burglary because of their known antiwar activities. The agents had a sketch of Bonnie, drawn from memory of the day of her bogus interview at the FBI office in Media, but were never able to connect it to her. She had left the house 10 minutes before the agents arrived. They spoke only to John. During the years following the break-in, all the burglars lived their normal lives, but feared that they might at any time be tracked down.

The statute of limitations for burglary takes effect 5 years after the crime. By March 1976, the burglars could no longer be prosecuted, yet they planned to keep their secret. It was revealed accidentally. The *Washington Post* reporter, Betty Medsger, to whom the stolen FBI files had been sent in 1971, had been an acquaintance of the Raineses when she worked as a reporter for the *Evening Bulletin* in Philadelphia. During a weekend visit to that city many years after the burglary, she had dinner at the Raineses' house. John Raines introduced Betty to the Raineses' teenage daughter: "Mary, this is Betty Medsger. We want you to know Betty, because many years ago, when your dad and mother had information about the FBI we wanted the American people to have, we gave it to Betty." Medsger was amazed to find out that her hosts and old acquaintances were among the Media burglars.

In 2014, during a question-and-answer session following a public presentation about the burglary, John Raines was asked what it was that had especially motivated him, unlike other civil rights and antiwar activists of the era, to move across such a hazardous line and become a burglar. After a long, reflective pause he said, "I have a background of belief in Jesus of Nazareth who took the fight for justice to the Cross."

The major sources for this chapter were:

Medsger, B. (2014). *The burglary: The discovery of J. Edgar Hoover's secret FBI.* New York, NY: Alfred A. Knopf.

Raines, J. B., & Raines J. (2014, July 22). *Recorded interview conducted and by D. Harris.* Personal collection.

LEARNING ACTIVITIES FOR "CRIME AFTER CRIME"

Facts of the Case

1. Why did William Davidon propose burglarizing an FBI office?
2. Why did Bonnie and John Raines agree to participate in the burglary?
3. What did the stolen Media, Pennsylvania files reveal about FBI operations?
4. Why did the *Washington Post* hesitate to publish the stolen secret FBI documents?
5. What changes in federal law were put in motion as a result of the Media, Pennsylvania burglary?

Historical Understanding

1. Describe the political climate in the United States during the year preceding the Media, Pennsylvania burglary.
2. Why did FBI Director Hoover believe it necessary to conduct extensive undercover surveillance?
3. Which constitutional rights did anti–Vietnam War activists believe the government was violating?

Expressing Your Reasoning

Should Bonnie and John Raines have participated in the burglary of the Media, Pennsylvania, FBI office? Why or why not?

Key Concepts from History

What do the following have in common?

1. In November 1872, Susan B. Anthony voted in Rochester, New York. Voting by women was against the law. Anthony believed that she had a right to vote. She was arrested, put on trial, and convicted of violating the law. The judge fined her $100, but Anthony declared in the courtroom that she would refuse to pay the fine.

2. On December 1, 1955, in Montgomery, Alabama, Rosa Parks refused to obey a bus driver's order that she give up her seat in the White section to a White passenger, after the Colored section was filled. Parks was arrested for violating Alabama's racial segregation laws and prosecuted in court. She had deliberately taken a seat in the White section of the bus to protest racial segregation.

3. In late 1971, Daniel Ellsberg released to *The New York Times* and other newspapers the so-called Pentagon Papers, a top-secret Pentagon study of U.S. government decisionmaking regarding the Vietnam War. Defense Secretary Robert McNamara commissioned the study from the RAND Corporation, a think tank formed to offer research and analysis to the U.S. armed forces. Ellsberg worked for RAND. In releasing the documents, he wanted to call attention to what he considered an unjust war that was going to continue and expand. He said, "I could no longer cooperate in concealing this information from the American public. I did this clearly at my own jeopardy and I am prepared to answer to all the consequences of this decision." He was prosecuted under the Espionage Act for revealing secret government documents.

Historical Inquiry

In 2014, John Raines lamented that the reforms adopted by Congress after the Media FBI burglary had become ineffective. He thought that the Foreign Intelligence Surveillance Act (FISA) court and congressional oversight committees no longer restrained government intelligence agencies as originally intended. He believed that the country had lapsed back to the conditions of 1971.

Using online and other sources, test John Raines's hypothesis and compose a short essay in which you accept or reject it, using evidence to support your decision. To begin your investigation, the following search terms will be helpful:

- National Security Agency (NSA)
- Edward Snowden
- Glenn Greenwald
- The Guardian
- Undercover operations
- FISA Court

Part X

CONTEMPORARY AMERICA
1990–2017

CHAPTER 37

Forty Acres and a Mule

Reparations for African Americans

Five Generations on Smith's Plantation, Beaufort, South Carolina, 1862

Photograph by Timothy H. O'Sullivan. Courtesy of the Library of Congress.

From 1517 until 1867, approximately 12.5 million enslaved Africans were shipped across the Atlantic Ocean to the Americas. Another 2 million perished while forced to walk from the hinterlands where they were captured to distant coasts, or while they were confined in coastal ports to await their transport in slave ships across the Atlantic. About 1.5 million of the enslaved, transported in overcrowded ships under horrific conditions, died during the Middle Passage.

It is called the Middle Passage because it was the middle part of a three-part voyage. The first part of the voyage started in Europe with ships carrying cargo, often including iron, cloth, brandy, firearms and gunpowder, bound for the West Coast ("slave coast") of Africa. On that coast, the cargo of goods from Europe was exchanged for a cargo of enslaved Africans. The voyage with human cargo from Africa to the Americas was the Middle Passage. In the Americas the slave cargo was exchanged for goods such as sugar, rum, and molasses, and the ships then departed home on their final passage.

When the Atlantic slave trade emerged, slavery already existed in Africa. Some of those enslaved were captured by other Africans, often from their enemies during war. Many of these captive slaves were sold to Western European slave merchants. Some slaves were captured directly by the Europeans. The Portuguese were the first to engage in the Atlantic slave trade, soon followed by the British, Dutch, French, Spanish, and Americans.

Ship owners regarded the slaves, branded with hot irons and shackled, as cargo to be shipped as cheaply as possible across the ocean. Those who survived were sold and forced to work on agricultural plantations, in gold and silver mines, as skilled laborers and domestic servants, at cutting timber for ships, and at construction. (Slaves would later build the White House and the U.S. Capitol.) In 1790, the first census of the newly independent United States recorded a total population of 3,893,635, of whom 694,280 (18%) were enslaved persons.

Most of the slaves shipped to the English colonies of North America came from the present-day African countries of Senegal, Sierra Leone, Liberia, Ghana, Benin, Nigeria, Congo, and Angola. The Atlantic slave trade was financially profitable for slave merchants, slaveholders, and for the African middlemen who sold captured people to the slave traders.

Enslaved Africans in the American colonies and in the states after independence were treated as a racial caste and forced into labor. Considered property, and under the complete control of their masters, slaves were beaten, raped, killed, and discarded. When slaves were bought and sold, husbands and wives were often separated, and children were often separated from their parents. Half of the interstate sales of the enslaved destroyed their nuclear families.

The wife and children of Henry Brown, an enslaved man in Richmond, Virginia, were sold away. Brown recalled the day his family departed:

> I stationed myself by the side of the road, along which the slaves, amounting to 350, were to pass. The purchaser of my wife was a Methodist minister, who was about starting for North Carolina. Pretty soon five wagon-loads of little children passed, and looking at the foremost one, what should I see but a little child, pointing its tiny hand towards me, exclaiming, "There's my father; I knew he would come and bid me good-bye." It was my eldest child! Soon the gang approached in which my wife was chained. I looked and beheld her familiar face; but O, reader, that glance of agony! May God spare me

ever again enduring the excruciating horror of that moment! She passed, and came near to where I stood. I seized hold of her hand, intending to bid her farewell; but words failed me; the gift of utterance had fled, and I remained speechless. I followed her for some distance, with her hand grasped in mine, as if to save her from her fate but I could not speak, and I was obliged to turn away in silence.

Although there were slaves in both cities and rural areas of the North, slavery was concentrated in the South. Nearly one-fourth of all White southerners owned slaves. In the seven cotton-producing states of the South, one-third of all income was derived from slavery. By 1840, cotton, produced by slave labor, amounted to 59% of the nation's exports. It was called King Cotton.

Prominent American institutions profited from slavery. For example, Georgetown, a Catholic university in Washington, D.C., has acknowledged selling 232 slaves, owned by the university, to keep the school financially afloat in 1838. The Aetna Insurance Company, based in Connecticut, has apologized for insuring slaveholders against the deaths of their slaves.

American industry was tied to the agricultural plantations where slavery was concentrated. Textile manufacture, for example, used slave labor extensively. Industries employing enslaved labor were more profitable than those employing free labor. Slave owners often hired out their slaves, including those with special skills such as tailors, carpenters, seamstresses, and mechanics. Some of these enslaved Black people working with metal, wood, or machinery developed new or improved technologies. Because they were not American citizens, however, they could not receive patents for their inventions. Their inventions contributed to American economic growth, but the patents went to slaveholders who profited from them.

There have been various attempts to quantify gains to Whites from exploitation of Blacks during slavery. Estimates in today's dollars range extremely, from $2.1 billion to $1.4 trillion.

There were short-term and long-term consequences of deprivations during slavery. For example, infants suffered from prenatal and postnatal nutritional deficiencies. These conditions, along with various prohibitions against, for example, learning to read or write, receiving health care, and owning property, hampered efforts of former slaves to accumulate wealth after emancipation. Such obstacles, resulting from systematic enslavement and exploitation of African Americans, ensured that money and other resources were channeled to Whites and denied to Blacks.

The end of The Civil War brought to freedmen (what former slaves, both men and women, were called) a new hope that they would now enjoy the fruits of their own labor. That hope began when, in January 1865, near the end of The Civil War, Union General William T. Sherman issued Field Order No. 15. President Abraham Lincoln approved the order. It issued 40-acre plots of land to newly freed slaves. The Union Army had seized 400,000 acres of tillable farmland abandoned by Confederate owners.

General Sherman's order was the result of his meeting in Savannah, Georgia, with Secretary of War Edwin Stanton and 20 African American ministers. The ministers advised that the land be redistributed to freedmen. By June, 40,000 freedmen had been settled on "Sherman Land." Sherman later ordered that the army could lend the new settlers mules; hence, the now proverbial slogan, "40 acres and a mule."

Congress created the Freedmen's Bureau to help former slaves and poor Whites. It provided food, housing, and medical aid; established schools; and offered legal assistance. In 1872, however, a shortage of funds and personnel, along with pressure from White southerners, prompted Congress to shut down the Freedmen's Bureau.

In 1865, the Thirteenth Amendment to the U.S. Constitution abolished slavery, thereby freeing approximately 4 million people. In 1865–1866, immediately following the end of The Civil War, many southern Whites tried to suppress the new freedom of emancipated former slaves. They enacted laws, called Black Codes, to restrict the freedom of African Americans and to compel them to work for low wages. These laws restricted Black people from owning property, conducting business, buying and owning land, and moving freely through public spaces. (Prior to The Civil War, some northern states—for example, Illinois, Indiana, Michigan, and New York—had enacted Black Codes to deter freed Blacks from residing in those states.)

Reconstruction (1865–1876), the era of rebuilding the South after The Civil War, raised other hopes for freedmen. Congress, over the veto of President Andrew Johnson, passed the Civil Rights Act of 1866. The act declared that all persons born in the United States were now citizens, without regard to race, color, or previous condition of servitude. As citizens they could make and enforce contracts; sue and be sued; give evidence in court; and inherit, purchase, lease, sell, hold, and transfer title to real estate and personal property. Under the act, persons who denied these rights to former slaves were guilty of a crime.

In 1867, again over the veto of President Johnson, Congress passed the Reconstruction Act. It temporarily divided the South into five military districts and mandated state governments based on universal male suffrage. The law also required southern states to ratify the Fourteenth Amendment to the U.S. Constitution before they could rejoin the Union. The Fourteenth Amendment granted "equal protection of the law," among other rights, to all citizens, including former slaves. The Fifteenth Amendment was adopted in 1870. It guaranteed that a citizen's right to vote could not be denied "on account of race, color, or previous condition of servitude."

By 1870, all former Confederate states had been readmitted to the Union, with new state constitutions guaranteeing interracial democracy. Blacks were elected to southern state governments and to the U.S. Congress. Reconstruction brought the first state-funded public school systems to the South, more equitable taxation laws, laws prohibiting racial discrimination in public transport and accommodations (for example, hotels and restaurants), and economic development programs, including aid to railroads and other enterprises.

At this time, former slaves and Black abolitionists called for land distribution to former slaves. One of them, Sojourner Truth, who had been born into slavery, argued that enslaved men and women had helped to build the nation's wealth and should be compensated:

> We have been a source of wealth to this republic. Our labor supplied the country with cotton, until villages and cities dotted the enterprising North for its manufacture and furnished employment and support for a multitude, thereby becoming a revenue to the government. Beneath a burning southern sun have we toiled, in the canebrake and the rice swamp, urged on by the merciless driver's lash, earning millions of money.

Calls for land distribution by Truth and others were unsuccessful.

African American hopes for a better future were soon dashed. As the result of an agreement following the contested presidential election of 1876, federal troops were withdrawn from the South and Reconstruction policies were dismantled. Soon, Reconstruction was replaced by Jim Crow, the term applied to the long period of racial segregation and discrimination that followed Reconstruction. (The term *Jim Crow* comes from a mid-19th century White actor's derisive song-and-dance caricature of Blacks.)

Jim Crow was enshrined in law by the landmark case of *Plessy v. Ferguson*, decided by the U.S. Supreme Court in 1896. In its decision, the Court ruled that separate facilities for Blacks and Whites were constitutional so long as they were equal.

The thin disguise of equality did not conceal the day-to-day reality. Facilities remained separate but were rarely equal. Public facilities for Blacks were nearly always inferior to those for Whites, when they existed at all. Blacks continued to be denied the rights of citizenship. Jim Crow and the Supreme Court's "separate but equal" doctrine made a mockery of the Reconstruction Amendments to the U.S. Constitution and of Reconstruction era policies.

White southerners, called "Redeemers," regained total control of southern legislatures. They adopted Jim Crow laws mandating segregation of Blacks and Whites in almost every aspect of daily life: schools, parks, libraries, buses, trains, restaurants, hotels, drinking fountains, and even cemeteries. "Whites Only" and "Colored" signs were constant reminders of the enforced racial order.

Poll taxes were used in southern states to deny Black citizens their recently gained right to vote. Poll taxes had to be paid before a person was allowed to vote, and some poor people could not afford to pay. Almost all southern Blacks were poor, so the poll tax affected them more than Whites.

Literacy tests were also used in southern states to exclude Blacks from voting. A citizen would be required to pass a test before he was allowed to vote. The tests were made more difficult for Blacks than for Whites. In some southern states there was a "grandfather clause" intended to discriminate against Blacks. Anyone who had voted before 1867, or whose father or grandfather voted before 1867, could skip the poll tax and literacy test. Almost no Blacks had been allowed to vote before Reconstruction, so they could not avoid the tax or the test.

Whites also denied economic opportunities to Blacks during the Jim Crow era. African Americans were refused jobs available to Whites. Land ownership by Blacks increased beginning with Reconstruction, but during the Jim Crow era, some Black people who had acquired land were forced illegally by Whites to abandon it, often under threat of violence. White farmers received credit from lenders to purchase farm equipment, seed, and fertilizer, but such credit was usually denied to Black farmers.

Many African Americans were driven into debt by sharecropping (a practice whereby laborers were given the use of property in return for a share in the crops produced), also called tenant farming. From 1900 to 1930 in the South 47% of all White farmers were tenants compared to 79% of all Black farmers.

Tenant farmers (sharecroppers) would incur debt from loans taken from the land owners to plant crops, and from credit given by company stores owned by the land owners for purchase of overpriced necessities. The sharecroppers often worked without compensation, sometimes until they died, to pay off debt.

Another form of unpaid labor was conducted in concert with southern state and county governments. Black men were picked up for minor crimes or on false charges. When faced with staggering fines and court fees, they were forced to work for a local employer who would pay their fines, but no wages. Southern states also leased their convicts to local companies that did not pay the prisoners for their labor.

The Ku Klux Klan (KKK), a Protestant male White supremacist organization, was formed to enforce segregation and racial discrimination through intimidation and terror, including lynching of African Americans. Although it was suppressed during Reconstruction, the KKK revived in 1915, targeting not only Black people but also Catholics and Jews, as well as recently arrived immigrants from Southern and Eastern Europe, many of whom were Catholic or Jewish. With 4 to 5 million members, the KKK flourished nationwide during the 1920s, including in urban areas of the Midwest and West. One of its ritual forms of intimidation was to assemble at night wearing hooded white costumes and set huge wooden crosses aflame. The KKK declined a second time in the late 1920s, but emerged again to oppose civil rights and racial integration during the civil rights movement of the mid-20th century. KKK groups endure at the present time.

During Jim Crow, Blacks were forced to behave subserviently toward Whites, for example, moving aside when a White person was walking past, and addressing

Whites with deference as "Sir" and "Ma'am." Most former slaves, and their descendants, were compelled to remain in a position of social, economic, and political exclusion.

There was organized White violence against Blacks during the Jim Crow era. Black churches and schools were burned to the ground. Black voters and those who tried to rally them were intimidated, and some were murdered. Thousands of Black people were lynched. At the end of World War I, Black veterans were assaulted for wearing their military uniforms. Blacks competing for scarce jobs after the war were attacked by Whites in cities across the country, including Long View, Texas; Chicago; and Washington, D.C.

The Social Security Act of 1935, part of President Franklin Roosevelt's New Deal, discriminated against African Americans. Under the act, old-age insurance and unemployment insurance excluded farm workers and domestics—jobs widely held by Blacks. Sixty-five percent of African Americans nationally, and between 70 and 80% in the South, were ineligible for Social Security benefits when the law was enacted.

Discrimination against African Americans was not confined to the Jim Crow South. It also prevailed in other regions of the country. From the 1930s through the 1960s, African Americans across the country were often segregated, and they were largely cut out of the housing market. Unable to get home mortgage financing from banks, Black people were driven to contract sales. A White seller would contract with a Black buyer to purchase a house. The seller kept the deed until monthly payments under the contract were paid in full. Unlike with a normal bank mortgage, the buyer would acquire no equity (financial value) in the house until the final payment was made. If a payment was missed, the down payment, all monthly payments, and the property itself were forfeited.

Blacks were segregated into Black neighborhoods, sometimes by threats of violence if they moved into a White neighborhood, and sometimes by a legally enforced restrictive covenant (a provision in the deed to a house prohibiting sale to Blacks or other specified people, and enforced by courts).

The federal government contributed to racial segregation of housing. The Federal Housing Administration (FHA), created by Congress in 1934, insured private mortgages. The insurance enabled buyers to secure lower mortgage interest rates and smaller down payments from banks. The FHA rated neighborhoods for insurance eligibility. Those where Black people lived were marked on FHA maps. The people who lived in those neighborhoods were considered ineligible and denied mortgage insurance.

Real estate agents used "redlining" to segregate neighborhoods by marking off Black neighborhoods with red lines on a map. Lenders would refuse to lend money or extend credit to borrowers in redlined areas. The Fair Housing Act of 1968 outlawed redlining. Like other discriminatory housing practices, however, it was used for decades to confine African Americans to center-city communities where investments in their homes deteriorated and lost value compared to homes in White areas.

During the middle of the 20th century, real estate agents in American cities used a practice called blockbusting that prompted "White flight." Unscrupulous agents would convince White home owners to sell their houses at low prices by promoting fear that Blacks would soon be moving into the neighborhood. Whites would sell at discounted prices. The agents would then sell the houses to Black people at inflated prices. As the neighborhoods became mostly Black, home values declined.

Black people were excluded from affordable housing in government-subsidized suburban communities developed across the country to address the housing shortage after World War II. The FHA insured mortgages for houses in these developments. The first model suburban community was Levittown on Long Island in New York. Between 1947 and 1951, the firm Levitt & Sons built more than 17,000 houses in Levittown.

The FHA guaranteed bank loans for construction and development in Levittown on condition that no homes were sold to African Americans and that every home had a clause in its deed prohibiting resale to African Americans. Clause 25 of the standard lease for the first Levittown houses, which included an option to buy, stated that the home could not "be used or occupied by any person other than members of the Caucasian race."

Even though the U.S. Supreme Court ruled restrictive covenants unenforceable in 1948, Levittown clung to its unlawful racial barrier. By 1953, the 70,000 people who lived in Levittown constituted the largest community in the United States with no Black residents. The 2010 census reported that 99.1% of Levittown residents were White.

Levittown homes sold originally for about $8,000, approximately $100,000 in today's dollars. Today, those homes sell for $300,000 to $400,000. In the ensuing two generations, the White families who moved into those homes gained $200,000–$300,000 in equity. Their descendants could inherit that wealth.

The racial discrimination in housing at Levittown was not unique. Racially explicit laws, regulations, and government practices combined to create a nationwide system of Black ghettos surrounded by White suburbs. Federal, state, and local governments purposefully created segregation in every metropolitan area of the nation, and its effects endure.

Another example of racial discrimination in housing comes from the Veterans Administration (VA). Title III of the G.I. Bill after World War II aimed to give veterans access to low-interest home loans. VA officials refused to insure loans to African American veterans, and bankers denied them mortgages.

Their restricted choice of neighborhood has contributed to the wealth disparity of African Americans compared to Whites. Sixty-two percent of Blacks have been raised in poor neighborhoods, compared to 4% of Whites. Generally, Blacks and Whites inhabit different neighborhoods.

Home ownership has been the major means of wealth accumulation for middle-class Americans. The wealth gap between Black and White Americans can be traced in part to housing discrimination in which the government was often complicit. Unlike Whites, Black people were historically prevented from accruing wealth in the value of their homes and then passing those gains on to their heirs.

In 1954, the U.S. Supreme Court reversed the "separate but equal" decision in *Plessy v. Ferguson*. In the historic case of *Brown v. Board of Education*, the High Court unanimously declared, "Separate educational facilities are inherently unequal." That decision to desegregate public schools accelerated a major movement for the civil rights of African Americans. Civil Rights Acts signed into law by President Lyndon Johnson during the 1960s prohibited racial discrimination in public accommodations (for example, hotels, restaurants, theaters, buses, and trains), voting, and housing. Resistance to these laws was fierce but, over time, they were upheld by the federal courts and gradually enforced.

In a historic speech delivered at the 1965 Howard University commencement, President Johnson, alluding to the unique national history of discrimination against African Americans, said: "Negro poverty is not white poverty." It was a premise for the civil rights and antipoverty legislation of his administration called "the Great Society."

Although African Americans continue to experience discrimination, in recent decades they have made gains in the exercise of legal rights. For example, there are no more "Whites Only" segregation signs, and state and federal laws now prohibit race discrimination in employment, housing, and public accommodations. There have also been socioeconomic gains. For example, the poverty rate for African Americans has declined, and levels of education and household income have increased

Yet, today, even after the successes of the civil rights movement, the African American population, on average, has higher infant-mortality rates, lower life expectancy, higher rates of unemployment, lower income, and higher rates of imprisonment than the White population. As of 2013, the median net worth of White households ($144,000) was 13 times greater than that for Black households ($11,200).

These disparities are a legacy of slavery and the century-long Jim Crow era that followed it. The effects of racial segregation, denial of the rights of citizenship, discrimination in employment and housing, and the many other forms of mistreatment of African Americans have carried over from the past to the present.

In the wake of the civil rights movement, some African Americans called for reparation for mistreatment during slavery and the Jim Crow era. (Reparation is the making of amends for a wrong that has been done by paying money to or otherwise helping those who have been wronged.) The recent calls for reparations are not the first appeal by African Americans for restitution of what had been taken or withheld from them.

The first movement requesting reparations emerged in the 1890s. It began amid racial segregation and the denial of civil rights to elderly former slaves, most of whom lived in extreme poverty. Spearheaded by the National Ex-Slave Mutual Relief, Bounty and Pension Association, the movement had approximately 600,000 members. One of its leaders was former slave Callie House, a mother of five who worked as a washerwoman in Nashville, Tennessee. Movement leaders lobbied Congress to create pensions for former slaves, and their children, as redress for the many years of unpaid labor provided during slavery. In support of a pension bill before Congress at the time, famed African American abolitionist Frederick Douglass wrote:

> The nation has sinned against the Negro. It robbed him of the rewards of his labor during more than 200 years, and its repentance will not be genuine and complete till according to the measure of its ability, it shall have made restitution.

No pension bill for African Americans was ever passed by Congress.

During the 1960s, some Black leaders revived the idea of reparations. In 1969, James Forman (then head of the Student Non-Violent Coordinating Committee) proclaimed a "Black Manifesto," demanding $500 million from American churches and synagogues for their role in perpetuating slavery before The Civil War. Other civil rights leaders, including the Reverend Jesse Jackson, expressed support for the manifesto. Several other Black organizations demanded reparations from businesses, government, or both.

In the 1980s, a new call arose for Black reparations. It was stimulated by two other movements that successfully secured payments from the U.S. government. The Supreme Court in 1980 ordered the federal government to pay eight Sioux Indian tribes $122 million to compensate for the illegal seizure of tribal lands in 1877. Then, in 1988, Congress approved the payment of $1.25 billion to 60,000 Japanese Americans ($20,000 to each victim) still alive from among the 120,000 who had been interned in prison camps during World War II. Advocates of reparations for African Americans also cited as a precedent payments by Germany to Holocaust victims and to the state of Israel for the atrocities committed against Jews by the Nazis.

In 1989, Representative John Conyers of Michigan introduced a bill in the U.S. House of Representatives called the Commission to Study Reparation Proposals for African Americans Act (now commonly known as HR 40). The preamble to the bill stated its purpose:

> To acknowledge the fundamental injustice, cruelty, brutality and inhumanity of slavery in the United States and the 13 American colonies between 1619 and 1865 and to establish a Commission to examine the institution of slavery,

subsequent de jure and de facto and economic discrimination against African-Americans, and the impact of these forces on living African-Americans, to make recommendations to the Congress on appropriate remedies, and for other purposes.

(*De jure* discrimination refers to discrimination mandated by law or established by government policy, whereas *de facto* discrimination refers to voluntary discrimination by private individuals or groups.) Representative Conyers's bill did not make it to a vote on the floor of the House. He reintroduced it at every new term of Congress between 1989 and 2017 but it was never brought to a vote.

The leading civil rights organization in the United States, the National Association for the Advancement of Colored People (NAACP), endorsed reparations in 1993. In 2001, the United Nations World Conference Against Racism, Racial Discrimination, Xenophobia, and Related Intolerance recognized slavery and the Atlantic slave trade as crimes against humanity.

Also in 2001, African American lawyer Randall Robinson published *The Debt: What America Owes To Blacks*. He did not call for direct cash payments to individuals. Rather, he proposed that the federal government set up a trust from which education, housing, and job training would be funded for African Americans.

Advocates assert that reparations are due to a people who for centuries were exploited, degraded, brutalized, persecuted, segregated, and killed. They point out that White supremacy was often imposed by state and local governments, and by the federal government, in schools, courts, employment, the armed services, lunchrooms, real estate, law-enforcement, housing, etc. They contend that the effects of these deprivations are still with us, and that justice requires compensating past injuries, not merely forbidding their repetition.

Many others, however, have voiced opposition to reparations. Among their arguments are:

- White people were not alone in conducting the Atlantic slave trade. Black African rulers and middlemen who participated in slavery and furnished enslaved captives to White slave merchants share in the responsibility.
- An estimated 3,000 slaveholders in the U.S. were Black. Would their descendants be eligible for reparations?
- There are no Black slaves living today. Slavery ended more than 150 years ago at the cost of several hundred thousand lives lost in The Civil War. It is unfair to ask American taxpayers, many of them from families that came to the United States after slavery ended, to pay for the wrongs of slavery.
- On almost all measures, socioeconomic disparities persist between Whites and Blacks in the United States. Yet, without financial reparations, conditions for African Americans have been on a trajectory of improvement. For example, between 1974 and 2014, the percentage of Blacks living in poverty declined

from 30% to 26%; between 1964 and 2012, the percentage of Blacks with college degrees increased from 4% to 23%; the rate of high school completion between 1964 and 2015 rose from 27% to 88%; median household income (in constant dollars) between 1967 and 2014 rose from $24,700 to $43,300; the unemployment rate dropped between 1967 and 2014 from 12.9% to 10.3%; in 1940 there were very few Black elected officials, whereas there are many thousands today.

- Federal and state governments have already spent billions of dollars on social programs such as welfare, public housing, health care, and employment, to redress the effects of past discrimination.

- Governments, universities, and companies have already addressed the legacy of slavery and Jim Crow through programs in hiring and college admission that favor African Americans.

- Local, state, and federal laws preventing future race discrimination have been enacted.

- A reparations program would expand to other groups who have been mal-treated in the United States: Native Americans whose lands were taken from them; Mexican Americans who were deprived by the Mexican-American War of the right to migrate to their former country; Chinese Americans whose labor was exploited and who were victims of the Chinese Exclusion Act; children whose labor was exploited; women who were denied political equality and property rights.

- African Americans would be better served to overcome the effects of discrim-ination through their own efforts rather than demand reparations that cast them as dependent victims. Identity as an aggrieved victim can undermine personal responsibility and can create perceptions of inferiority.

- Our nation's resources are not unlimited. Reparations payments amounting to billions of dollars each year would limit the country's ability to address worthy demands on the federal budget. Cost estimates for reparations range beyond a trillion dollars, some as high as trillions. As a *New York Times* edi-torial lamented in response to the Black Manifesto: "There is neither wealth nor wisdom enough to compensate in money for all the wrongs in history."

- Any reparation plan would lead to perplexing questions of fairness regarding how it would work: Three-fourths of Black people do not live in poverty. Who would qualify for reparations? Would well-off African Americans receive payments? Would Black people who emigrated from African, Latin American, or Caribbean countries in recent times receive payment? Who would qualify as Black? Who would pay? What amounts would be paid?

- Race-conscious reparations would be resented by many among the dwindling majority of White people in the United States and would thereby compound racial conflict in the country.

- The precedent of reparations payments to Japanese Americans interned during World War II is not comparable. Those payments were made directly to the individuals actually interned. Reparations for African Americans would be paid not to those directly wronged but to their descendants, and to some whose ancestors were not wronged.

- The analogy of German government reparations to Israel and individual Jewish victims of the Nazis is not parallel. Those payments were made to a nation-state and to actual victims, not to generations that followed them.

Whether Americans of African descent should receive compensation for 250 years of bondage and a century of Jim Crow that followed persists as a vexing public controversy. Referring to the nation's racial history during his 2008 campaign for president, then Senator Barack Obama quoted American novelist William Faulkner: "The past is never dead. It's not even past."

The major sources for this chapter were:

Araujo, A. L. (2017). *Reparations for slavery and the slave trade.* London, UK and New York, NY: Bloomsbury.

Bittker, B. I. (2003). *The case for Black reparations.* Boston, MA: Beacon Press.

Coates, T-N. (2014, June). The case for reparations. *The Atlantic.* Available at http://www. theatlantic.com/features/archive/2014/05/the-case-for-reparations/361631/

Frum, D. (2014, June). The impossibility of reparations. *The Atlantic.* Available at: https://www.theatlantic.com/business/archive/2014/06/the-impossibility-of-reparations/372041/

Rothstein, R. (2017). *The color of law.* New York, NY: Liveright Publishing.

LEARNING ACTIVITIES FOR "FORTY ACRES AND A MULE"

Facts of the Case

1. Briefly describe the conditions experienced by those enslaved in the American colonies and later in the states.
2. How did Whites in the American colonies, and later in the states, benefit from enslavement of Black people?
3. What is the origin of the slogan "40 acres and a mule"?
4. Briefly describe the following: sharecropping, convict leasing, restrictive covenant, redlining, and blockbusting.
5. Describe ways that racial discrimination prevented African Americans from gaining wealth.
6. What is HR 40?

Historical Understanding

1. Briefly describe the Atlantic slave trade.
2. What were the Black Codes?
3. What were major changes brought about during Reconstruction?
4. What is the Ku Klux Klan (KKK)?
5. In what ways did the federal government deny equality to African Americans?
6. What kinds of racial discrimination were prohibited by the Civil Rights Acts of the 1960s?

Expressing Your Reasoning

Should Representative John Conyers have introduced HR 40 in Congress? Why or why not?

Key Concepts from History

What do the following have in common?

1. The Philadelphia Plan was a federal program established in 1967 to remedy the effects of past discrimination. The plan mandated timelines and goals for building contractors in Philadelphia to hire members of minority groups.
2. In 2003, a case involving the University of Michigan Law School policy of giving special consideration to applicants from minority groups reached the Supreme Court. The law school's intensely competitive admission process aimed for "a mix of students with varying backgrounds and experiences who will respect and learn from one another." Test scores and undergraduate performance were the most important criteria in selecting applicants for admission, but the law school also examined other factors in making its admissions decisions, including the race and ethnicity of the candidates. "Underrepresented" racial and ethnic minority applicants (African Americans, Latinos, and Native Americans) were looked upon favorably because they helped achieve the school's mission of student diversity. The consideration of race and ethnicity in admissions increased the number of students from minority groups enrolled in the law school.
3. In 1977, New Jersey adopted a state law, the Casino Control Act, for licensing casinos in Atlantic City. The act requires that casino licensees take steps "to ensure that women, minorities and persons with disabilities are recruited and employed at all levels of the operation's work force." Those holding a license to operate a gaming casino are required to increase the representation of women and minorities in job titles within categories established by the federal Equal Employment Opportunities Commission in which the casino licensee is below the goals established by the Casino Control Act.

Historical Inquiry

In the 1968 case of *Regents of the University of California v. Bakke,* the U.S. Supreme Court ruled that "affirmative action" in college admissions was permitted under the Constitution. Affirmative action in that case referred to a higher education institution's choice to consider race as part of the application process. Has college enrollment of Black students increased since the ruling in the Bakke case?

Using online and other sources, test the hypothesis that enrollment of Black students at colleges has increased since the *Bakke* decision. Compose a short essay in which you accept or reject the hypothesis, using evidence to support your conclusion. To begin your investigation, the following search terms will be helpful:

- *Regents of the University of California v. Bakke*
- *Grutter v. Bollinger*
- Abigail Fisher affirmative action case
- Affirmative action in college admissions
- Effects of affirmative action in college admissions

CHAPTER 38

Bake Me a Cake
Wedding Cakes and the Constitution

Groom Figurines on Wedding Cake

It was not possible for David Mullins and Charlie Craig, two gay men, to marry in their home state of Colorado in 2012 (it was made legal in 2014). They planned to marry in Massachusetts, a state that allowed same-sex marriage. Following the wedding, they would have a reception in Colorado that family and friends could attend.

In July 2012, Mullins, Craig, and Craig's mother visited Masterpiece Cakeshop in Lakewood, Colorado. The three wanted to order a beautiful cake for the two men's wedding reception after their return from Massachusetts. Even before Mullins and Craig could describe the design, colors, and decorations for the cake they wanted to order, Jack Phillips, the owner of Masterpiece Cakeshop, refused their order. He said he would gladly make brownies or other items for the reception—anything except a cake. He explained that his religious beliefs prevented him from making a wedding cake for same-sex couples. It was his "standard business practice not to provide cakes for same-sex weddings."

Phillips described his refusal more specifically in an interview after the incident became a media story: "If gays come in and want to order birthday cakes or any cakes for any occasion, graduations, or whatever, I have no prejudice against that whatsoever. It's just the wedding cake—not the people, not their lifestyle." He also said cake decoration is an art form that he practices to honor God.

Phillips is not alone in refusing to provide services for lesbian, gay, bisexual, and transgender (LGBT) customers. Some service vendors (usually businesses with a single owner) defend this practice. They claim that the laws prohibiting discrimination against LGBT customers violate their First Amendment right to freedom of speech by compelling them to engage in speech they don't agree with. Further, they claim that forcing them to "honor," "celebrate," or "participate in" a same-sex marriage violates their right to "free exercise of religion," also guaranteed by the First Amendment to the Constitution.

Masterpiece Cakeshop's policy was not limited to celebrations by same-sex couples. Phillips also refused cake orders that celebrated Halloween, that were made of alcohol, or featured anti-American themes. He even refused to make a celebratory half-cake for a man getting a divorce. In defense of Phillips, Kristen Waggoner, senior counsel for the Alliance Defending Freedom (ADF), an American Christian nonprofit organization that supports religious freedom, the sanctity of life, and marriage and family, explained:

> The First Amendment protects Jack's right to create artistic expression that is consistent with his core convictions. Individuals can support both same-sex marriage and Jack, and people should have the right to disagree on critical matters of conscience. The same government that can force Jack to violate his faith and conscience can force any one of us to do the same.

Mullins and Craig left the shop—stunned and humiliated. Mullins later described the 20-second exchange with Phillips: "It was the most awkward, surreal, very brief encounter." Mullins's post on Facebook about the experience generated a great deal of attention. As the result of reviews on Yelp, the shop's ratings plunged from 4 (of possible 5) to below 1. A small crowd protested outside the shop. Some of their signs read: "Love is sweeter" and "Let the gays eat cake."

Mullins and Craig then filed a complaint with Colorado's Civil Rights Commission. The American Civil Liberties Union (ACLU), a nonpartisan, nonprofit organization that defends the rights and liberties of Americans, represented the two men. The ACLU files lawsuits on behalf of clients and attempts to influence or persuade regulators and legislators by lobbying for actions, policies, and decisions. The ACLU argument in the Mullins and Craig complaint was that Phillips had violated Colorado's Anti-Discrimination Act (CADA).

The Colorado legislature passed CADA in 1951. The act established Colorado's first fair employment law for employees of government agencies. A 1957 amendment to the act repealed the ban on interracial marriage and extended the fair employment law to employees of private businesses. Another amendment, passed in 2008, banned discrimination on the basis of sexual orientation in housing sales and rentals, in public accommodations (such as hotels, restaurants, and theaters), and by all businesses that offer "goods and services" to the public. Although Focus on the Family, an American Christian conservative organization, fiercely opposed the 2008 amendment, Colorado Governor Bill Ritter signed the anti-discrimination bill into law.

Federal law prohibits discrimination in several areas. The Civil Rights Act of 1964 outlawed discrimination based on race, color, religion, sex, or national origin. The Civil Rights Act does not mention sexual orientation. Various federal appeals courts have ruled on the issue of whether sex discrimination applies to claims based on sexual orientation; the rulings from these courts are inconsistent.

In December 2013, Judge Robert Spencer at the Colorado Office of Administrative Courts concluded that Masterpiece Cakeshop had violated the state law, CADA, in its treatment of Mullins and Craig. The Colorado Civil Rights Division reached the same conclusion. After this ruling, David Mullins stated: "Being denied service by Masterpiece Cakeshop was offensive and dehumanizing especially in the midst of arranging what should be a joyful family celebration. No one should fear being turned away from a public business because of who they are."

Masterpiece Cakeshop appealed the decision to the Colorado Court of Appeals. In the appeal, Jack Phillips claimed the government was forcing him to approve same-sex marriage. He argued that cake decoration is "a form of art" that he practices to honor God, and that creating cakes for same-sex marriages "would displease God."

In August 2015, the Colorado Court of Appeals agreed, in an unanimous decision, that Masterpiece Cakeshop had discriminated against Mullins and Craig. The court stated that Phillips could not use his religious beliefs to refuse service to same-sex couples. The court also stated that Phillips would be fined if the shop continued to discriminate against same-sex couples. Phillips was also ordered to offer his employees "comprehensive staff training" on the new policy and to provide the court with quarterly reports on the shop's customer dealings. In April 2016, Masterpiece Cakeshop again appealed the decision; the Colorado Supreme Court declined to take the case, and thereby affirmed the lower court's decision. The next (and last) chance for Masterpiece Cakeshop was to appeal to the U.S. Supreme Court, and in July 2016, Masterpiece Cakeshop, with the support of the Alliance Defending Freedom, petitioned the U.S. Supreme Court for a review of the case.

On June 26, 2017, the U.S. Supreme Court announced that it would hear the case, *Masterpiece Cakeshop, Ltd. v. Colorado Civil Rights Commission*, during the 2017–2018 term. The issue in the case is the following, as stated in the petition for a writ of certiorari (a legal order for the lower court to send the records of the case for the justices to review) filed on July 22, 2016:

> Whether applying Colorado's public accommodations law to compel Phillips to create expression that violates his sincerely held religious beliefs about marriage violates the Free Speech or the Free Exercise of Religion Clause of the First Amendment.

The U.S. Supreme Court receives, on average, 10,000 petitions a year for review of cases that have been previously decided in the lower courts. To be granted review by the Supreme Court, a case must involve an issue of federal law or fall within the jurisdiction of the federal courts. The justices generally do not accept cases that involve only state law. They are more likely to accept cases in which their decision will have a constitutional impact, cases that deal with important legal questions, cases that present issues on which lower federal court decisions are in conflict, and cases that affect the entire population rather than just the petitioners and the respondents in the cases. There are no juries and no witnesses in cases heard by the Supreme Court. The justices have three choices when they review a petition for review of a case: (1) decline to take the case, (2) affirm the lower court's decision without hearing arguments, or (3) decide to hear the case. If at least four of the nine justices decide to hear the case, they issue a writ of certiorari. Typically, the court hears about 75 to 85 cases a year.

The nine justices are appointed to the U.S. Supreme Court for life. When appointed to the U.S. Supreme Court, the justices take two oaths: one oath to support the U.S. Constitution and a second oath to administer justice equally and impartially. Each justice has an equal vote on all cases that are decided by majority vote. (A case might be decided on a 5–4 vote). It is assumed that the justices reflect their judicial views, personal ideologies, and political philosophies in their decisions. Of the nine justices on the U.S. Supreme Court at the time of this writing, four justices are assumed to represent the "liberal wing" of the Court: Associate Justice Stephen Breyer, Associate Justice Ruth Bader Ginsburg, Associate Justice Elena Kagan, and Associate Justice Sonia Sotomayor. Four justices are assumed to represent the "conservative wing" of the Court: Associate Justice Samuel A. Alito, Jr.; Associate Justice Neil Gorsuch; Chief Justice John G. Roberts, Jr.; and Associate Justice Clarence Thomas. Associate Justice Anthony Kennedy is often the "swing vote" because he sometimes votes with the conservative wing and sometimes with the liberal wing.

The U.S. Supreme Court has reviewed a number of cases related to LGBT rights. In the 2015 case *Obergefell v. Hodges*, the Court ruled in a 5–4 decision that same-sex couples were guaranteed the fundamental right to marry by both the due process clause and the equal protection clause of the Fourteenth Amendment to the U.S. Constitution. Four Justices dissented from the majority opinion in *Obergefell v. Hodges*: Alito, Roberts, Scalia, and Thomas. According to a 2017 survey by the Pew Research Center, the majority of Americans think same-sex marriages should be legal (62% in favor, 32% opposed).

Although gay rights activists and supporters saw the case generally as a victory, they were concerned about the following statement in the opinion, which was written by Justice Kennedy: "[T]hose who adhere to religious doctrines may continue to advocate with utmost, sincere conviction that, by divine precepts, same-sex marriage should not be condoned." This statement may have implications for future "public accommodation" cases, including the pending case of *Masterpiece Cakeshop, Ltd. v. Colorado Civil Rights Commission*.

In June 2017, in *Pavan v. Smith*, the U.S. Supreme Court ruled in a 7–3 decision that the U.S. Constitution requires the states to list married same-sex couples on their children's birth certificate. LGBT rights advocates claimed a victory. Justices Alito, Thomas, and Gorsuch dissented from the majority opinion.

The U.S. Supreme Court has heard many cases related to the religious freedom clauses of the First Amendment to the U.S. Constitution. Some of the recent cases relate to the Religious Freedom Restoration Act (RFRA) of 1993. This federal law "ensures that interests in religious freedom are protected." However, in a 1997 case, *City of Boerne v. Flores*, the U.S. Supreme Court ruled that the RFRA was unconstitutional because it was not a proper exercise of Congress's enforcement power under Section 5 of the Fourteenth Amendment. The Supreme Court ruled that RFRA overstepped Congress's authority. The High Court held that although Congress could enact legislation such as the RFRA in order to prevent abuses of religious freedom, it did not have the authority to determine ways that states could enforce the legislation. In response, 21 states have passed state Religious Freedom Restoration Acts that apply to state governments and local municipalities. Colorado has not passed such an act.

Although the RFRA was ruled unconstitutional in its application to the states (because it was seen as an overreach of Congress's authority), it continues to be applied at the federal level. In a 2014 case, *Burwell v. Hobby Lobby*, the U.S. Supreme Court ruled in a 5–4 decision that private companies could be exempt from an Affordable Care Act regulation that owners objected to on the grounds that it violated their free exercise of religion. In this case, the High Court held that Hobby Lobby, a private corporation of arts and crafts stores, could not be required to pay female employees' birth control costs under its health-care plan.

The U.S. Supreme Court has also heard many cases related to the freedom of speech clause of the First Amendment to the U.S. Constitution. One case that is relevant for *Masterpiece Cakeshop, Ltd. v. Colorado Civil Rights Commission* is the 2005 case *Rumsfeld v. Forum for Academic and Institutional Rights, Inc.* In this case, some law schools, represented by the Forum for Academic and Institutional Rights, argued for the right to refuse military recruiters access to their campuses.

Their justification was the official U.S. policy on military service: the "Don't ask, don't tell" (DADT) policy of 1994.

Under the DADT policy, discrimination and harassment against closeted homosexual or bisexual service members were forbidden. DADT, however, barred non-closeted lesbian and gay persons from serving in the military. Because they objected to the military's discrimination against openly gay people, some law school administrators and deans tried to restrict military recruiting on their campuses.

In response, Congress passed the 1996 Solomon Amendment, which required colleges and universities that received federal funds to allow military recruiters onto their campuses. In 2006, in *Rumsfeld v. Forum for Academic and Institutional Rights, Inc.*, the Supreme Court ruled 8–0 that the Solomon Amendment was constitutional and that the federal government could withhold funding from colleges and universities that denied access to military recruiters. The Court explained that by allowing recruiters onto their campuses, the law schools were not endorsing the military's policy. Chief Justice Roberts, who authored the opinion, wrote that the Solomon Amendment regulated conduct, not speech, and was therefore constitutional.

Individuals and organizations referred to as *amici curiae* ("the friends of the court") can submit briefs (written arguments) concerning cases before the U.S. Supreme Court. *Amici curiae* are individuals and organizations who are not parties to cases but who have relevant information about cases and a strong interest in them. In the *Masterpiece Cakeshop* case, in 2017 the U.S. government entered an *amicus curiae* brief arguing that "The more fundamental question is the power of a government to compel Americans to frame or speak messages against their conscience." On the other side, James Esseks of the ACLU has stated:

> If businesses get to say, "We're not going to serve you or you or you, because my religion tells me I shouldn't," that undermines every non-discrimination law we have in the country. It's not limited to gays or weddings or bakeries or florists. It allows any business to turn people away based on the business owner's religious beliefs. This is not a small accommodation for religion. This is a serious body blow for civil rights across the country.

Oral arguments for the *Masterpiece Cakeshop* case were heard on December 5, 2017, with a decision expected in spring 2018. Mullins and Craig are represented by the American Civil Liberties Union, a national organization that works to defend individual rights, and liberties and the Colorado Civil Rights Commission is represented by the Colorado solicitor general. Jack Phillips is represented by the Alliance Defending Freedom, an American Christian nonprofit organization that supports religious freedom.

For constitutional scholars, attorneys, politicians, religious and nonreligious people, business owners, the LBGT community, and many others, the case is about much more than a wedding cake. They think the case raises fundamental issues about religious freedom, the role of religion in public life, freedom of speech, citizen equality, and discrimination based on sexual orientation. The decision in *Masterpiece Cakeshop, Ltd. v. Colorado Civil Rights Commission* will have far-reaching effects in all these areas.

The major sources for this chapter were:

Alliance Defending Freedom. (n.d.). Jack Phillips' stand for faith and freedom. Available at https://www.adflegal.org/jack-phillips

Eckholm, E. (2015, March 31). Context for the debate on "religious freedom" measures in Indiana and Arkansas. *The New York Times*. Available at: http://www.nytimes.com/2015/04/01/us/politics/context-for-the-debate-on-religious-freedom-measures-in-indiana-and-arkansas.html?emc=eta1

Green, E. (2015, August 13). Christian bakers gotta bake, even for gays. *The Atlantic Monthly*. Available at: http://www.theatlantic.com/politics/archive/2015/08/in-colorado-christian-bakers-have-bake-even-for-gays/401249/?utm_source=atl-daily-newsletter_

Liptak, A. (2017, June 26). Justices to hear case on religious objection to same-sex marriage. *The New York Times*. Available at: https://www.nytimes.com/2017/06/26/us/politics/supreme-court-wedding-cake-gay-couple-masterpiece-cakeshop.html

Masterpiece Cakeshop, Ltd., v. Colorado civil rights commission: case files. SCOTUSBlog. Available at http://www.scotusblog.com/case files/cases/masterpiece-cakeshop-ltd-v-colorado-civil-rights-commn/

Pew Research Center. (2017). Changing attitudes on gay marriage. Available at: http://www.pewforum.org/fact-sheet/changing-attitudes-on-gay-marriage/

Riley, J. (2015, August 13). Court: Colorado cake shop cannot refuse service to gays. *Metro Weekly*. Available at http://www.metroweekly.com/2015/08/court-colorado-cake-shop-cannot-refuse-service-to-gays/

Riley, J. (2017, June 26). Supreme court to hear case of Colorado bakery that denied service to gay couple. *Metro Weekly*. Available at http://www.metroweekly.com/2017/06/supreme-court-hear-case-colorado-bakery-denied-service-gay-couple/

"S. M." (2017, July 7). Can a baker refuse to make a gay wedding cake? *The Economist*. Available at https://www.economist.com/blogs/democracyinamerica/2017/07/just-desserts

Same-sex couple denied wedding cake by bakery. (2012, July 30). *CBS News*. Available at https://www.cbsnews.com/news/same-sex-couple-denied-wedding-cake-by-bakery/

Torrez, A., & Smith, T. (2017, September 18). OA105: More gay wedding cakes. *Opening Arguments* [podcast]. Available at: http://openargs.com/oa105-gay-wedding-cakes/

LEARNING ACTIVITIES FOR "BAKE ME A CAKE"

Facts of the Case

1. What happened when David Mullins and Charlie Craig tried to order a wedding cake?
2. Why did Jack Phillips refuse to make a wedding cake for David Mullins and Charlie Craig?
3. Who represents Mullins and Craig and the Colorado Civil Rights Commission, and who represents Phillips in *Masterpiece Cakeshop, Ltd. v. Colorado Civil Rights Commission*?

Historical Understanding

1. Describe the rulings in two early 21st-century U.S. Supreme Court cases that relate to gay rights: *Obergefell v. Hodges* and *Pavan v. Smith*.
2. When was same-sex marriage legalized in Colorado and in the United States?
3. What is Colorado's Anti-Discrimination Act (CADA)? How was it amended in 2008?
4. What is the Religious Freedom Restoration Act (RFRA) and how might it apply to *Masterpiece Cakeshop, Ltd. v. Colorado Civil Rights Commission*?
5. Describe the process the U.S. Supreme Court follows when it selects cases for review.

Expressing Your Reasoning

Should Jack Phillips be free to refuse to bake a wedding cake for a gay couple? Why or why not?

Key Concepts from History

What do the following have in common?

1. In the 1942 case *Chaplinsky v. New Hampshire*, the U.S. Supreme Court (in a unanimous decision) upheld the arrest of Walter Chaplinsky, a Jehovah's Witness. Chaplinksy had used a public sidewalk as a pulpit to criticize organized religion as a "racket." His preaching attracted a large crowd and caused a commotion. After a police officer removed him from the scene, Chaplinksy called the town marshal a "God-damned racketeer" and "a damned Fascist." He was charged with "offensive speech" under a New Hampshire law forbidding such speech in a public place. Chaplinsky claimed that the city law violated the First Amendment. The Supreme Court upheld the arrest. Justice Frank Murphy wrote the unanimous decision for the Supreme Court, which reads in part:

There are certain well-defined and narrowly limited classes of speech, the prevention and punishment of which have never been thought to raise any constitutional problem. These include the lewd and obscene, the profane, the libelous, and the insulting or "fighting" words—those which by their very utterance inflict injury or tend to incite an immediate breach of the peace. It has been well observed that such utterances are no essential part of any exposition of ideas, and are of such slight social value as a step to truth that any benefit that may be derived from them is clearly outweighed by the social interest in order and morality.

2. In 1971, Marvin Miller, the owner/operator of a California mail-order business specializing in pornographic films and books, mailed a brochure advertising books and a film that graphically depicted sexual activity between men and women. One recipient of the brochure was a restaurant in Newport Beach, California. The restaurant owner and his mother opened the brochure and then called the police. Miller was arrested for violating a California state law. The case went to the Supreme Court. The question before the Court in *Miller v. California* was whether the sale and distribution of obscene material was protected under the First Amendment's guarantee of freedom of speech. The Court ruled that it was not. It indicated that "obscene material is not protected by the First Amendment." The Court ruled, 5–4, against Miller; in doing so, it redefined obscenity, whose legal definition had been in a confused state for a decade and a half. The Supreme Court developed a three-prong standard, the "Miller Test," for obscenity. In order for material to be declared obscene, a court must determine the following: (1) the average person, using contemporary community standards, would find the work designed to excite lustful thoughts; (2) the material depicts or describes, in an offensive way, sexual conduct prohibited by state law; and (3) the work, as a whole, lacks serious literary, artistic, political, or scientific value.

3. In 1977, former President Gerald Ford contracted with Harper & Row Publishers, Inc., to publish his memoirs. Harper & Row negotiated with *Time Magazine* to publish 7,500 words from Ford's account of his pardon of former President Richard Nixon, prior to the release of the memoirs. Before the *Time Magazine* article was published, however, *The Nation* published a 300-word excerpt from the memoirs. Harper & Row sued *The Nation* for copyright infringement. In the 1985 Supreme Court case *Harper & Row v. Nation Enterprises*, the Court ruled, 6–3, that *The Nation*'s use of the copyrighted material was infringement.

Historical Inquiry

Jack Phillips claims that requiring him to bake a wedding cake for a gay couple would violate his religious liberty guaranteed by the First Amendment to the U.S. Constitution. The First Amendment begins: "Congress shall make no law respecting an *establishment of religion*, or the *free exercise* thereof (emphasis added)." Using online and other resources, test the hypothesis that there can be conflict between the free exercise and establishment clauses of the First Amendment. Compose a short essay in which you explain the meaning of both clauses and then accept or reject the hypothesis that they can conflict with each other. Use evidence to support your conclusion. To begin your investigation, the following search terms will be helpful:

- Free exercise versus establishment clauses
- In God We Trust and establishment clause
- Under God and establishment clause
- Chaplains Corps and establishment clause
- *Aronow v. United States*

CHAPTER 39

Accord Discord

The Paris Climate Accord of 2015

Paris Climate Accord Cartoon

Illustration by Steve Hunter.

On June 1, 2017, President Donald Trump announced he intended to withdraw the United States from the Paris Climate Accord (PCA), an agreement that had been signed by 196 countries in December 2015. On August 4, 2017, the United States Department of State gave formal notification by email to the United Nations that the United States would leave the PCA as soon as possible. According to the signed agreement, the earliest a country could officially withdraw from the PCA is November 2020.

There was intense national and international reaction to the withdrawal statement of President Trump. Many world leaders expressed great disappointment with the withdrawal decision. Environmentalists in the United States believed the withdrawal was a grave mistake. The opponents of the accord were pleased with the president for keeping his campaign promise of taking the United States out of what he had called "a very bad deal."

The Paris Climate Accord is an agreement within the United Nations Framework Convention on Climate Change (UNFCCC) that aims to combat climate change by reducing the global emission of greenhouse gas, adapting to the effects of climate change, and providing a financial means for assisting developing countries (unindustrialized countries with a low standard of living) in these efforts.

The PCA requires that participating countries voluntarily determine their own targets for greenhouse gas reduction and the amounts of their own financial contributions to the fund that assists developing countries. Because both the emission and financial targets are voluntary and nonbinding, countries are able to adjust the targets as they see fit.

Each country is required by the PCA to issue regular reports on its own progress in reducing greenhouse gases. According to the U.S. Environmental Protection Agency, greenhouse gas emissions in the United States increased by 7% from 1990 to 2014, but decreased by 7% from 2005 to 2014. Much of this later improvement was the result of using natural gas, which is found deep underground in large quantities and emits one-half the greenhouse gas that coal does.

Greenhouse gases are various compounds that trap heat in the Earth's lower atmosphere keeping the planet warmer than it would be otherwise. The molecular composition of the compounds allows the gases to absorb solar heat and then reflect it toward Earth. This process is called "the greenhouse effect" because, as in a greenhouse, solar energy is trapped, causing higher temperatures.

Greenhouse gases enter the Earth's atmosphere as a result of human activity such as the burning of fossil fuels, including coal and natural gas. Fossil fuels were formed from the decomposition of living organisms in the distant geological past. Intensive livestock production, use of fertilizers, and industrial processes all add greenhouse gases to the atmosphere. Deforestation also contributes by removal of trees that would have removed carbon dioxide, a greenhouse gas, from the atmosphere.

The principal compounds found in greenhouse gases are carbon dioxide (CO_2), methane (CH_4), nitrous oxide (N_2O), and fluorinated gases (gases created by humans that can remain in the atmosphere for centuries, such as those found in refrigeration and air conditioning systems).

Many questions swirl around the growing emission of greenhouse gases: What is climate change? Is it really happening? If so, to what extent, if any, is it the result of human activity? Can the natural processes of the Earth's atmosphere effectively manage the effects of greenhouse gases?

Climate is the pattern of weather in a region over an extended period of time. Global warming refers to the increase in the average temperature of the Earth. Climate change refers to the effects of warming, over time, on regional and global weather patterns.

At least 95% of climate scientists believe that current climate change is a result of the increased use of fossil fuels during the 20th century. Less than 5% of climate scientists are skeptical of both the extent of climate change and the degree to which it is being caused by human activity. The skeptics attribute change in the climate to natural fluctuations of temperatures on Earth, and they believe the Earth and its atmosphere can adapt naturally, and harmlessly, to the increased levels of greenhouse gases.

One of the first warnings of climate change came in the 1988 testimony of scientists before a congressional committee. National Aeronautics and Space Administration (NASA) scientist and climate change expert Dr. James E. Hanson testified that increase in global temperature was not the result of natural processes, but rather of greenhouse gases, especially carbon dioxide. For many people, Hanson's widely publicized testimony marked the first time they had heard the expressions "global warming," "climate change," and "the greenhouse effect."

The scientific debate over climate change and its extent, causes, and effects has taken on political, economic, and social dimensions. Many Republicans have been skeptical of climate change and resist government efforts to control it. Most Democrats believe that it is occurring, largely as a result of human activity, and that it is dangerous. They tend to favor laws and policies to counteract climate change.

During the presidential campaign of 2016, Republican candidate Donald Trump pledged to remove environmental regulations that limited coal production and employment in the coal industry. Most climate scientists agree that burning of coal is the largest contributor to greenhouse gas emissions. Candidate Trump called climate change a "hoax" that benefits China's economic competitiveness over that of the United States.

Some business leaders resist costly regulations by the federal government to control greenhouse gas emissions. Those skeptical of claims about the effects of climate change oppose government mandated solutions. Other companies—for example, Shell, Exxon, Apple, and Facebook—maintain that climate change threatens great harm, and they support PCA. Like many environmentalists, leaders of these companies and other company leaders also support use of newer, cleaner energy sources that they expect will become less expensive than coal and oil.

Convinced that PCA is socially and environmentally responsible, some companies want to be able to compete with foreign corporations in the development of energy innovations that are encouraged by the accord. These companies suspect that the withdrawal from the PCA could put them at a disadvantage when competing with companies from other countries whose governments provide subsidies to help meet their own PCA emission reduction targets.

Many workers in the coal, oil, and gas industries fear government regulation to control greenhouse gases. They believe that newer, clean energy sources, such as solar and wind power, will result in the loss of jobs in the fossil fuel industries.

Environmentalists, and many others, believe climate change is real and will cause harmful effects on humans. A Yale University climate change poll in 2016 found that 70% of Americans believe that climate change is occurring. In the poll, 58% of Americans said they are worried about the effects of climate change. The poll also found significant majorities supporting more government action to reduce these effects.

As part of the PCA, President Obama pledged in 2015 to reduce the U.S. greenhouse gas emissions by 26–28% by 2025. He also pledged $3 billion to the Green Climate Fund that is to be used by developing nations to combat the causes and effects of climate change. China and the United States, the first and second largest contributors to greenhouse gas emissions, worked closely in the Accord's development and adoption.

Obama pledged the United States' commitment to the PCA through executive order rather than seeking a formal adoption by the U.S. Senate. The president justified his decision by claiming the terms of the agreement were voluntary and not binding, and therefore it did not have to be treated as a treaty requiring Senate confirmation. Both executive orders and treaties are official agreements between the United States and foreign nations. A main difference between the two is that a treaty must by approved by two-thirds of the U.S. Senate. It was unlikely that President Obama, a Democrat, would have been successful in having the accord approved by a Senate controlled by Republicans with a majority of 54 Senators.

President Trump proclaimed, "In order to fulfill my solemn duty to protect America and its citizens, the United States will withdraw from the Paris Climate Accord." Because the U.S. committed to the PCA through executive agreement, President Trump was free to remove the country from the agreement without approval from Congress. He offered these reasons for withdrawing from the accord:

- PCA is unfair to the United States because greenhouse emission targets established by China and India gave these countries a competitive edge. As the president put it:

  While the current agreement effectively blocks the development of clean coal in America, China will be allowed to build hundreds of additional coal plants. So we can't build the plants but they can. According to the agreement, India will be allowed to double its coal production by 2020. Think of it. India can double their coal production. We're suppose to get rid of ours.

- The accord would result in the loss of 2.7 million American jobs by 2025, according to a study by the National Economic Research Associates (NERA, a conservative economic consulting firm whose reports were relied upon by President Trump in announcing the withdrawal form PAC).

- The accord would only reduce the Earth's temperature by a minuscule two-tenths of 1° Fahrenheit.
- The accord would reduce the gross domestic product (GDP), an overall measurement of the nation's wealth, by $3 trillion. It would result in the average household income being reduced by $7,000 a year.
- The accord's reduction in the use of fossil fuels would create an energy demand crisis that would cause energy companies to have periodic losses or reductions of electricity (blackouts and brownouts, respectively) for their customers.
- The accord's pledge of $3 billion by the United States to the fund is twice the amount any other nation committed.

Vice President Mike Pence called the Paris Climate Accord "a transfer of wealth from the wealthiest country to others." Republican congressional leaders called the withdrawal a victory for the middle class, workers, businesses, and coal miners.

The critics of President Trump's PCA withdrawal wasted no time in responding to his reasons for leaving the agreement. Critics claimed that instead of reducing jobs, the PCA would create more jobs as the result of developing clean-energy innovations like solar and wind power. In addition, the World Resources Institute cited the NERA study as flawed. The study maintains it did not account for greenhouse gas reductions that would take place in non-industrial sectors of the economy. The study further did not allow for clean-energy innovations that would take place by 2025.

The president's critics discounted his China and India argument by claiming that both countries are moving away as fast as possible from coal as a source of energy and will likely reach their targeted emission goals early. PCA supporters maintained that a reduction in the increase of the Earth's temperature by less than 2° Celsius (3.6° Fahrenheit) would not be trivial and would help reduce the impacts of climate change on the planet.

As additional rebuttal to the president's reasoning, his critics maintained that the cost of upholding the accord would be less than three-tenths of 1% of GDP and would not damage the economy. Moreover, critics of the president's claim that blackouts and brownouts are most often caused by natural events like inclement weather and heat waves that are made worse by global warming.

Finally, critics addressed the cost of remaining within the accord. Acknowledging that the U.S. contribution to the Green Climate Fund was expensive, they pointed out that the United States accounts for one-third of all greenhouse gas emissions. They also cited the cost per capita. When computed this way, the cost to the United States' contribution would amount to $9.30 per person. By comparison, Sweden's per capita pledge was $60.54 per person.

Because countries that initially agreed to the accord cannot formally withdraw until 2020, the United States is required under the provisions of the accord to continue to report regularly on its greenhouse gas emissions. The State

Department also announced in August 2017 that it will continue to attend meetings of the UNFCCC so it can look after the interests of the United States.

In May 2017, at the Group of Seven (G7) meeting, President Trump was the only national leader who did not reaffirm a commitment to the Paris Climate Accord and to fostering clean energy development. The G7 is a forum for highly industrialized democracies to coordinate economic, security, and energy policy. The seven nations of the G7 are Canada, France, Germany, Italy, Japan, the United Kingdom, and the United States. (The European Union is also represented.) Other leaders expressed great disappointment with President Trump's position. Over his objections, they adopted a strong Climate and Energy Action Plan for Growth. The plan reconfirms the commitment to the Paris Accord, describes action to implement the accord, and sets forth specific ways of helping all countries reach their targeted goals.

President Trump's PCA withdrawal decision was a victory for the Cooler Heads Coalition. The coalition is a politically conservative group that is operated and financed by the Competitive Enterprise Institute. It represents nonprofit organizations pursuing a 2-decade campaign to convince the public and members of Congress that the seriousness of climate change has been greatly exaggerated. Members of the coalition have opposed state and federal efforts to address climate change. Some of them refer to climate change as a "hoax" and environmentalists as "global-warming alarmists."

The coalition has collected millions of dollars from the coal and oil industry, as well as from non-profit foundations that are skeptical about climate change and its causes and effects. The coalition is not legally required to report sources of revenue because it claims it is a nonpartisan educational organization that does not have lobbying of Congress as a primary purpose or method of operation.

The Cooler Heads Coalition was consulted on environmental issues during the Trump campaign. As part of the presidential transition following President Trump's election, Myron Ebell, head of the coalition, served as the director for issues relating to the Environmental Protection Agency. Ebell believes that climate change debate is about ideology. The coalition maintains that unless environmental regulations are curbed, they will undermine free enterprise and the economy.

Although he acknowledges that climate change is real and that humans are playing a role in it, Ebell believes it is a "scam" by climate researchers hoping to continue their work by obtaining government research grants for the study of climate change. Ebell and several of his colleagues were invited to the briefing at the White House for President Trump's withdrawal announcement.

Some climate change scientists who support the reduction of greenhouse gases question whether the PCA will have a positive impact on climate change. They believe the accord's provisions are too weak and would have a very small chance of succeeding. Worldwide industrialization with expanded burning of fossil fuels, they maintain, will doom the accord, as it is, to failure. Others, for example

Adrian Rafferty, a climate change expert from the University of Washington, believe PCA's call for a temperature increase of less than 2° Celsius (3.6° Fahrenheit) is both realistic and ambitious, but will be inadequate. His research suggests global warming may well grow to between 2° and 4.9° Celsius by 2100 (3.6° and 4.82° Fahrenheit, respectively). He notes, "If we want to avoid climate change we have very little time left."

Those who believe that climate change is real and has been significantly caused by human activity identify five main adverse and interrelated causes and effects on the Earth's climate. Climate change skeptics (and remember, only 5% or less of scientists in the field are skeptical) have a rebuttal for each:

1. **Human Involvement.** Studies show that more than 95% of climate scientists believe that human activity is causing climate change. Skeptics maintain that climate change is mostly the result of natural causes and that the planet is capable of adapting to climate changes caused by human activity.

2. **Temperature.** Studies of tree rings, ice cores, and corals over the past millennium show the Earth is getting warmer, as much as 2.5° Fahrenheit over the past 250 years and 1.5° Fahrenheit over the past 50 years. Skeptics argue that increases in carbon dioxide will eventually saturate the atmosphere and reduce infrared radiation that causes warming, and that fluctuations in the intensity of the sun contribute to global warming.

3. **Oceans.** Sea-level temperatures, levels, and acidification (an increase in acid content due to the ocean's increase absorption of carbon dioxide from the atmosphere) are rising at an unprecedented rate because of global warming. Increases in sea levels threaten to flood low-lying areas in the world. Rising temperatures and acidification threaten marine species and coral reefs. Skeptics reply that sea levels have been rising for thousands of years, and assert that the acidity increases are the result of natural fluctuation. They also assert that claims of rising sea levels are based on faulty computer models.

4. **Polar Regions.** In the two polar regions of the world, glaciers are melting. There has been a reduction in Arctic Sea ice, and both ice sheets and permafrost (a thick subsurface layer of soil that remains below freezing throughout the year) are melting. Skeptics counter that over the past 16 years the Earth has not warmed significantly even though there has been a substantial increase in greenhouse gas emissions. In addition, much of the melting in the polar regions, they claim, is due to naturally occurring changes in ocean currents.

5. **Extreme Events.** Droughts, heat waves, heavier storms, and the decline of snow cover in many places are all attributable to climate change caused by humans. This includes their intensity, frequency, and duration, as well as the number of Category 4 and Category 5 hurricanes. Climate change skeptics reply that these are all the result of naturally occurring weather patterns and not activity by humans.

Although President Trump is a climate change skeptic who declared, "I was elected to represent Pittsburgh, not Paris," he did not close the door permanently on the Paris Climate Accord. He said he was open and willing to a renegotiation that resulted in a better deal for America, one that was "more favorable to its business, its workers, its people, and its taxpayers."

The major sources for this chapter were:

Is human activity primarily responsible for climate change? (n.d.). *ProCon.org*. Available at https://climatechange.procon.org/

Kessler, G., & Lee, M. Y. H. (2017, June 1). Fact-checking President Trump's claims on the Paris climate change deal. *The Washington Post*. Available at https://www.washingtonpost.com/news/fact-checker/wp/2017/06/01/fact-checking-president-trumps-claims-on-the-paris-climate-change-deal/?utm_term=.788e139a7920

O'Harrow, R., Jr. (2017, September 5). A two-decade crusade by conservative charities fueled Trump's exit from the Paris climate accord. *The Washington Post*. Available at https://www.washingtonpost.com/investigations/a-two-decade-crusade-by-conservative-charities-fueled-trumps-exit-from-paris-climate-accord/2017/09/05/fcb8d9fe-6726-11e7-9928-22d00a47778f_story.html?utm_term=.8946e431cec3

Shear, M. (2017, June 1). Trump will withdraw U.S. from Paris Climate Agreement. *The New York Times*. Available at https://www.nytimes.com/2017/06/01/climate/trump-paris-climate-agreement.html

Varinsky, D., Mosher, D., & Schwartz, A. (2017, June 1). 5 claims Trump used to justify pulling the U.S. out of the Paris Agreement—and the reality. *Business Insider*. Available at http://www.businessinsider.com/fact-check-trump-reasons-for-leaving-paris-agreement-2017-6

Worland, J. (2017, July 8). Why Trump pulling out of the Paris Agreement led to a stronger Climate Change Plan. *Time*. Available at http://time.com/4850421/g20-trump-paris-agreement-climate-change/

LEARNING ACTIVITIES FOR "ACCORD DISCORD"

Facts of the Case

1. What are the aims of the Paris Climate Accord (PCA)?
2. What are greenhouse gases and what is the greenhouse effect?
3. How are the PCA targets for emission reduction and financial contributions to the Green Planet Fund determined?
4. What is the relationship between global warming and climate change?
5. What were the primary reasons President Trump offered for withdrawal of the United States from the PCA?

Historical Understanding

1. What role is played by electoral politics in environmental protection?
2. Why did President Obama use an executive agreement to enter into the PCA?
3. What are the primary concerns of environmentalists about climate change?
4. What are the primary arguments of PCA skeptics about climate change?

Expressing Your Reasoning

Should President Trump have withdrawn the United States from the Paris Climate Accord? Why or why not?

Key Concepts from History

What do the following have in common?

1. Rachel Carson wrote *Silent Spring* in 1962. The book describes the harmful effect on the environment of synthetic pesticides (chemicals designed to kill living organisms, such as insects). Her book accused chemical companies of spreading disinformation about the safety of pesticides, and public officials of blindly accepting the untruths. Her book helped create environmental concern among citizens and led to the creation of the Environmental Protection Agency of the federal government.
2. Earth Day is celebrated each year on April 22 by 193 countries around the world and coordinated internationally by the Earth Day Network. Earth Day began in the United States in 1970 to demonstrate support for environmental protection. The founder of Earth Day was Gaylord Nelson, then a senator from Wisconsin. Senator Nelson had just witnessed a massive oil spill off the coast of Santa Barbara, California. Each year, events, such as demonstrations and education forums, are held to advance environmental protection causes; in recent years, they have focused on global warming and climate change.
3. The Dakota Access Pipeline protests began in early 2016. The protests were in opposition to a 1,200-mile underground oil pipeline that would extend from North Dakota to Illinois. A number of Native American tribes objected to the construction of the pipeline as a threat to their sacred burial grounds and a threat to the quality of their water if the pipeline were to leak. Thousands of Native Americans were joined by other environmentalists in occupying the land where the pipeline was being constructed. In the end, the pipeline developers were able to get all the necessary environmental and construction permits. The demonstrators were cleared from the area they had been occupying. The pipeline went into full operation in June 2017.

Historical Inquiry

In 1997, the Kyoto Protocol Treaty was signed. The protocol is an international agreement linked, like the later Paris Climate Accord, to the United Nations Framework Convention on Climate Control. The protocol went into effect in February 2005. The objective was to reduce greenhouse gas concentrations in the atmosphere that interfere with the world's climate systems. Has the Kyoto Protocol Treaty been successful in reducing the emission of greenhouse gases into the atmosphere?

Using online and other sources, test the hypothesis that the Kyoto Protocol Treaty has been successful in reducing the emission of greenhouse gases into the atmosphere. Compose a short essay in which you accept or reject the hypothesis. To begin your investigation, the following search terms will be helpful:

- Greenhouse gas emissions since 2005
- The United States and the Kyoto Protocol
- Kyoto Protocol emission targets

Permissions

Chapter 22

"A National Game That Is Played Out" reprinted with permission of *Harper's Weekly*.

Chapter 29

Excerpts from pp166–8, 186, 208–9, 233–7 from BLACK BOY by Richard Wright. Copyright 1937, 1942, 1944, 1945 by Richard Wright; renewed © 1973 by Ellen Wright. Reprinted by Permission of HarperCollins Publishers.

Chapter 33

United States Holocaust Memorial Museum, courtesy of the National Archives and Records Administration, College Park.

Chapter 34

Photograph provided courtesy of the Museum of History & Industry, Seattle, WA, P-I Collection.

General Jacob L. Devers Presenting American Flag to the Mother of Private First Class Fumitake Nagato at Arlington National Cemetery, 1948. Courtesy of Special Collections, California State University, Sacramento Library.

Chapter 38

Groomsmen on top of cake courtesy of Sirtravelot/Shutterstock.

Chapter 39

"Pop it out by the roots" by Steve Hunter.

About the Authors

David E. Harris is a retired professor of teacher education at the University of Michigan. Before holding that position, he was the social studies education director for the school districts of Oakland County, Michigan, and an American history teacher at James Madison Memorial High School in Madison, Wisconsin. With Alan Lockwood of the University of Wisconsin, he coauthored the first edition of *Reasoning with Democratic Values*. He lives in northern Michigan adjacent to the Sleeping Bear National Lakeshore with his wife, Marcia, a retired kindergarten teacher. Their children and grandchildren visit often. David wrote several of the chapters of this book while overlooking the splendor of the lakeshore.

Anne-Lise Halvorsen is an associate professor in the Department of Teacher Education at Michigan State University. Her research and teaching interests are elementary social studies education, historical inquiry, project-based learning, the history of education, the integration of social studies and literacy, and teacher preparation in the social studies. Her publications have appeared in *Journal of Curriculum Studies*, *Teachers College Record*, and *Theory and Research in Social Education*. She is the author of *A History of Elementary Social Studies: Romance and Reality* (Peter Lang, 2013) and the co-author of *Powerful Social Studies for Elementary Students* (Cengage, 2012). In 2017, Anne-Lise won the Michigan Council for the Social Studies College Educator of the Year Award. She is a former kindergarten teacher and a former curriculum writer for the state of Michigan. She resides in Detroit, Michigan, with her husband, Bil Lusa, and their three children.

Paul F. Dain is a retired teacher from Bloomfield Hills, Michigan, where he taught American government, Advanced Placement American government, and Advanced Placement comparative government at Andover High School. He received his undergraduate degree in political science from Western Michigan University and his master's degree in the teaching of social studies from Wayne State University. In 1983, he received the Outstanding Social Studies Teacher Award from the Michigan Law-Related Education Organization. In 1987, he received the Master Teacher designation by Bloomfield Hills Schools. In 1997, he received the Newsweek-WDIV Michigan Outstanding Teacher Award. In 1984, he authored the *Detroit Free Press Elections Workbook*, an advanced-level workbook for high school teachers to use in teaching about presidential elections. Paul resides in Florida with his wife, Jane, and continues to be engaged in educational, community, and civic activities.